TRAVELING THROUGH SINAI

TRAVELING THROUGH SINAI

From the Fourth to the Twenty-first Century

Edited by
DEBORAH MANLEY
and SAHAR ABDEL-HAKIM

With illustrations by W.H. Bartlett

The American University in Cairo Press
Cairo New York

The editors and publisher are grateful to the following for permission to use material in this book: Methuen Methuen Publishing Ltd. for permission to use material from *Through the lands of the Bible* by H.V. Morton; and Canon John Wilkinson for permission to use material from *Egeria's Travels*. Every reasonable effort has been made to contact copyright holders. We apologize and thank any authors or copyright holders who we have not been able to properly acknowledge. If a work in copyright has been inadvertently included, the copyright owner should contact the publisher.

The American University in Cairo Press
113 Sharia Kasr el Aini, Cairo, Egypt
420 Fifth Avenue, New York, NY 10018
www.aucpress.com

First paperback edition 2009

Dar el Kutub No. 23747/08
ISBN 978 977 416 281 7

Dar el Kutub Cataloging-in-Publication Data

Manley, Deborah
Traveling through Sinai: From the Fourth to the Twenty-first Century / Edited by Deborah Manley and Sahar Abdel-Hakim.—Cairo: The American University in Cairo Press, 2008
p. cm.
ISBN 977 416 281 1
1. Egypt—description and travel 2. Egypt—Antiquities I. Abdel-Hakim, Sahar (jt. ed.)
II. Title
913.23

1 2 3 4 5 6 7 8 14 13 12 11 10 09

Designed by Joanne Cunningham/AUC Press Design Center

Contents

Introduction

Sinai is unique in human history both in terms of the events that took place on this land and the recording of its history. To learn about the land and know its history, one needs to know both what travelers thither scribbled on paper and what they engraved on Sinaitic stone. A record of the land is inscribed on the land itself as events that remain as elusive as any narrative, at once narrating a history and refusing to disclose it. History still asks these questions:

Which is the peak on which Moses received the Ten Commandments from God and *which* is the peak from which the Prophet Muhammad's horse, Boraq, ascended to heaven? *Where* did the Children of Israel pass by on their exodus from Egypt—or did they pass this way at all? *Who* were the Pharaohs who mined turquoise from Serabit al-Khadem and carved representations of themselves on the entrances of the mining galleries? *Who* are the people whose graffiti are engraved on the walls of St. Catherine's Monastery? *What* was the purpose of the carving in the 'Written Valley'—Wadi Mokkateb? *Is* the fountain of Moses the well that supplies St. Catherine's Monastery with water or is it Oyun Musa on the western coast of the peninsula? *Who* are the people who built the circular tombs or *nuwamis* on a rocky headland south of Jebel Musa? *Who* are the thousands of unnamed pilgrims who came this way over a thousand years ago—and have come ever since and still come today—leaving no mark except the mark of experience within them?

In many respects the story of Sinai is both solid and illusive, bringing together fact and perception, shifting from one book to another but rarely drastically changing. Such is the allure of Sinai: the land of histories that would not be fixed, of steep mountains and deep valleys, of deserts and oases, of fortifications and revelations, of old towns and ancient monasteries.

Just like the journeys of the history of Sinai, physical travel in the peninsula is not easy. Many travelers over the centuries traversed its mountainous desert for different purposes, but following the routes it allows. Most of Sinai's visitors were passersby who crossed it on their routes from Africa to Asia or from Europe to Asia, and vice versa. Pilgrims heading for or coming from Jerusalem and Mecca were—apart from the Bedouin people of the land—the most frequent travelers to Sinai. Merchants, traders, explorers, and the fascinated traveler followed.

Who were these travelers, we asked, and what were their reasons for travel? They were the pilgrims—changing their itineraries with the changes in history and means of transport; traders carrying their goods between countries and customers; explorers and surveyors and the adventurous—wanting to know what lay there; and, today, the leisure travelers are the most frequent visitors, especially to southern Sinai, but, always the pilgrims are there, drawn in from all over the world to this hub of history.

Our own journeys thither were not dissimilar. In this historic land people have run away from each other and run to meet each other, always with a plan, human or divine. Our time there was a few hours of getting together. As creators of this book we are connected by friendship and common interests. We met together in Sinai fashion—on the land and on the pages of a book. Despite the distance apart of our homes—in Cairo and Oxford, we traveled to the historic meeting place of Sinai. We came from different places, different cultures, and different generations, followed different itineraries—but we were both bound for the same destination.

One of us flew into the tourist spread of Sharm al-Sheikh and gladly left its pleasures to approach, across the arid, almost empty landscape, the steep hills and dramatic mountains. It took less than an hour in modern transport to come among them—a distance that would have taken a traveler on camel-back a long, weary day as the mountains drew slowly, very slowly, closer. The first sight of Jebel Musa—the Mountain of Moses—where the Laws were given—and of Mount St. Catherine, where the saint was believed to have come to Sinai, is still today a moment of thrill. Less than an hour from the monastery are the mysterious *nuwamis*—the well-built circular constructions atop a lonely, rocky hill. Known to be tombs, they still remain mysterious—another link in this land between human travelers and a power they believe to be beyond themselves.

As one of us flew north to south, reaching Sinai through one of its modern gateways, the other traveled west to east, from Cairo to Suez, Sinai's ancient portal. But is the Suez of the earlier travelers the same place today's travelers encounter?

Centuries of geographic inscription on the land have left their mark. The Suez of today is neither the one celebrated nor the one dismissed for its ruinous state by some early travelers. It has shifted place. Today's Sinai travelers do not visit the city any more but simply touch its outskirts and hasten to cross the Ahmad Hamdy tunnel into Sinai. The newly built tunnel connects east and west by land and runs under the older Suez Canal, the waterway connecting north and south. At this juncture of land and water people from all over the world meet, some head towards Sinai, others sail down its western mountainous coast.

The car pulled out of the tunnel following the new asphalt road constructed over the ancient tracks, passing historic villages built around wells, springs, and water resources. Signs on the road point to historic places of renown, concealed behind the majestic mountainous peaks, at once inviting and hidden. Uyun Musa, Ras Sudr, Wadi Gharandal, Abu Zeneima, Sarabit al-Khadim, Abu Rudeis, Wadi Serbal, Wadi Feiran—every spot in Sinai has a name, an identity, and many stories. The signs pointing to these places recall the complex history of the peninsula just as they narrate the story of present day life. Lampposts lighting the asphalt road, satellite dishes hanging over the Bedouin's houses, a kelim factory, a gift shop, all suggest that yesterday's stories are not much different from today's, that the land accommodates its nomadic people and the sedentary traveler, records and narrates their existence, experiences, and inscriptions.

Such are the modern itineraries. Historically, people came from different directions but could only tread the passes that Sinai allowed. Tradition says the Israelites reached Sinai from the west, Mary and Jesus crossed northern Sinai, moving east to west, Muhammad miraculously flew in. The roads traversed by so many travelers are still largely trodden by those who prefer to travel by land. With its distribution of mountains, wadis, and wells, it is the land itself that charts the travelers' itineraries. Sinai has created its own road map from time immemorial. Across the centuries, some travelers took the northern coast road from Farma to Arish to Rafah, following the wells and escaping the mountains. This was the chosen road of Ibn Battuta and Alexander Kinglake. Those who chose to take the southern mountainous paths traversed the desert and were led through historic tracks imposed by the land's own topography and known almost instinctively by their Bedouin guides.

Today's travelers to Sinai arrive through old doorways such as Suez or new ones like Sharm al-Sheikh. But once there, they follow the tracks of generations and generations of travelers, passing historic villages and oases created around wells. In every respect, Sinai strikes its visitors as an old-new land, a place spacious enough to hold past and present, ancient and modern, stories of believers, disbelievers, and converts either way, and fairy tales and folk tales and stories of war and peace. Its stories of Moses and Pharaoh, of Mary and Jesus, of Ibrahim and Sarah, of Muhammad and Boraq, are known to children all over the world. These typical Sinaitic stories are believed to be true but remain illusive, are told and retold in different versions as they flow in a steady passage of narrative, intersecting with other more solid stories of fortifications and garrisons, of walls that were built and eventually abandoned.

At the heart of Sinai is the fortress Monastery of St. Catherine where Orthodox monks have lived for many hundred years. Here pilgrims and travelers have come over the centuries. The monastery houses a library and is itself a volume on human history, which tells its story with a conglomeration of buildings, in the library holdings and on the monastery's walls. It narrates the tale of the travelers' minds and sentiments, of trips undertaken in pursuit of earlier journeys. St. Catherine is said to have traveled to this spot miraculously from Alexandria and since then has invited numerous travelers, both religious pilgrims and curious adventurers. The monastery is said to have been created on the site of the Burning Bush—and that bush or its continuing representative still flourishes and is still visited there.

The monastery is a composite of buildings—rooms for living, rooms for storage, and rooms for worshipers—the magnificent Church of the Transfiguration, smaller chapels, and the mosque. This composite of buildings is a place for visitors and for residents, of passersby who leave a trace and of dwellers who eventually depart to their heaven. Testimony to this regular flow into St. Catherine's and Sinai is visible in the Charnel House, seen as today's visitors leave the monastery. The skulls and neatly laid bones in the Charnel House are only different versions of the narratives inscribed in the tomes and volumes in the library of the monastery.

To these narratives travelers have contributed writings of their own lives and Sinaitic experiences, some of which they left behind, on leaving the peninsula, in the visitors' books of the monastery; others they recorded on their return to their homelands and these have been accumulated in libraries across the world. Now St. Catherine's Monastery is sending out to the world some of its own precious writings and illustrations for the world to share.

Whether as traders, pilgrims or explorers, no traveler traversed Sinai without the help of its people, the *Bedu*, who, very much like the land itself, figure prominently in the travelers' accounts, although they were seen differently by different travelers. Very much like their mode of life, the general perception of them seems to have been on the move. It shifted and changed across the centuries and according to the writer's personal inclinations. In the texts, the *Bedu* move from one mental image to another, evoke different sentiments and shape different relations between the travelers and their guides. Some travelers loved the *Bedu's* 'exoticism,' others did not—but all traveled in their company. Some trusted them—some did not—but all realized their dependence on them and admired their independence, and their lack of involvement in the world beyond the peninsula. This volume contains voices descriptive of these different sentiments and relationships between the travelers and their guardian guides. Readers will hear the famed traveler, Isabella Bird, in a little known account, tell how her guides rescued her from thirst. They will encounter E.H. Palmer who took a further step to meet the *Bedu* by studying their culture and traditions and retelling their stories.

These are the oases in this book, of which the focus shifts from the place and its entrenched history to the history that was being written by the travelers and now is passed on in these chapters. Here are accounts of the journey travelers followed, and the routines, pleasures, hardships, and encounters which accompanied these journeys. Readers traveling on board this book will have the chance to rest from the tough journey in the wilderness of Sinai to encounter their traveling companions around a desert fire at a watering place and listen to tales of other travelers and of the *Bedu*. They will share the meals—meager or grand—and the nights' rest and numerous suns traversing the sky and marking days and nights where every day is a new birth, every journey a fresh story written in the book of travel to Sinai.

This book is a record of both the place with its history and geography and its visitors. It reflects the land's history and the travelers' reflections, revealing moments of happiness and sadness, of human aspirations and frailties, ideas, beliefs, impressions—thoughts packed in the travelers' luggage and others acquired from his or her interaction with the land and its people. Some liked it; others did not, but both valleys and mountains were crossed. . . .

Note: We have retained the travelers' spellings of place names and people. While they have little consistency, they are still recognizable.

1
To Sinai and Back

Over the centuries the remote reaches of the Sinai Peninsula have drawn pilgrims and fascinated travelers. Over those centuries the tales told by those people of what they achieved have been built on and refined. These stories have been told and retold, losing and gathering angles in their telling. Perhaps, one may judge, the would-be traveler was repeating and interpreting the experiences of others who had gone before.

The preparations for the journey to Sinai for many started across Europe and into Russia. For many the actual journey started in Egypt—either at Cairo or on the Red Sea. An important event for the start of any journey is significant, but for those who were following their beliefs, the journey bore even more significance. Well into the twentieth century travelers to Sinai carried their Bible with them and compared it with the land through which they passed.

In 1425 an English poem described the chief sites of pilgrimage in about 1500 lines—here are the lines on Sinai from Purchas: His Pilgrims.

In That Mount Up High, 1425

Anon

In that mount up high
Is a minster of our Lady:
The minster of the Bush, men call it,
Wherein the body of St Katherine was put.
Also behind the high altar
Is where Jesus did appear
In that church to Moses,
When he kept Jethro of Midian's sheep truly.
In the midst of that hill is a place
Where did penance the prophet Elijah;
One the height of that hill
God gave to Moses both the Laws
Written in tables, without miss.
Plenary remission then it is.
A garden there is at no distance
Where Onorius did his penance.
Another hill also is there,
To which angels did bear
The blessed body of St Katherine,
She was a holy virgin.
Under that hill trust thou me.
There runneth the Red Sea.

At each of these places, that I told,
Is VII years, and VII 'lentones' (Lenten pardons) be thou bold.
Thus from Sinai would I skip
And tell of the pilgrimage of Egypt . . .

Why People Go There: Pilgrims to Sinai, 1835

Leon Laborde

As soon as Christianity began to extend itself, and was established in some parts of the holy city which had been the principal theatre of its mysteries, pilgrimages were at first made to the nearest, and afterwards to the more remote provinces, in proportion as the new religion made progress. About the third century Europe took a part in these pilgrimages, and the devotion of the Emperor Constantine, and of his mother Helena, as well as the care with which they collected the more interesting relics connected with Christianity, and enshrined them in magnificent edifices enriched by the most sumptuous presents, excited universal attention, and powerfully stimulated the zeal of the primitive Christians.

From that period commenced those innumerable pilgrimages which seem to have increased in proportion as the difficulties attending them were augmented. The first Christian travellers landing in the East, set out from Cairo or Jerusalem, reached Sinai, scrupulously visited all its celebrated localities, and then proceeded to their different destinations: that is to say, those who set out from Jerusalem went to Cairo to visit the hermits of the Thebiad and the lakes of Natro; whereas those who took their departure from Cairo terminated their pilgrimage at the Holy Sepulchre (Jerusalem). In the fourth century Saints Jerome and Eusebius went to Egypt to admire the austerities of the hermits of the Thebiad, and of the desert of Nitrice. Antoninus in the year 560 visited Sinai; he found . . . in a convent, which had already been constructed there, and on the summit of the mountain he observed the chapel, of which remains are still to be seen.* In the following years several other pilgrims ascended to that hermitage to pay their respects to the pious anchorites, who led there a life of expiation and suffering, of which we can scarcely form any idea.

Then in the eighth century, Jerusalem's internal dissensions allowed it to fall to the Muslim invasion. This, however, does not seem to have "subdued the ardour for these pilgrimages which then prevailed."

The relations which Charlemagne established with Haroun-el-Raschid, and the wise rule of the latter, enabled the Christians of the East to enjoy a degree of liberty and repose which they had not known since the conquest. They had then at Jerusalem twelve houses or inns, and in the valley of Josaphat some fields and vineyards. In the peninsula of Sinai, besides the monastery of St Catherine, several lesser convents were built in different valleys, and attended by monks. Pilgrimages . . . became customary, and entered into the manners of the time.

A Version of the Story, 1437

Pero Tafur

The journey to Mount Sinai endured for fifteen days. This mountain is very lofty and stands quite alone, about half a league from the Red Sea. On the summit of this mountain there was formerly a monastery, where the body of St Catherine was kept, and they say that one year, when there was great scarcity of bread, the monks on that account, and also in view of the great labour in climbing those heights, went to Babylonia (Cairo), leaving the monastery and the holy body unattended. Thereupon the blessed St Catherine appeared to them and told them to return, and that they would find provisions and a convenient place to live in, and that where they should find a great heap of wheat, and there, thanking God

* These remains were still visible into the nineteenth century, although they may well have been restored over the centuries.

and the Virgin St Catherine for the blessings they had received, they erected their monastery which is still a most notable place. The monks ascended the mountain and brought down the body with great honour, and placed it in the monastery at the foot, where they now live, not, indeed, neglecting what is on the mountain itself, for there are many holy places there, it being the place where God gave the tables of the law to Moses, and where he appeared to them in the burning bush. Here also is the place where he bade Moses strike the rock with his rod, and the water gushed forth, which to this day runs down to the foot.

A Monk's Tale, 1836

Joseph Wolff

March 24: Neophytes, the Superior, introduced me to Gedeon, an old monk, one hundred and five years of age, who has lived above sixty years in the Convent. This Superior made me a present of the History of their Convent. Many Christian monks lived around Mount Sinai, either in the caves of rocks, or in tents, a long time before the reign of Emperor Justinian, but on account of their vexation they frequently had to suffer from the Arabs, they wrote to the Emperor Justinian to assist them in building a Convent. He sent them one thousand Christians, with wives and children, from Servia, who were called by the Arabs, *Subhian*, from the Arab word 'Sabe' (boys or slaves); and other masons came from Mattarea, a village near Heliopolis. With their assistance the Convent was built A.D. 527.

In the time of Diocletian, a woman, Catherine by name, had suffered martyrdom at Alexandria, when her body was carried to Mount Sinai, where she was watched by them three hundred years, and after the Convent was built she was interred there with great magnificence, by order of Justinian. This is the legend of St Catherine, which I relate as Herodot [sic] dies his history: as I heard it, without making any comment upon it.

The Convent was in possession of an impression of the hand of Muhammed, which, as the story goes, they received in the following manner. When Muhammed was a youth he came near the Convent of Mount Sinai, lay down in the road, and slept in the sun. The monks observed that a large bird, spreading his wings over him, protected him against the sun; the monks perceived by this that he would one day become a great man; they invited him to the Convent, and told him as they had perceived that one day he would become a great man, they requested him to leave behind him a mark of favor and protection, on which account he stamped the mark of his hand upon a piece of wood; when he made his appearance as the Prophet of God, many years after, he passed again the Convent, they produced the mark of his hand, for which he granted to them a firman.

In the time of Sultan Selym, Melindar, one of Selym's generals, destroyed 360 Convents, which were built around Mount Sinai. On his approaching Mount Horeb, the monks went out to meet him, and besought him to spare them, and when they produced the hand and firman of the Arabian prophet, he granted protection to the Convent on condition of their making a Mosque in the Convent, which they agreed to and which Mosque is still in existence, and which I have seen. The monks made the successors of Selym believe that it had been built by Muhammed himself; and till now, the Muhammedan performing his pilgrimage to Mecca, and passing Mount Horeb, stops, dismounts his horse, and performs his devotion in the same Mosque to the God, the most merciful, and pitiful, and then continues his journey. The hand of Muhammed, however, was taken possession of by Sultan Selym.

For many this was not only a pilgrimage, it was also a journey into lands they had never seen before. The desert wilderness experience was one they would never forget.

The Peninsula of Sinai, 1864

Arthur Penryn Stanley

The great limestone range of Syria, which begins in the north from Lebanon and extends through the whole of Palestine, terminates in the south in a wide tableland, which reaches eastward far into Arabia Petraea, and westward far into Africa. At the point where this rocky mass descends from Palestine, another element falls in, which at once gives it a character distinct from mountainous tracts in other parts of the world; namely, that waterless region of the earth, which extends from the shores of the Atlantic to those of the Persian Gulf, under the familiar name of the Desert.

But similar in character, both as a wilderness, and as a mountain country, is broken by three great clefts, which divide the several portions from each other. The westernmost of these clefts is the deep valley, which descending from the mountains of Abyssinia contains the course of the solitary, mysterious, and majestic river, with the green strip of verdure lining its banks, which forms the land of Egypt. The second runs almost parallel to this—the bed not of a fertilising stream, but of a desolate sea—the Arabian Gulf of the Greeks, the Gulf of Suez in modern geography. The third and easternmost cleft at its southern extremity is similar in character to the second, and forms the Elanitic Gulf of the Greeks, the modern Gulf of Akaba; but further north it passes into the deep and wide valley of the 'Arabah, which in turn communicates with the still deeper valley of the Jordan, running up into the heart of the mountains of Lebanon, the original basis from which the whole of the system takes its departure.

It is between those two gulfs, the Gulf of Suez and the Gulf of Akaba, that the Peninsula of Sinai lies. From them it derives its contact with the sea, and therefore with the world; which is one striking distinction between it and the rest of the vast desert of which it forms a part. From hardly any point in the Sinaitic range is the view of the sea wholly excluded; from the highest points both of its branches are visible; its waters blue with a depth of colour more like that of some of the Swiss lakes than of our northern or midland seas, its tides imparting a life to the dead landscape. . . . It must always have brought to the mind of those who stood on its shores, that they were on the waters of a new and almost unknown world.

The Wadis, 1872

Paul Lenoir

In its general configuration, the Sinaitic peninsula forms a singular agglomeration of mountainous chains, running almost parallel one with the other, and which meet in a kind of cluster at the extremity of the peninsula. Between each of these gigantic walls, placed in such strange juxtaposition by nature, are the natural beds of the torrents that originate in the rains or the melting of snow. These narrow valleys, which are just like corridors, are called by the Arabs *wadis*. The word 'valley' does not accurately reproduce the sense of the Arab word, considering the narrowness of the passage which the traveller has to thread for a space of sometimes several kilometres. The light, striking only the horizontal planes presented of the fretted sides of the two mountains, gives these ravines the same partially dark effect as that of a cellar which depends on a long slit for daylight. The power of sound is extraordinary in these *wadis*: the strange multiplied echoes enabled us to make, with very little effort, noise enough for an entire population. For two days, while labouring through sand and pebbles, we kept these magnificent chains in sight; but they seemed to retreat before us as if they were in a mirage, and our joy was great indeed when we entered the first of the series of corridors. *Wady Beiyanah* was the first into which we plunged.

The Climate, 1873

Murray's Handbook

The climate of the Peninsula, especially of the mountain parts, is very healthy. The old hermits, to whom tradition assigns an almost fabulous longevity, believed that men needed in the desert "hardly to eat, drink, or sleep, for the act of breathing will give life enough". One of its most remarkable features is its intense dryness, observations with wet—and dry—bulb thermometers showing a difference of 20° and even 30°. In winter it is very cold in the mountains, and snow often falls, though it is never seen lower than 4,000 feet. The heat in summer is proportionately intense, especially in the limestone districts; and the khamseen winds, which occur generally in the spring, rend the usually clear atmosphere stifling and oppressive. There is a great difference between the temperature of the day and the night, especially in the winter, the thermometer sometimes falling below freezing point at night, to go up as high as 70° in the day. This change is not so great in the plains. The prevailing winds are from the north and the east. As a rule the air is very still, with only a gentle cooling breeze, but now and then heavy gales suddenly spring up. The rainfall is very slight, unless there occurs one of those storms already alluded to. Slight shocks of earthquake are said to be occasionally felt. Heavy dews are common in the winters.

The astonishing history of this place awed travelers, whether they were convinced this was the place where the Children of Israel passed with Moses or whether they saw it as a step back into a history long past.

The Foundation of the Convent, 7th century

Procopius

In what was formerly called Arabia and is known as 'Third Palestina', a barren land extends for a great distance, unwatered and producing neither crops nor any useful thing. A precipitous and terribly wild mountain, Sinai by name, rears its height close to the Red Sea, as it is called. . . . On this Mount Sinai live monks whose life is a kind of careful rehearsal of death, and they enjoy without fear the solitude which is very precious to them. Since these monks have nothing to crave—for they are superior to all human desires and have no interest in possessing anything or in caring for their bodies, nor do they seek pleasure in any other thing whatever—the Emperor Justinian built them a church which he dedicated to the Mother of God, so that they might be enabled to pass their lives therein praying and holding services. He built this church not on the mountain's summit, but much lower down. For it is impossible for a man to pass the night on the summit, since constant crashes of thunder and other terrifying manifestations of divine power are heard at night, striking terror into man's body and soul. It was in that place, they say, that Moses received the Law of God.

And at the base of the mountain this Emperor built a very strong fortress and established there a considerable garrison of troops, in order that the barbarian Saracens might not be able from that region, which, as I have said, is uninhabited, to make inroads with complete secrecy into the lands of Palestine proper.

The earliest pilgrims to Sinai traveled from Jerusalem—the first important destination of their pilgrimage—and from there passed southward to Mount Sinai.

From Jerusalem, 384

Egeria

January: From Jerusalem to the holy Mount Sinai it is twenty-two staging posts. . . . Before you reach the holy Mount Sinai you come to the fort of Clysma [Suez] on the Red Sea, the place where the children of Israel crossed the sea dry-shod. And the tracks of Pharaoh's chariot are permanently marked across the sand; its wheels were a good deal further apart than the chariots that we now have in the Roman Empire, since it measured twenty-four feet from wheel to wheel, and its tracks are two feet broad. Pharaoh's chariot tracks reach right down to the sea-shore at the point where he entered the sea in his efforts to catch the children of Israel. And at the point where they entered, where his tracks finish, two marks like small columns stand to right and left. This spot is not far from Clysma fort.

Not all travelers linked the same places in their own times to the Biblical sites, and many travelers, no doubt, used each other's identifications for places along the Old Testament route. One thus finds discrepancies between one writer and another. They were after all looking back over a period of three millennia. . . . One thing is certain: the great majority of travelers had a thorough knowledge of the Bible and most carried their Bibles with them.

The Routes of the Journey, 12th century

Peter the Deacon

Shur, the desert where they [the children of Israel] went for three days without water (Exodus 15.22), is of an enormous size. No one has ever seen a bigger desert, and no one could guess the quantities of sand. Between the Desert of Shur and Marah (Ain Musa) there is one staging-post next to the sea, and at Marah itself there are some palm trees (very few), and the two springs which holy Moses made sweet.

From there on for three days' journey there is an endless desert to the left. Then you reach Arandara, the Arandara which was called Elim (Wadi al Gharandal; Exodus 15.27) There is a stream there, and, though it dries up from time to time, there is water to be had from its bed or from near the bank. In that place there is plenty of grass and a great many palm trees, all the way from Shur where we crossed the Red Sea there is no place as pleasant as this, or with such good plentiful water. The next staging-post is beside the sea, and it is halfway [modern Abu Zanima].

Next, two mountains come into sight on the left, and, before you reach them, there is the place where the Lord rained manna on the children of Israel. They are lofty mountains, and very steep. On one side of the mountains the valley is perfectly flat and like a colonnade about two hundred yards wide, with the steep high mountains of either side. But where the mountains open out the valley is six miles wide and a good deal longer.

All around the mountain caves have been carved out (such caves are mainly around about Wady Mukattib), and if you just took the trouble to put up some curtains, they would make marvellous bedrooms. Each bedroom is inscribed with Hebrew letters. At the far end of the valley is good water in plenty, but it is not the equal of Elim. This is called the Desert of Paran, and it was from here that Moses sent out spies to explore the land. It is protected by mountains on both sides, but it has no fields or vineyards, and there is nothing there but the water and some palm trees.

Close to the village of Paran—a mile and a half away—the mountains converge to make a valley. It is the place called Rephidim, and it is where Amalek met the children of Israel, where the people murmur for water, and where Moses was met by Jethro, his father-in-law. The very lofty steep mountain which overhangs Paran is the place where Moses prayed while Joshua defeated Amalek; a church has now been built on the spot where Moses prayed (there are ruins here today), and you can still see the place where he sat, and how he had the stones under his couch. When Amalek was defeated, Moses built up an altar there to the Lord (Exodus 17.15). And for half a mile there it is all so steep that you would think you were going up a wall.

From Paran there is a thirty-five mile journey before you reach the holy Mount Sinai. . . .

All the way to the holy Mount Sinai the valley running between the mountains is full of monuments to the right and left, and near the holy Mount the place called The Graves of Craving is full of tombs.

The fourteenth century English knight, Sir John Mandeville, according to his own accounts, traveled in the Near East and published the learning of the area that he acquired. It is not known whether this was his own experience or a collage of the knowledge of others. 'Babylon' was at that time the name of Cairo. His description of the journey—well by well—is the definition of the journey which a Bedouin guide would have given. And much that Mandeville recorded continues to be recorded in other's accounts over the centuries.

Babylon to Mount Sinai, 1322

Sir John Mandeville

Now shall I say you also the way, that goeth from Babylone to the Mount if Synay, where Mount St Kateryne lieth. He must pass by the deserts of Arabye; by the which deserts Moyses led the people of Israel; and then pass men by the well, that Moyses made with his hand in the desert, when the people grudged, for they found no thing to drink. [Ain Musa] And then pass men by the well of Marache [Ain Hawarah] of the which the water was first bitter; but the children of Israel put therein a tree; and anon the water was sweet and good for to drink. And then go men by desert unto the Vale of Elyn; in the which Vale be twelve wells, and there be seventy two trees of palm, that bear the dates, the which Moses found with the Children of Israel. And from that valley is but a good journey to the Mount of Synay.

And wit well, that from Babylone [Cairo] to the Mount Synay is well a twelve good journeys [days's journey]: and some men make them more: and some men hasten them and pain them; and therefore they make them less. And always find men Latiners to go with them in the countries, and farther beyond, into time that men con the language. It behoveth man to have victuals with them, that shall dure them in the deserts, and other necessaries for to live by.

And the Mount of Synay is clept the desert of Syne, that is for to say, the bush burning: because there Moyses saw our Lord God many times, in the form of fire burning upon that hill; and also in a bush burning; and spake to him. And that was at the foot of the hill. There is an abbey of monks, well builded and well closed with gates of iron, for dread of the wild beasts. And the monks be Arrabyenes, or men of Greece: and there is a great convent; and all they be heremytes; and they drink no wine, but if it be on principal feasts: and they be full devout men, and live poorly and simply, with gourds and with dates: and they do great abstinence and penance. There is the Church of St Kateryne, in which be many lamps burning. For they have of oil of olives enough, both for to burn in their lamps, and to eat also. And that plenty have they be the miracle of God. For the ravens and the crows and the choughs, and other fowls of the country assemble them every year once, and fly thither as in pilgrimage, and every of them bringeth a branch of the bays or of olive in their beaks, instead of offering, and leave them there; of the which the monks make great plenty of oil; and this is a great marvel.

Also behind the altar of that church is the place where Moyses saw our Lord God in a burning bush. And when the monks enter into that place, they do off both hosen and schoon or boots always; because that our Lord said to Moyses, *Do off thy hosen and thy shoon: for the place that thou standeth on is land holy and blessed.*

And beside the high altar, three degrees of height, is the Feretrum of alabaster, where the bones of St Kateryne lie. And the prelate of the monks showeth the relics to the pilgrims. And with an instrument of silver, he rubbeth the bones; and then there goeth out a little oil, as though it were a manner sweating, that is neither like to oil nor to balm; but it is full sweet of smell. And of that they give a little to pilgrims; for there goeth out but little quanity of the liquor. And after that they show the head of Saint Kateryne, and cloth that she was wrapped in, that is yet all bloody. And in that same cloth so y-wrapped, the angels bore her body to the Mount Synay, and there they buried her with it.

In that abbey ne entereth not no fly ne toads ne newts, ne such foul venomous beasts, ne lice ne fleas, by the miracle of God and of our Lady.

Murray's Handbook—*created by and carried by many later nineteenth-century travelers—gave two routes to St. Catherine's: Both routes assume that one started from Ain Musa—the 'Wells of Moses'—up to a day's journey by land or sea beyond Suez. Mileages are given from Suez. Some travelers came or went across the Red Sea from Kosseir to the port of Tor.*

The Routes of the Journey, 1873

Murray's Handbook

Route (a) via Wady Mukatteb and Feiran	Miles
Ain Musa (Marah)	21
Wady Amarah (Marah)	20
Ain Hawarah (Marah)	6
Wady Ghurandel (Elim)	7
Wady Useit (Elim)	6
Wady Ethal	7
Wady Shebeikeh (mouth of)	4
Wady Taiyibeh (mouth of) (Encampment by the Sea)	4
Jebel el Markhah	7
Seih Bab'a	6
Nugb Buderah	4
Wady Igne (mouth of, leading to Magharah)	5
Wady Mukatteb (the Written Valley)	5
Wady Feiran	4
Feiran (El Maharrad) (Rephidim)	14
Wady esh Sheykh (mouth of)	6
Wady Solaf (head of) and mouth of Nugb Hawa	15
Nugh Hawa (summit of)	5
Jebel Musa & Monastery of St Catherine	5
Total 153 miles	

Route (b) via Sarabit el Khadim	
Ain Moosa to Wady Shebekeikeh (Route a.)	Miles
Sarboot el Jemel	71
Wady Sawig (mouth of)	7
Sarabit el Khadim	13
Debelat Sheyk Ahmed	6
Erweis el Ebereig	7
Wady Solaf (head of) and mouth of Nugb Hawa	21

Jebel Moosa etc via Nugb Hawa (see Route a)	12
Total 147 miles	10

If the traveller does not intend returning to Cairo, but means to continue across the desert to Hebron, he had better, unless Egyptian antiquities are especially his object, choose Rte. a as affording the most general objects of interest.

Lady Catherine Tobin was less precise in her measurement of distance but perhaps this reflects more directly on the length of the journey—dreary long days measured in Bedouin terms of time.

The Routes of the Journey, 1853

Catherine Tobin

			Hrs.	Miles
1853				
Dec.	24	Left Cairo (on camels) towards Suez		
"	28	At Suez, arrived at Ayun Moussa by water	5	15
"	29	In the Wilderness	4	9
"	31	The same	8	24
1854			8	26
Jan.	1	The same		
"	2	The same	9	27
"	3	The same	9	27
"	4	The same	8	26
"	5	Arrived at Mt. Sinai	8	26
"	6	Remained at Mount Sinai—ascent by Gebel Musa	5	15
"	7	Remained at Mount Sinai—visited Convent of Forty Martyrs		
"	8	Remained at Mount Sinai		
"	9	Left Mount Sinai		
"	10	In the Wilderness	6	15
"	11	The same	9	27
"	12	The same	9	27
"	13	The same	9	27
"	14	Arrived at Nakhel (en route to Aqaba)	9	27
			9	28

On the Sinai Road, 1882

Sir Flinders Petrie

The traditions of travelling and working in Sinai are very different from those of life in a fertile country such as Egypt, and are still further from the ways of any European land. In Egypt most long distances can be traversed on the railway, and to go a few miles from a station means only an hour or two of donkey ride; whereas in Sinai the tedious camel is the only vehicle, and you may well spend six days on a distance which would be crossed in two or three hours in a train. In Egypt there is always water of some quality near at hand, and it only needs boiling before use; In Sinai the water sources are a day's journey apart, and you may be glad to be within such a distance that a camel can go to the water and back in the day. The beginning is the worst of all, for on the road down is the serious bar of three days without water. In Egypt the rich fertility of the land provides an abundance everywhere: excellent birds, fish, good native bread, eggs, milk, and vegetables are almost always to be had. But in Sinai grim nature gives you the stone and the serpent instead of the bread and the fish, and the utmost that can be obtained from the desert valleys is an occasional tough sheep or goat.

Early travelers knew their Bible almost by heart. Often in their minds was the question, "Which route was followed by the Children of Israel as they escaped from Pharaoh's wrath?" Many scholars sought to determine the answer. . . .

Which Route Did the Israelites Take? 1877

Samuel Manning

A yet further difficulty in the way of tracing the course pursued by the fugitives arises from the character of the only historical document we possess on the subject. The Mosaic narrative is one of remarkable precision and accuracy. It is in fact an itinerary giving the journeys day by day, and the halting places night by night. But, as Dean Stanley has remarked, it was written by and for those who were so well acquainted with the localities that they required no explanatory details. The names being familiar and the places known, no further indication was thought needful. This, whilst it affords a strong incidental corroboration of the authenticity of the narrative, deprives us of those helps to identify that stations on the route which might otherwise have been afforded. The names having disappeared, or being only handed down by doubtful and obscure traditions, we are left to work out a conjectural line of march from insufficient data.

But whatever perplexities we may feel in the endeavour to trace the precise course followed by the Israelites, the general outlines of the scenery remain unchanged, and we can realise with the utmost vividness and certainty the general aspect of the country through which they passed.

It is fascinating to recognize how for some travelers this was undoubtedly the route of the Israelites, yet others at an earlier period doubted that the Old Testament account was truly factual—or, if factual, whether it really related to Sinai. This argument and comparison between the Bible and the landscape and its configuration continues to this day.

Plain Er-Rahah

Did They Go This Way at All? 1845

Richard Lepsius

The tradition of Jebel Musa being the Mount of the Law, became gradually more decided and exclusive for this view after the time of Procopius in the sixth century; mainly, no doubt, on account of the church founded at that spot in the reign of Justinian. I am not aware that there are any modern travellers and savants who have thrown doubts on the correctness of this assumption. Not even Burckhardt,* although from the numerous inscriptions on Serbal he was led to infer that that mountain might have been at one time incorrectly regarded by the pilgrims as Sinai. The words of this distinguished traveller are as follows: "it will be recollected that no inscriptions are found either on the Mountain of Moses, or on Mount St Catherine; and that those which are found in the Ledja valley at the foot of Jebel Catherine, are not to be traced above the rock from which the water is said to have issued, and appear only to be the work of pilgrims who visited that rock. From these circumstances I am persuaded that Mount Serbal was at one period the chief place of pilgrimage in the Peninsula; and that it was then considered the mountain where Moses received the tables of the law; though I am equally convinced, from a perusal of the Scriptures, that the Israelites encamped in the Upper Sinai, and that either Jebel Musa, or Mount St Catherine, is the real Horeb.

* The Swiss traveler John Lewis Burckhardt, who traveled to Sinai in 1816.

It is not at all impossible that the proximity of Serbal to Egypt, may at one period have caused that mountain to be the Horeb of the pilgrims, and that the establishment of the Convent in its present situation which was probably chosen from motives of security, may have led to the transferring of that honour to Jebel Musa. At present neither the monks of Mount Sinai nor those of Cairo consider Mount Serbal as the scene of any of the events of sacred history; nor have the Bedouins any tradition among them respecting it, but it is possible, that if the Byzantine writers were thoroughly examined, some mention might be found of this mountain, which I believe was never before visited by any European traveller."

More recently the remarkable book of travels by E. Robinson* forms a marked epoch in our knowledge of the Peninsula as well as of Palestine. With reference to the position of Sinai, he for the first time especially urges the favourable facility of the great plain of Raha, to the north of Jebel Musa, in which there was ample space for the encampment of the people of Israel. In his determination, however, of the actual Mount of the Law he deviates from the previous tradition, since he endeavours to prove that Moses did not ascend Jebel Musa, but the mountain ridge jutting out from the south, above the plain, which is now called Horeb by the monks, and whose highest point is named Sefsaf. Unfortunately he did not visit Wadi Firan and the adjoining Serbal.

Mount Sinai! All Change! 1938

Louis Golding

The last candle had only just gone out in my high-hung cell in the Convent of Mount Sinai, when the first camel entered.

He entered not by the door, but by the right hand wall, and though it was a small room, he found no difficulty in picking his way between the foot of the bed and the washstand. His head high in the air, he padded contemptuously towards the left hand wall, and disappeared. Another camel came and another followed him; the caravan was stretched out along the steel-grey horizon. Without pause the tawny river, humped with yellow waves, heaved along its uneven channel. Then it reached the lee of a high mountain, which was altogether on smoke, because the Lord descended upon it in fire: and the smoke thereof ascended as the smoke of a furnace, and the whole mount quaked greatly.

And a voice at the head of the caravan cried out: Mount Sinai! Mount Sinai! All change! This way for Hezoreth and all stations for the River Jordan! All change!

Then the cloud that had hung stationary over the head of the leading camel moved, the trumpeters blew their silver trumpets, the standards went forward; and the host went after the standards, and the four winds of heaven blew; and, as they blew, all the valleys were filled with the odours of myrrh and frankincense.

So the host moved out of the plain of Er Rahah into one of the narrower wadis, and the tumult died down, saving only for the sound of the camel-bells.

* Reverend Edward Robinson, an American minister, in Sinai in the mid-nineteenth century.

Far and delicate, like rocking pin-points of sound, the voices of the camel-bells thrilled through the cold air.

The cold air . . . I became aware of a sudden that my shoulders were slabs of ice. With the dream still heavy on my eyes, I reached out to lift the bedclothes over me, but they had slipped, they were not there. I was awake now. I was aware that the door of my room was wide open. I had not latched it properly and the stark wind from the summit of Gebel Ed Deir had swung it open. I was aware also that I heard the sound of bells, though they were not the camel-bells of my dream.

It was not many bells but one bell – the bell that summons the monks of the Convent of Mount Sinai from their cells for their first devotion. It rings at two-thirty in the morning, first three notes, low pitched, then louder, again three times, five minutes later.

It was bright hot morning when I awoke again. The strip of sky raced like a blue river between the tops of the rust-red cliffs.

2
The Place, the People, and the Travelers

No person took the journey into Sinai lightly, whether their expedition was spiritual or a personal adventure. Until recently the Sinai Peninsula was one of the most isolated places on Earth with no road except a track made by the plodding feet of camels, and even now the modern tourist is impressed by the isolation and the awe that centuries of history bring. Today the remoteness is only comparative—we know there is an easy way back to the world from which we came. Well into the twentieth century, travelers faced a real challenge since there was no easy way back to the world they knew. But alongside all the pilgrims and travelers were the people of the desert without whom the stranger could not penetrate this least friendly of lands.

The Land, 1937
Joan Plowden

Sinai is a curious country: geographically it forms a giant's stepping-stone between Africa and Asia; politically it is a province of Egypt; historically and racially it has affinities with Arabia; geographically it is unique. Considering its accessible position it must be one of the least-travelled and least-known regions in the world. Except in the case of certain monastic groups and a few coastal villages there had been no attempt to live in it, for without a regular water-supply there can be no settled life. Nearly all the interior is filled by a huge limestone plateau called et Tih, the traditional Desert of the Wanderings—such a bleak forbidding district that until a few years ago it was not even properly surveyed, and is by no means now even fully explored.

Below et Tih comes a belt of rugged low-lying country; this again rises tier after tier of brilliant red granite mountains piled up in chaotic confusion, which are crossed and drained by a perfect labyrinth of *wadis* or dry ravines. In this almost inaccessible region is found some of the great scenery of the world, and three amongst the mountains have been identified at different times by tradition or by expert opinion as the veritable and ancient Mount Sinai. Beside one of them—Jebel Musa—stands isolated at a height of five thousand feet the splendid and renowned old Convent of St Catherine, which by its long existence as custodian of the traditions revolving around the Mount of the Law has for fourteen centuries been the goal of every traveller and the focus of interest in Sinai. In fact, but for the amenities created and preserved by the Greek monks in their desolate surroundings, the Peninsula might have remained to this day hardly better known than the lonely central highlands.*

Circumstances of geography and climate have restricted the history of Sinai to a series of unrelated events, the actors in which had only a transient interest in the land. One was of outstanding importance: Scriptures and tradition alike point to Sinai as the scene of the Exodus and of the promulgation of the Ten Commandments. Once and once only a great tide of people surged across the empty landscape, and the strange tale of their passing and the spiritual adventures that befell them here became the heritage of half the world. But the Israelites, like other nomads, passed on leaving no trace behind them; man, the cultivator and builder, has had no hand in the shaping of this land, and it is still unchanged after thirty centuries.

There are no rivers; the mountains are bare rock; nature has carved out with frost and flood the watercourses which serve the Bedouin as highways and there are practically no others. The climate is wonderful: the air is dry and pure, and so invigorating that it fills a traveller with energy and takes the edge of every hardship. The winter though short is very hard in the high country, while soon after April the heat becomes insupportable for the average European. A rare good fortune had launched me in Sinai in time for the brief and magical spring, when grass and flowers are conjured from the rock, when days are pleasantly warm and the nights not too cold, when winter floods are over and the wilderness wears such a serene and gracious aspect that to wander there for forty years were not an unwelcome condemnation.

* Her reference is to the central highlands of Scotland.

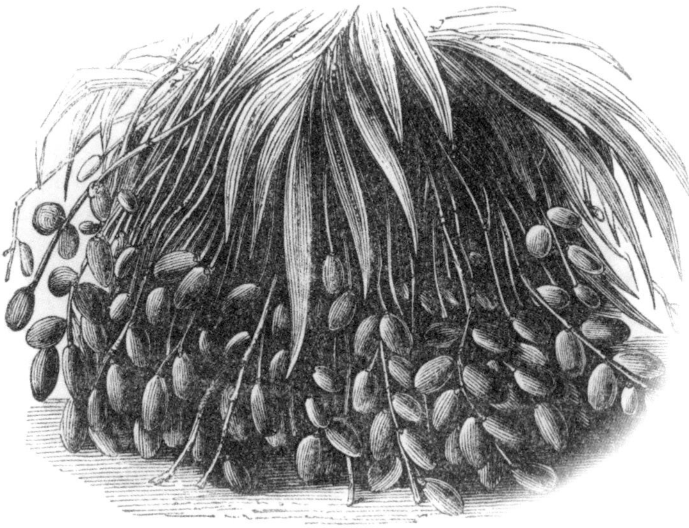

The Land, 1920

Lina Eckenstein

Sinai, generally speaking, is a country of stern desolation. Its mountains are bare, its plains are swept by the wind, its river beds are to all appearance waterless. But clusters of bushes that follow the valley floors or rise from the plains, show that moisture percolates the soil beneath the surface, and is procurable by digging down to the harder subsoil (i.e. "striking the rock"), as was done in the time of the passage of the Israelites. Such digging is done by the Bedawyn at the present day, the holes for water being called *hufrah* in Arabic. In some places, however, the water along the valleys is thrown up and forms natural oases as in the Wadi Gharandel, the Wadi Feiran, and at Tor. In others it is raised by means of the mechanical device of a water-wheel and by a *shaduf.*

According to Arab tradition the land along the shores of the Mediterranean was of great fruitfulness before it was invaded by sand drifts. It was the same with the numerous fruit and vegetable gardens which were once cultivated by the monks and hermits. With the exception of the garden of the convent, they have passed away

The herds of gazelles which were numerous as late as the Middle Ages, are few and far between. Pasture lands which formerly fed sheep and goats were encroached upon by the introduction of the camel. The transport of goods and pilgrims which gave occupation to the owners of camels during the Middle Ages has practically ceased.

A history of Sinai deals with the people who visited the peninsula at different times, rather than with its permanent inhabitants, who, in the course of the centuries, seem to have undergone little change. They still live the life of the huntsman as in the days of Ishmael, sleeping in the open, and adding to their meagre resources by carrying dates and charcoal to the nearest centres of intercourse, in return for which they receive corn.

The Story of the Convent, 1739

Richard Pococke

On the 11th [April], the Dr. arrived at Mount Sinai, passing over a square spot, encompassed with loose stones, whereon the architect of the convent intended first to have erected that building; but was by miracle prevented, and pointed to the place whereon it now stands.

The convent is dedicated to the celebrated St Catherine, and stands at the foot of the mount; our author entered it by a window thirty feet from the ground, being drawn up to it in a machine by a windlass; and this is the common entrance. The chief of the convent attended withinside to receive him, and gave him his choice, either to retire first to his apartment, or to visit the church; he choosing the latter, was conducted to the shrine in which the body of the saint was deposited; where the monks sang a hymn.

Mount Sinai has two summits; it is called by the Arabs Jebel Musa, or the mountain of Moses, because that here many remarkable things happened to that holy prophet. It was here that God appeared to him at the burning bush; and the fathers show a bramble, which they say is of the same sort, though it is plainly one of a very common kind, brought from Europe; here, however, it is an exotic. Here he also fed the flock of his father-in-law Jethro; and not far off he struck the rock, out of which water immediately flowed; the stone is of red granite, about fifteen feet long, ten broad, and twelve high; the opening does not resemble any thing done by a tool, and is something like the mouth of a carved lion; into this aperture the Arabs put certain medicinal herbs, which they afterwards give to their camels, in case of disease, to the expelling which, the administration of them, as they think, considerably contributes.

Near at hand is Mount St Catherine, whither the body of that saint, after her martyrdom under the tyrant Maxentius, was brought by angels, and kept, till the convent in which it is preserved, was finished. This is by much the highest mountain in the neighbourhood; it over-tops Sinai, which appears to the N.E. of it but low; the foil is a species of speckled marble, in which may be seen beautiful configurations of trees, and other vegetable representations.

The Building of the Convent, 933–40

Said ibn Batrick, Eutychius, Patriarch of Alexandria

The monks of Sinai hearing of the piety of Justinian, and the delight that he took in building churches and monasteries, went to him and described how the Ishmaelite Arabs harmed them by plundering them of their food stores, invading and emptying their cells, and entering their churches where they devoured the eucharist. When the emperor inquired into their wishes, they said: "We beg for a monastery in which we shall be safe." For at that time there was no convent building in which the monks could congregate. They dwelt scattered in the mountains and along the valleys near the Bush from which the Lord spoke to Moses, having only a large tower above the Bush which is standing to this day, and a church dedicated to the Virgin, where they sought protection when those approached whom they dreaded.

The emperor despatched them with a legate with full authority to the prefect of Egypt, asking that he should be supplied with building materials, with men and provisions in Egypt. He was charged to build a monastery at Kelzem (Clysma), and a monastery at Raya (Riathou), and one on Mount Sinai, this to be so fortified that no better could be found.

The legate came into Sinai, where he found the Bush in a narrow valley with the tower near it, also bubbling springs and the monks scattered along the valleys. He intended building the monastery on the summit of the mountain, leaving the Bush and the tower below, but he altered his plan because of the lack of water on the mountain, and built the monastery near the Bush enclosing the tower, and a church on the summit of the mountain, where Moses accepted the Law. . . . But the change of plan so annoyed the emperor that it cost the legate his life.

Who Was St. Catherine? 1938

H.V. Morton

The association of Catherine with Sinai is a remarkable story, and from this remote mountain fastness the fame of the saint went out all over Europe, particularly to Belgium. St Catherine was a virgin of Alexandria who died for her faith during the reign of Maximianus. Among the tortures devised for her was that of being strapped to four spiked wheels, which, we are told, revolved without tearing her flesh. Her executioners then carried her to a headsman who struck off her head. Five centuries after her martyrdom, it was revealed to a monk of Sinai that St Catherine's body had been transported by angels to the summit of Jebel Katherin, the companion peak to Mount Sinai. The monks ascended the mountain and discovered her bones, which they interred in a church on the summit of Mount Sinai.

The saint's bones exuded oil, which was periodically gathered in glass phials by the monks, who took turns for the privilege of performing this task. One day, about the year 1026, a monk called Simeon was drawing off the oil on the top of Mount Sinai when three saintly finger-bones became detached, which he took with him when he descended to the monastery. Now it had been the custom for the monks of Sinai to make journeys to the courts of Europe to request alms from the kings and princes. Among the generous benefactors to Sinai were the Dukes of Normandy. Monks journeyed every year from Sinai to Rouen, never failing to return loaded with gifts of gold and silver.

In the year 1026, or thereabouts, it fell to the lot of the monk Simeon to make this journey, and he took with him the three finger-bones of St Catherine, which, after many adventures by land and sea, he presented to Duke Robert of Normandy, the father of William the Conqueror. As Simeon arrived at Rouen just after Robert's accession, the future conqueror of England was at that time probably an infant of twelve months. . . .

In an amazing way the cult of this saint swept through Europe. Returning crusaders brought it back with them from the East; Latin versions of her life began to appear; a new flood of pilgrimage was directed towards Sinai, where the monks were obliged to ring down the relics from the top of Mount Sinai and inter them in a chest in the church, where they remain to this day.

A Building With History, 1865

E.H. Palmer

The Convent of Mount Sinai, according to popular tradition, owes its origin to the Byzantine Emperor Justinian, who fortified and endowed the little church, built by Helena, the mother of Constantine, "on the spot where God spake with Moses". It was at first dedicated to the Transfiguration, until the removal thither of the relics of St Katherine gave that lady a share in the patronage; and it has since then been generally called the Convent of St Katherine. . . .

It is an ancient castellated building, the eastern side, which faces the valley, presenting a flat wall composed of large blocks of hewn granite, partly original masonry and partly restored. About thirty feet from the ground is a small wicket covered with a penthouse, like those seen in English mills; through this travellers were formerly drawn up into the Convent, though they are now admitted by a side door.

A little farther to the south is a buttress tower built by General Kleber, the commander of the French troops during their occupation of Egypt. A white tablet let into the wall commemorates the restoration of the building by that officer. In the angles which this buttress forms with the wall are some small niches chiselled out in the stones, and these contain rude pans of incense placed there by the Arabs, who venerate the Prophet Khidhr (or Elias) at this spot.

On the north side is a large door, now blocked up, called Bab er Rais, or the Abbot's gate. By it the bishops used to enter, and from it a distribution of clothes and food to every member of the Jibaliyeh tribe was made on his arrival. It is now finally closed, but the practice of distributing alms, on the appointment of a new superior or the arrival of an archbishop, is still kept up.

The Mountain of Moyses, 1322

Sir John Mandeville

From that abbey men go up the mountain of Moyses, by many degrees: and there men find first a church of our Lady, where that she met the monks . . . and more high upon that mountain is the chapel of Hekye the prophet. And that place they clep Oreb, where of Holy Writ speaketh, *And he went in strength of that Meat, unto the Hill of God, Oreb.* And there nigh is the Vine that Saint John the Evangelist planted, that men clep raisins. And a little above is the chapel of Moyses, and the rock where Moyses flew to, for dread, when he saw our Lord face to face. And in that rock is printed the form of his body; for he smote so strongly and so hard himself in that rock that all his body was dolven within, through the miracle of God.

And there in the cave beside is the place where our Lord took to Moyses the ten commandments of the law. And there is the cave under the rock, where Moyses dwelt, when he fasted forty days and forty nights. And from that mountain men pass a great valley, for to go to another mountain, where Saint Kateryne was buried of the angels of our Lord. And in that valley is a church of forty martyrs: and there sing the monks of the abbey often time. And that valley is right cold.

Moses before the Exodus, 1846

Harriet Martineau

In travelling from the Nile to Mount Sinai, the chief interest is in following the track of the Israelites; and the person one thinks of most is Moses.

In the island of Roda [in Cairo] we had seen the spot where, according to tradition, his bulrush cradle was found. At Memphis, we had seen the place of his abode; and at Heliopolis, that of his education. According to a Mohammedan tradition, he was a learned priest of Heliopolis. . . . At all events, the early part of his life, up to mature manhood, was passed in ease and in the leisure of learned pursuits, in the neighbourhood with which we are now familiar, and whose natural features were deeply impressed upon our minds by our grateful and admiring interest in his history. Its natural features (from which it is impossible now to exclude the Pyramids) were, however, all we had. . . . But we were now going into the region where his purposes were born, reared and accomplished.

We were to see objects which he saw, and as he saw them; - the scene unchanged, and the people the same, (one may say) that he met; - the same races, living in the same manner, and presenting the same aspect. For some weeks to come, we might look about us with his eyes, and become able, day by day to enter more into his mind.

Travelers' observations of inhabitants and inhabitants' observations of travelers naturally refute each other.

The People, 1920

Lina Eckenstein

Some of the pilgrims supply information on the Saracens or Bedawyn, who all through showed an independent spirit. During the whole of the Mameluk dynasty (1250–1517), they were complete masters of Suez. William de Baldensi, calling them Ridelbim, stated that they lived on their camels and goats, neither sowing nor reaping, and eating such bread as they procured in Syria and Egypt. They were brown, fleet-footed, and carried a shield and a spear, rode on camels, wrapped themselves in linen, and acknowledged the authority of the Sultan, who, however, gave them presents since they could easily expel him and occupy Syria and Egypt. . . .

The attitude of these Bedawyn in matters of religion was perplexing to the Europeans, who began with looking upon Mohammad the Prophet as the incarnation of all wickedness, and then realised that his followers had a standard of dignity and hospitality which were by no means despicable. Ludolf, in 1341, noted that the Saracens did homage to St Katherine and Frescobaldo remarked that the Saracens held the mountains of Sinai in veneration. "And be it known," he continued, "that the Saracens reverence Virgin Mary, St John the Baptist, St Katherine, and all the patriarchs of the Old Testament, and hold that Christ was the great prophet previous to Mohammad; also that Christ was not born of the flesh, but that the Divine Father, through the lips of an angel, sent the Divine Word, and that in many ways they approximate our faith."

The People of the Land, 1935

G.W. Murray

The Towara (sing. Turi), or 'Arabs of Tor', that is to say all the tribes living in the true Sinai Peninsula, south of the Jebel et-Tih, are a confederation of tribes, perhaps seven hundred and fifty tents strong, united not by blood relationship, but merely by community of interest. Confined within an alpine labyrinth of jagged peaks and tortuous ravines, these mountaineers have lost, or perhaps, never gained the franker traits of the wanderers over the steppes. They may fairly be called shy, shifty and suspicious—especially of one another. He who will not trust others is seldom worthy of trust himself, yet in days gone by when I found it necessary to have considerable sums in gold brought long journeys, often by a single Bedouin, to pay the monthly hire of the caravan, there was never a piece lacking. In their continual wrangles about money, they lay hands on their swords and scream at one another like fox-terriers, but self-control is never really lost. Blows are not struck, nor is gross personal abuse exchanged.

Also the presence within their borders of a monastery which distributes free bread twice daily, and the tradition of centuries of extortion practised on pilgrims, have demoralized them from stalwart thieves to shameless beggars. The modern traveller to St Catherine realises this whenever his car halts at Wady Feiran. Yet there is a sort of Irish charm about the Towara that endears them to everyone, who has known them well. In spite of what I have written above, I like the Towara. Perhaps Lupus the soldier, came to repent of the hasty judgement he scratched on the sandstone of Wadi Mukattab.* I hope he did.

Making a Living, 1860

William Beamont

After passing the cemetery, we met a dozen Arabs on their way to Cairo with charcoal, their only merchandise, and on which they pay a tribute to the Viceroy in kind. To make it the Bedouins burn seyal, a kind of acacia, and the shittah or shittim tree of Scripture, which is found in some of these wadys. The Suez railway, which has already begun to affect this trade, will ultimately destroy it; and although, while the transition is going on, the people will suffer some hardship, it is to be hoped that in the end civilization will be advanced and their comforts increased. . . .

This morning the aromatic sheah, which is possibly the thyme wood of Scripture, filled the air for a great distance with its perfume, making the sandy waste like the waste of water's in the poet's simile. . . .

The charcoal burners resort to the wady of Barak for the sake of its large seyal trees; and as they never plant a tree in the place of any they cut down, their trade, even if it escaped destruction from the railway, must cease in time for want of raw material.

A Harsh Life, 1882

Sir Flinders Petrie

On March 20th we went on and rejoined our old route in the Wady Shebeikeh, reaching Wady Gharandel that night. The *retem* bushes were in full flower, covered with small white blossoms; the plant is a white bloom and very bitter. The various protections of vegetation from the hunger of animals in this wilderness are notable. The *retem* has become so bitter that camels will not eat it, and I only saw it attacked by groups of kids, standing on end around it and eating the flowering branches. The more general defence is thorns, and the acacia, or *seyyal*, grows thorns like spike-nails, which might be thought to defy attack. But the camel has grown a mouth to correspond, and browses placidly on the thorns without hindrance. Indeed, our fire of dead thorn-bushes needed to be protected, and we had to drive away a camel who walked up to the smouldering heap and dragged off the dry branches to eat them.

* "An evil race! I, Lupus, a soldier wrote this with my hand." (Greek inscription in Wadi Mukkatab)

We pity the dullness of a people without art or literature; for such as their race may have, they have not the knowledge to enjoy. But conversation is their pleasure and constant delight. The steady stream of words which I have heard pouring out hour after hour from a group of Bedawyn, the excitement, the passion, the layer over layer, two or three deep going on at once, is an artistic activity of which we have but a faint reflection left in our lives. It is the same with most nomads, whether the wilds be in Asia, Africa or America; the use of rhetoric and oratory is one of their greatest powers and pleasures. This is their fine art, this is their literature, this is their politics. And a dreary and clumsy thing the printed page must be when thrust upon such people, who scarcely need it, as their memories have not been atrophied by its use. Even still the spoken word is more effective than the printed, to all lower types of intelligence among ourselves. They have not learned to distrust its fallacies of feeling, of inattention, and of artifice, nor to prefer a diagram of argument to a flow of heart.

In his family, also, the Bedawy has his advantages. He does not denaturalise his children by putting them into a distant cramming machine (the boarding schools of Britain), and finding them nuisances in the few weeks he ever sees them. The girl or boy takes charge of the family herds, guides and cares for them, and knows them closely. Without fear they spend their days in the remotest places. Once I nearly stumbled over a little goat-herd of perhaps ten years old, sitting high up on the desert, almost indistinguishable from the stones around. He never moved, and would not condescend to notice me except with his eyes. The children grow up in all the work of the family—quiet, dignified, reserved, occupied with what their age can do. The close and integral family affection which this joint life produces is certainly a large part of an Oriental's happiness.

The Arab and the Modern World, 1931

C.S. Jarvis

To the Arab, civilization is hateful because it means he must live in a house and is not free to wander at his will; it necessitates also adherence to a time-table and, except for the question of prayers, there is no such thing as time to a Bedouin, and even in his devotions he is fairly lax; and last but not least he might become so soft and dependent that he could not set forth on a month's journey in the clothes he stands up in and nothing else. The average Bedouin, if the occasion arises, will cheerfully start on a journey across the desert without carrying even water or food, a change of clothing, or notifying his relatives of his departure. He does not even trouble to fill his tobacco pouch; he hopes he will meet people by the wayside who will provide him with his wants, and if they do not materialize, going without water or food for a day or two will not worry him unduly. When a race has perfected absolute freedom in this fashion one can more or less understand the mentality that causes them to struggle against all temptation to fetter it in any way.

We ourselves have been so hopelessly tied up by the bonds of civilization from birth that this type of freedom is beyond our ken and moreover would not attract us if it meant going without our daily bath and only eating a meal when some passing wayfarer provided the food. Nevertheless, I have felt sometimes a sneaking longing to be as free as an Arab and to be able to "walk out" on the bonds of our rather intricate existence.

One may ask a passing Arab if he has seen a certain man of a certain tribe and he will answer at once that the individual in question passed that way eight months ago with two camels, three goats and his *sitt* (wife). He may not have seen the man himself, but he has heard the news round the camp fire and made a note of it in his subconscious mind. If by any chance, however, the man about whom one is inquiring should happen to be a malefactor or wanted by the police for some misdemeanour it is a quite different state of affairs—not a soul has seen him or even heard of him, and in fact one feels that to suggest such a thing is lacking in taste and decent feeling. I do not know whether this is a wish to protect a brother-Arab, or an instinctive desire not to be mixed up in anything of police-court nature for fear of repercussions. I rather suspect the latter reason.

Pilgrims began to come into this bleak and uninviting land less than four centuries after the death of Christ.

The Route Thither and the People Who Followed It 1, 1878

Philip Schaff

A dragoman, a waiter, a cook, sixteen Bedoween and sixteen camels loaded with baggage, chicken and turkey coops, water-barrels, tents, bedding, all sorts of provisions, and a cooking apparatus, form the caravan of four passengers. The journey lasts thirty days from Suez to Gaza or Hebron, via Sinai and Nakhl and costs each passenger a little over two pounds ($10 a day). Some go only to Mount Sinai and back again to Suez, which takes three weeks. Others take the route to Akaba, Petra, and the Dead Sea, which is more interesting, but requires from forty to forty-five days, and an extra *bakshish* of ten pounds per person for permission of the Bedaween to pass through Petra. We could not make this route because of war among the Bedaween tribes, and thus missed the pleasure of seeing the Gulf of Akaba, the wonderful rock-hewn city of Petra and ascending Mount Hor where Aaron died.

Let me first make you acquainted with our company. It consists of two American clergymen, and two English laymen. The former are unarmed, the latter carry pistols. One of the Americans is a teetotaller, a vegetarian, and enthusiastic botanist, always in pursuit of rare plants; and although he touches no wine, no meat, no butter, he keeps well and never complains of his diet. One of the Englishmen, formerly an officer of the Royal Engineers, is silent and somewhat absent-minded, but well posted in geography and geology, kind, courteous and amiable. The other Englishman, who is hardly out of his teens, takes special delight in natural history, and would like above all things to see a live hyena and jackal. He keeps the Bedaween bush hunting and bottling snakes, scorpions, chameleons, and lizards, which he generously intended to present to the museum of his native town; but unfortunately his camel broke the bottles after carrying them safely to the gates of Gaza. He barely saved the horns of an ibex which the Bedaween shot on Mount Sinai. Upon the whole, the company is congenial, and gets along without a family quarrel, which is so apt to break up in a miscellaneous party of travellers to the East.

The Route Thither and the People Who Followed It 2, 1937

Joan Plowden

We were now well launched on the immemorial track travelled by all those who from the dawn of history have found their way into southern Sinai. It is a well-documented route, and from the records that have come down to us we can picture in considerable detail the daily routine no less than the adventures of the widely differing classes of wayfarers. Earliest of all were the ancient Egyptians, who sent expeditions both by land and sea to mine for copper and turquoise. If tradition speaks truly, the most famous migrants of history, the fleeing Israelites, moved southward into the wilderness this way, and the scenes they saw and the landscape through which they toiled have changed no whit from that day to this.

Then in the Christian era began a small and steady influx of hermits and holy men from Egypt; they came by twos and threes, meekly and on foot, and they came to remain, yet one can hardly call them settlers, for with few exceptions they were content to inhabit holes like the coneys their prototypes: to live humbly and to die as inconspicuously. One little cluster of hermits aspired to a fuller communal life and so formed the nucleus of the Convent.

This brings us to the next large class of travellers . . . the pilgrims who in the Middle Ages journeyed from all parts of Christendom to Mount Sinai. At Suez they paused to overhaul stores and equipment before embarking upon the more perilous section of their peregrination; horses and mules were exchanged for camels and the narratives become especially interesting because the usages of camel-travelling differ hardly at all from one century to the next, so that the pilgrims' quaint and vivid descriptions are for the most part equally applicable to the same form of journeying today.

After the pilgrims came the explorers and students, the archaeologists and surveyors of the nineteenth century, a very few of whom pressed on beyond the Convent to the lesser known eastern seaboard. Prominent among these early explorers were Koller, Ruppell, Seetzen, Burckhardt, Laborde, and Lord Lindsay; and somewhat later Ritter and Dr. Robinson.

Finally among travellers must be mentioned what we might call the residual category of persons who enter Sinai with individual motives unconnected with the Convent—the ibex hunter, the manna enthusiast, the stray prospector, and the police seeking for fugitives and smugglers.

No Pleasure Trip, 1878

Philip Schaff

A journey through the wilderness is no pleasure trip. It costs more for discomforts than we pay for comforts in civilized lands. The romance of camp-life among the wild Bedawin lies in anticipation and reminiscences, rather than actual experience. The intense heat, the vile insects, the growling of camels, the barbarous habits of the Arabs, the occasional sand-storms, and the many inevitable inconveniences take away the rainbow colour from the poetry. The journey is a weariness of the flesh from beginning to end, and ought not to be attempted except by persons of vigorous constitution.

And yet it impresses itself more deeply on the memory than most parts of an Eastern journey. It is instructive to the geologist, the botanist, the archaeologist, and the Biblical student. It is a great satisfaction to pass over the route of the Israelites on their way to the land of promise, and to ascend the mount from which God made his greatest revelation before the coming of Christ. It brings the early Bible history nearer and makes it clearer. It imparts life and reality to the books of Exodus, Leviticus, Numbers, and Deuteronomy. . . .

I Could Go On a Journey, 4th century

Ammonius

It occurred to me as I sat in my little cell near Alexandria . . . that I could go on a journey and thus escape the persecutions of the faithful. . . . I was, moreover fired by the desire to see memorable places, including the Holy Sepulchre, the place of the Resurrection, and others that were associated with our Lord Jesus Christ. After worshipping at these places, I decided to seek the holy mountain called Sinai, going the desert journey together with others who were bent on the same purpose, and I journeyed thither (from Jerusalem) with the help of God in eighteen days. And when I had prayed I remained with the holy fathers in order to visit their several cells to the profit of my soul.

3
Preparations for the Journey

Neither pilgrim nor traveler set off into the wilderness of Sinai without careful preparation. Once one left the doubtful comforts of Suez, there was little chance to add to one's provisions. The first necessity was a pass, without which travelers and pilgrims could be turned back at the very door of the Convent of St. Catherine. This pass was obtained from the Monastery of the Archbishop in Cairo and continued to be required for travelers well into the twentieth century. Having acquired this document, one had to negotiate with a local who could speak on your behalf with the Bedouins of the desert. Bedouins wishing to undertake this mission waited in Cairo for the next set of travelers visiting their lands. With the advice of their guide, they packed bedding, food, supplies, medicines, water, and headcoverings. Everyone took their Bible and many found that it became ever more meaningful as they traveled slowly through the bleak landscape.

Obtaining Permission, 1843

George Fisk

It is needful that all travellers intending to make a sojourn in the convent of Santa Katerina at Mount Sinai, should take with them a letter of introduction from the superior of the Greek convent at Cairo. For the purpose of obtaining such a credential, we resolved on paying a personal visit to the worthy superior. Having arrived at the outer gate, we found several brethren seated on a dewan, within, dressed in the graceful costume of their order, and with fine flowing beards, and hair streaming over their shoulders. They performed the office of porters, or janitors. They received us respectfully; and when Hassenein (their dragoman) informed them of the purport of our visit, we were immediately admitted; and one of them led the way through several passages or corridors, in which were sundry other brethren variously occupied, till at length he ushered us into the chamber of audience, at the further part of which was a raised dewan, and at the right hand corner of it, on the floor, a separate set of cushions and carpets—with a low table and writing materials near at hand. The apartment was delightfully cool; and its whitewashed walls were decorated with curious old and rudely executed pictures of scripture subjects, and crucifixes. One of the pictures, and apparently the most ancient, was intended to represent Mount Sinai, Horeb, and the Convent of Santa Katerina, in which every rule of perspective was most amusingly set at nought.

We had but little time for observation, ere the superior made his appearance; and, after receiving us with every token of respectful attention, bade us seat ourselves on the dewan, and took his own place on the low cushions beside the writing table; while near him, sat one of the brethren, a fine, intelligent looking, white bearded old man of about sixty, as Arabic interpreter. The superior was a younger man, and of a very kind and prepossessing countenance.

Our dragoman was desired to step up upon the dewan, and to open the conference. He informed the superior that we were two English gentlemen, making a pilgrimage to Jerusalem, by way of Mount Sinai and Akabah, and desiring to share the hospitality of the brethren of Santa Katarina. The superior courteously replied, that he should be gratified in giving us a letter of recommendation; inquired our names, which he took down in writing, and promised that the letter should be ready for us on the morrow.

A lay brother then entered the room, bearing a salver, on which were presented to us preserved cherries, spring water, and arakee—a pleasant spirit distilled from dates, of which we partook; and having conversed briefly about England and English travellers, the aged brother, who sat near the superior, handed us delicious coffee. When we had finished it, he rose again from his seat to receive the empty cups, with great humility of manner. I presume this is one of the usual formalities of their hospitality. It was altogether a simple and primitive scene. There we were—two English clergymen, in the midst of Grand Cairo—strangers—yet received with all hospitality by those simple monks, as if we had been known to them from our youth. I could not but think of the words—"I was a stranger, and ye took me in." We soon afterwards rose to depart, expressing in the best way we were able, our sense of obligation for the kindness we had experienced. The superior and brethren cordially bade us farewell and a "bon voyage".

Booking 1, 1816

John Lewis Burckhardt

The Arabs of Mount Sinai usually alight at Cairo in the quarter called El Djemelye, where some of them are almost constantly to be found. Having gone thither, I met with the same Bedouin with whom I had come last year from Tor to Cairo; I hired two camels from him for myself and my servant, and laid in provisions for about six weeks consumption. We left Cairo on the evening of the 20th of April, and slept that night among the ruined tombs of the village called Kayt Beg a mile from the city (the tombs of the caliphs). From this village, at which the Bedouins usually alight, the caravans for Suez often depart; it also the resort of smugglers from Suez and Syria.

The Bedouins of Sinai, or, as they are more usually denominated, the Towara, or Bedouins of Tor, formerly enjoyed the exclusive privilege of transporting goods, provisions and passengers, from Cairo to Suez, and the route was entirely under their protection. Since the increased power of the Pasha of Egypt, it has been thrown open to camel-drivers of all descriptions, Egyptian peasants, as well as Syrian and Arabian Bedouins; and as the Egyptian camels are much stronger, for a short journey, than those of the desert, the Bedouins of Mount Sinai have lost the greater part of their custom, and the transport trade in this route is now almost wholly in the hand of the Egyptian carriers. The hire of a strong camel from Cairo to Suez, was at this time about six or eight Patacks, from one and a half to two Spanish dollars.

Isabella Bird was traveling from the Far East to Cairo up the Red Sea and through the Suez Canal. At Suez she took the advice of* Murray's Handbook *and made arrangements for her pilgrimage to Sinai.

Booking 2, 1878

Isabella Bird

On my first visit to Suez I had ascertained that the journey to Sinai and back might be accomplished by a lady alone without any real risk; and the Director of the P. and O. hotel, and Mr Andrews, the P and O* superintendent, had so kindly furthered my wishes that when I returned I found that Sheyk Barak, four camels, four Bedouin Arabs, and one Arab servant for myself were already engaged, and that I

* P and O or P & O stood for Pacific and Orient Steamship Company, the shipping company which carried passengers between Britain and India by way of the Overland Route through Egypt and later through the Suez Canal.

was to start on the following evening. My reason for taking a servant only and not a dragoman (professional guide-interpreter) was that I preferred freedom both as to my equipments and manner of proceeding en route, and Hassan, the servant, besides knowing very little English, was quiet and fairly trustworthy.

The advice given in 1906 by the Baedeker guide could have been useful for any traveler in the previous centuries. Only when cars began to be used for the journey to Sinai did the advice need to change.

Advice, 1906

Baedeker's *Palestine and Syria*

This expedition is usually undertaken from Suez and takes at least 15–17 days, including those spent at the monastery. The traveller should procure through his consul a letter of introduction from the monastery of the Sinaites at Cairo to those of the Monastery of St Catherine. All the preliminaries of the journey must be arranged at Cairo. The first thing to be done is to enter into relations with a trustworthy tourist-agency or to engage a good Dragoman, who provides camels, tents and provisions. . . .

A written Contract is exceedingly desirable and this should be signed at the consulate. Express stipulations should be made for an adequate supply of water, both for drinking and for washing. With regard to personal equipment . . . strong shoes are necessary, as the rocks are very sharp and angular. Warm rugs should be taken to fold over the saddle and to be used at night. Arabian saddle-bags are very convenient for carrying the requirements of the toilet, books, and other articles. The traveller should have his own drinking-cup and water-bottle, which latter can be filled from time to time from the small cask in which the general supply of water is carried. No one should attempt to make the trip without a Dragoman and tents, unless he is experienced in Oriental travelling and is master of the Arabic language.

Along with the dragoman, a guide to the Peninsula was a necessity.

Our *Ghafir* or Guard, 1762

Carsten Niebuhr

Any person, whether Christian or Mahometan, who travels either by sea or land along the coast of Arabia Petraea, chooses a *Ghafir*, a guide, or protector, to whom he makes presents, either from time to time, or at least upon his safe return. He thus travels secure and unmolested. If the vessel in which he sails happens to be shipwrecked, it is plundered by the Arabs; but his *Ghafir*, if present, saves his goods from pillage. If the person who he names as his *Ghafir*, be absent, his property is, however, set apart. But if he have no *Ghafir*, or names a fictitious one, he is plundered, without regard to his rank or character. The Turkish merchants, from avarice, to spare a trifling present, or from pride, to avoid associating with an Arab Schiech, seldom take *Ghafirs*, but they suffer for the neglect. For these rights of hospitality and friendship are held sacred among those Arabs.

We therefore took with us three Schiechs, to guide us to Mount Sinai. They supplied us with camels for us and our servants. To prevent disputes, we had our contract written out by the Cadi of Suez, in the presence of the Governor.

Sheich Hussein, 1839

John Kinnear

Sheich Hussein is a fine-looking old man, and very courteous in his manners. He was once renowned as a warrior and a hunter; and although time has grizzled his beard, and tamed a little his fiery spirit, his eye has lost none of its brightness; and there is an independent bearing about him which shows that he is still able, if need were, to lead his tribe to battle among the fastness of his native Desert.*

A few travelers, including Isabella Bird, went alone with their guides; some travelers went in pairs or groups. Harriet Martineau in 1846, though traveling with three friends, joined a large group. William Turner traveled with a stranger.

Companions 1, 1815

William Turner

My only companion, besides my servant George (who was well pleased to perform so meritorious a pilgrimage, free of expense) was a Greek tailor from Adrianople, who had come to Egypt, solely to make this pilgrimage, and meant to indemnify himself for the expense of the journey by selling in Cairo.

Mary Dobson traveled in the party of Rendell Harris, which included sixteen people in addition to servants and guides. She described them all.

Companions 2, 1912

Mary Dobson

Miss Morton had the capacity for riding a camel gracefully, an achievement which one seldom sees in a woman, save in imaginary pictures of Rebekah meeting Isaac.

* Kinnear was travelling with the Scottish artist David Roberts and one may assume that it is Sheick Hussein who appears in Roberts' pictorial record of their journey.

Mrs Chamberlain of Toledo, Ohio, USA, and Miss Cutler of New York, were both connected with the Young Women's Christian Association. Miss Cutler had specialised in Old Testament exegesis, and was also a good Greek scholar. Both were keen on studying every possible aspect of the Israelitish wanderings for the sake of their work. Mrs Chamberlain's cheerfulness kept the Camp alive.

Miss Mabel Western was the VAD [nurse] of the party, who washed for us, sewed for us, fetched hot water for us, as well as doing many other things, until we felt ashamed of letting her do so much, but she gloried in her office, which finally included helping to photograph, on a private camera in the Library, a long manuscript that some of us wanted.

Miss Edna Emerson had spent twelve years as a missionary in Arabic-speaking countries, and was therefore invaluable in haranguing camel men, and reading manuscripts in the Library which were often inclined to be ineligible.

We represented many different schools of thought; and came from different quarters of the globe; and we were happy all together, and there was never a touch of bitterness in our lengthy discussions.

What to take on this journey into the harsh wilderness was a study in itself. Other travelers would pass on advice, either by word-of-mouth or through their accounts of the journey. Later guidebooks included lists of what was required. Some travelers took the minimum and lived as simply as possible, others were accustomed to comfort. Some people took a small pile of luggage, others took a mountain of belongings. The Bedouin profited from this extravagance since the camels to carry these loads had to be hired from them.

Preparations 1, 1547

Pierre Belon

Their provisions were water of Nilus, a camel's load of Bisket, and many muttons killed, and the flesh shred (the bones being taken out) into small gobbits, and boiled with Onions and Suet till all the liquor was consumed, then seasoned with Salt and Spices, and put up in Vessles, which continued so fresh, that 15 days after, being heated with Onions, they seem as fresh as if they had been first dressed.

Preparations 2, 1835

John Lloyd Stephens

Early in the morning I went into the bazaars, and fitted out Paul (his dragoman) and myself with the necessary dresses. Paul was soon equipped with the common Arab dress, the blue cotton shirt, the tarboosh, and Bedouin shoes. A native of Malta, he was very probably of Arab descent in part, and his dark complexion and long black beard would enable him readily to pass for one born under the sun of Egypt.

For myself, I could not look the swarthy Arab of the desert, and the dress of the Turkish houaja or gentleman, with the necessary arms and equipments, was very expensive; so I provided myself with the unpretending and respectable costume of a Cairo merchant: a long red, silk gown with a black abbas of camel hair over it; red tarboosh, with a green-and-yellow-striped handkerchief rolled around it as a turban; white trousers; large red shoes over yellow slippers, blue sash, sword and a pair of large Turkish pistols.

Stephens had safely in his care a letter to the governor of Aqaba assuring him of safe conduct to Petra, though it had been problematical to obtain.

My caravan consisted of eight camels and dromedaries and, as guide and camel-drivers, three young Bedouins from nineteen to twenty-two years old. My tent was the common tent of the Egyptian soldiers, bought at the government factory, easily carried, and as easily pitched; my bedding was a mattress and coverlet; and I had, moreover, a couple of boxes, about eighteen inches high, and the width of my mattress, filled with eatables, which I carried slung over the back of the camel, one upon each side, and at night, by the addition of two pieces of board, converted into a bedstead. My store of provisions consisted of bread, biscuit, rice, macaroni, tea, coffee, dried apricots, oranges, a leg of mutton, and two of the largest skins containing the filtered water of the Nile.

Preparations 3, 1873

Murray's Handbook

It must be remembered that absolutely nothing can be bought after leaving Suez, except sheep, which may sometimes be had from the Bedaween near Sinai. In addition, therefore, to any preserved meats and other things, it is necessary to take stock of five fowls, turkeys and pigeons, for the whole journey. Fresh bread may be baked at Sinai. Good tea will be found a very grateful and refreshing drink after a hot day's ride. One of the best pick-me-ups after a hot and wearying day's ride is a tumbler of tea *a la russe*, with a slice of lemon, some sugar and a spoonful of brandy. Milk can only be procured regularly if there happens to be among the camel one with a newly dropped young one: it is better, therefore, to take some preserved milk—Aylesbury, Lion Brand, is the best . . . [having recommended brandy and water "as the best beverage on the desert journey," but "many people will prefer to take claret."] . . . though, as 3 bottles of claret will hardly go as far as one of brandy, an extra camel will be required for its transport.

A party of 4 should have 2 large tents, one for feeding and sitting in, and one for sleeping in, and one smaller one for the kitchen and servants. Beds (iron that fold up), tables, chairs and all the inside appurtenances of a tent should be examined, and seen to be strong and sound. . . . All water for drinking should be carried in barrels kept strictly locked, and the Arabs never allowed to draw from them. In addition to this, each person should have a small water-skin, called a *semzemeeyah*, to hang at his saddle; these if new should be filled and emptied several times, to get rid of the disagreeable taste that they give to the water. Water for washing may be carried in a goat-skin called *girbeh*; but the following description will show the traveller who does not care about roughing it too much, that he had better not be dependent on the *girbeh*, and the water that is generally to be met with in the Peninsula. "To the traveller in these thirsty limestone deserts, his dependence upon brackish and unpalatable water for his only supply is one of his greatest hardships. To be constantly imbibing a fairly powerful solution of Epsom salt is an amusement one soon grows tired of. We used to try all sorts of plans to disguise the flavour, - lime-juice, brandy, strong tea, or Arab coffee as thick as cream; but neither these, nor boiling, nor filtering, nor anything we could do, were really of much avail. Then again, the system of carrying it in the *girbehs*, or prepared goat-skins, though externally convenient in some respects, does not improve its flavour or the relish with which you drink it. The appearance of a filled girbeh is very much like that of a small black pig which has met with a watery grave; so that, what with the naturally villainous taste of the water, its strong purgative properties, the little extra goatish flavour imparted to it by the *girbeh*, and the notion of the drowned pig, you have to become pretty well hardened before you can be said to enjoy it."

Captain H.S. Palmer

Clothing 1, 1873

Murray's Handbook

A flannel shirt and a suit of tweed of moderate texture, not too thin, forms the best clothing. It is a great mistake to wear very thin clothing, as the direct rays of the sun are felt through it in the daytime, and the evenings are often quite cold. A rug and great coat should be taken: an extra covering is often required at night, and they are useful in adding to the comfort of the seat on the camel.

The head must be well protected from the sun: a pith helmet or white or grey felt hat well wrapped round with a puggery are perhaps the best coverings; but special care should be taken that the nape of the neck is protected. It is a good thing to cut the hair pretty short, and always wear underneath the helmet or hat one of the white cotton caps (*tagheeyeh*) worn by the natives under the tarboosh. A tarboosh itself will be found useful to wear in the tent at night.

Those who intend to do much walking and climbing among the Sinaitic hills must have at least one, if not two, pair of very stout strong boots, as the granite rocks destroy leather in an incredibly short space of time. A loose white *burnous*, or abbayeh, to wear while camel riding, is is a great protection from the heat and dust.

The ordinary Arab saddle-bags will be found very useful for carrying things in daily use. The best portmanteau is a tin travelling bath of moderate size, with an inside that takes out, and a wicker covering: and this arrangement allows the luxury of a bath, when water is to be had, without carrying extra luggage.

Clothing 2, 1839

John Kinnear

We shall all wear the Arab costume, both on account of its superior comfort and convenience, in travelling, and because Sheich Hussein declares that the Frank (foreign) dress is an abomination in the eyes of the Bedaween.

In Wadi-Schilla, Paul Lenoir's companions confronted "the first insects with which we had hitherto been called upon to do battle, and with which one always has to do war in the East unvictoriously, because they are not to be defeated or routed in the end."

Clothing 3, 1842

George Fisk

The experienced traveller in a high temperature, will take care to keep the head thickly covered, so as to be protected against the severity of the vertical sun. Hence, I believe, the adoption of the folds of the turban, as an item of oriental costume. It is the most comfortable thing imaginable. It is desirable to wear flannel, and to have the body well covered, so as to keep up, if possible, a continuous perspiration; for the slow pace of the camel affords but little inducement to that natural process; and the sun, if suffered to act upon the surface, parches the skin, and produces fever. I would clothe myself as thickly for a Desert route, as for a winter journey in Europe.

Preparations 4, 1872

Paul Lenoir

I had foreseen this danger, and in a provident spirit had purchased at Suez one of those little ivory hands with an elastic handle, which are common objects in the chateaux in the south of France. I had been very much laughed at, but when the horrid little wretches swarmed about us, every one was enviously eager to get hold of my hand. If I had put it up to auction, I should have made my fortune; but I preferred letting it out to subscribers, six hours at a time. The subscriptions were paid in pickles, of which I am extravagantly fond. Bank-notes and coin temporarily lost their value, in the desert.

Preparations 5, 1878

Isabella Bird

I took one baggage-camel, a riding-camel for myself, one for my servant (Hassan), and one for the sheikh. I hired a large tent for myself and a small one for Hassan; a mattress, blankets, and cooking utensils were lent to me at the hotel, and as a luxury I took a folding chair. Disregarding the suggestion of Murray's Handbook, I reduced my stores to a minimum, taking only two tins of condensed milk, two of cocoa-and-milk, some raisins, some flour, a pot of raspberry-jam, some rice and some Liebeg's extract of meat, having found by considerable experience that such a diet is amply sufficient for the support of strength while leading an open-air life. A white umbrella, a washing basin, a goat-skin filled with Nile water, a lamp, and a canvas roll containing clothing completed my equipment, and I lacked nothing. My books were a Bible, Murray's Handbook, and 'The Imitation of Christ', and in case of need, I took some brandy and a few simple medicines.

Sheyk Barak signed a contract, arranging for my journey to Sinai and back and my safe conduct, the route only being partially specified. Eighteen days were allowed for the journey, including a halt of four days at Sinai. The contract stipulated for tobacco and coffee for the Bedaween, and the hire of the four camels and the escort came to £16. The whole cost of the expedition, including backsheesh, was £28. . . .

Eight sheiks of the Towarah Arabs have arranged to undertake the escort of travellers in turn, so that the unseemly strifes which used to be the worry of travellers are now at an end, and no journey is safer than the one through the desert.

C.W. Wilson was a member of the team sent to draw up a full and official record of the Sinai Peninsula.

Preparations 6, 1868

C.W. Wilson

Our travelling observatory was simply a provision box, with its sides knocked out and replaced by strips of wood nailed across, the instruments were fixed to a stand, which stood in the centre of the box without touching its sides, and over all thick matting was stretched, to keep off the direct rays of the sun. The barometer always stood in one of our tents.

Servants and Staff, 1762

Carsten Niebuhr

A traveller, although he knows a little of the language, cannot want servants, who must previously have been in those parts that he wants to visit. With such, we were ill provided. Our Swedish servant was as much a stranger as ourselves; we had a

Greek cook who had lived long enough in Cairo, but had never been out of Egypt; an interpreter to assist our physician in his practice, who was a renegado* Greek, and had never travelled before; and a young Jew of Sana, who had before travelled the same road upon which we were entering, but was regarded with sovereign contempt by the Mahometans, on account of the nation to which he belonged. None of these could be of much service to us, in our intercourse with the Arabs.

What to Read?

While Isabella Bird took the Bible, **The Imitation of Christ,** *and* **Murray's Handbook,** *different travelers took different books depending on the purpose of their journey. For early travelers there was only one guidebook—the Old Testament. John Lloyd Stephens in 1835 regretted carrying no guidebooks but like others used the Bible as his guide.*

No Guidebook, 1835

John Lloyd Stephen

In one respect I was very unlucky in this journey. I had no guidebooks. Having formed no definite plan in my wanderings, I never knew with what books to provide myself, and therefore carried none, when I needed them most it was utterly impossible to obtain any; and from the borders of Egypt to the confines of the Holy Land I was in some measure groping in the dark; the Bible was my only guide; and though the best a man could have in his pilgrimage through life, and far better than any other in this particular journey, yet others would have been exceedingly valuable, as illustrating obscure passages in the sacred book; and particularly as referring, besides, to circumstances and traditions other than scriptural, connected with the holy mountain.

Guided by the Bible, 1846

Lord Lindsay

Mr Manuely conducted us to the shore of the Red Sea, and saw us embark for Asia. We crossed in half an hour. I read the sublime description of the Passage of the Israelites, the song of Moses, and the seventy-seventh Psalm, with the scene before my eyes; for it was a little to the south of Suez that they crossed the gulf. It was a strange and thrilling experience to look down on these waters, now so placid, and remember their division—to look up at the azure and spotless sky, and figure to oneself the cloud by day and the pillar of fire by night that guided the chosen race to the Land of Promise.

---

* Renegado means a Muslim convert.

Traveling with the Bible, 1823

Joseph Wolff

In the afternoon at two o'clock, Mr Carne, Mr Clarke, and myself, mounted upon camels, and left Cairo; my servant Franz Six, and the servant of Mr Carne, and six Arabs accompanied us. I took with me Hebrew, Greek and Arabic Bibles and testaments. On our way to Suez, we met with a caravan of Arabs, who rested on the plain of the desert with our camel-drivers; I sat down with the Arabs, and began to talk with them in Arabic, and recited the Psalms and some verses of the Sermon on the Mount (Mathew v).

Reading Burckhardt, 1843

Stephen Olin

None were to be had in Cairo but 'The History of Arabia. Ancient and Modern' in the Edinburgh Cabinet Library. This I found to be worthless. An English gentleman had Mr Stephen's 'Incidents of Travell', which, lively and interesting as they are known to be, deal but little in details. I was indebted to an intelligent Bohemian, a Captain in the Austrian army, for an occasional reference to a German edition of Burckhardt, which he was so obliging as to read into English for my benefit. The Bible, too, was always at hand, and it certainly proved the most useful as well as the most interesting book that can be taken by the traveller upon this route. It was pleasing to see with what avidity it was consulted in questions of history and nomadic customs by those least addicted to its perusal. In the matter of names, however, I was left mostly to my Towarah guides, from whose pronunciation I wrote them as well as I could.

Reading Laborde, 1937

Joan Plowden

I also bethought me to buy an Old Testament, for Laborde had little to say concerning the historical connexions of Sinai with the Exodus of the Israelites from Egypt. Honesty compels me to state that my own knowledge was very hazy. I had no idea to what extent the identification of the Peninsula with the scene of the Biblical history had been scientifically established. I had determined to consult no topographical authority beside Laborde, but since I had no reason to believe that the Israelites' wanderings had led them to el Aqaba, my acquisition was a very modest form of cheating.

Here I was wrong: the Israelites did go to the ancient counterpart of el Aqaba, but they called it Ezion-Geber then. As for the Bible helping me to find a way around the Peninsula my scruples were misconceived, for historians and antiquarians after more than a century of research still disagree upon the route that the Israelites followed.

In the train (from Cairo to Suez) I passed the time in reading and found my childish recollection of a straightforward narrative much at fault. I had forgotten, if I ever knew, that there are three sources for our knowledge of this part of Jewish history—the books of Exodus, Numbers, and Deuteronomy, but they do not relate a consecutive story: some episodes appear twice with variations, others in faulty chronological order; many parts are mutually contradictory, while the geographical references are so fragmentary and puzzling that even as a supplement to Laborde the Old Testament cannot be regarded as a route-book through Sinai.

The Moment of Departure, 1835

Leon de Laborde

A small path, traced on the border of a branch of the canal, leaving on our right a mosque, which was formerly converted into a fortification by the French, and is now entirely abandoned, led us from Cairo towards our encampment. Here each person carefully re-arranged his equipment, just as the voyager settles himself in the berth of a vessel, or the traveller in his carriage between Paris and the first stage where he is to change horses. To us it was of particular importance to look after our provisions, and the other peculiar resources which we required on our journey. The strict necessity of attending to these preparations at the moment of departure serves, more than any other circumstance, to recall the ancient comparison of the camel to a ship, of the desert to the sea, and of such a journey to an adventure on the ocean.

4
From Cairo to Suez

The great majority of travelers after the Middle Ages set out from Cairo across the desert to Suez. The first days from Cairo to Suez were a preparation for the rigours of the journey ahead. The travelers became accustomed to the task of riding a camel and began to appreciate the hardships of the desert.

Setting Out from Cairo, 1845

W.H. Bartlett

At length, everything is ready, the camels blockading the door, and the usual clamour of the Arabs filling the street, I left the hotel to pay one or two farewell visits, and joined my little caravan to the cemetery outside the Bab-en-Nusr, or Gate of Victory, where the splendid domes of the tombs of the Memlook sultans—the perfection of Arabian architecture—rise like an exhalation from the lonely waste. By unusually good management the camels, often reloaded here, were already provided with their respective burdens and I had nothing to do but to start.

It was so much earlier than I had expected to be ready, that no one was found to give me a parting convoy; and I stood in the dead, oppressive heat of noon, alone on the verge of the Desert. The hot film trembled over the far-stretched and apparently boundless sands; and though I had looked forward with delight to the time of setting off, the journey now for the first time seemed formidable; and with not even a friendly shake of the hand, or a parting God-b'w'e—within a stone's throw too of the grave of poor Burckhardt, I could not repress a feeling of melancholy.

But the Arabs cut this short, by suddenly leaping up out of the shade of a ruined tomb, and mechanically bringing forward my dromedary, over whose wooden pack-saddle mattress, carpet, and saddlebags were spread, so as to make a broad and comfortable seat; the growling animal was forced upon its knees; and leaping on, and holding firm by the pegs of the saddle as he suddenly rose up on his hind legs, I achieved (more fortunate than some others) my first ascent without pitching head foremost upon the sands, which I accounted a good omen; the others were ready, and we paced off on our noiseless track over the broad expanse, as a vessel spread its sail and slips quietly out to sea; while the minarets of Cairo grew fainter and fainter, till we lost them in the red and dusky haze of an Egyptian atmosphere.

Like most travelers, Harriet Martineau set off from Cairo. She had already spent some weeks in Egypt and gone up the Nile. With a group of travelers who had been gathered together into a large party, she was now on her way to Sinai, and from there to Petra and Jerusalem.

Cairo from a Camel, 1846

Harriet Martineau

From my high seat, I saw more of the deep, dim, wide interiors of the Cairo dwellings, and of the people at their trades, than I ever did before. This last view of the streets was the best: but there was something mournful in passing for the last time those picturesque alleys, and imposing mosques, and busy bazaars, and the captivating groups of oriental figures of which the eye never tires. We passed out near the citadel, traversed the bazaar or market which was formed outside the gates, and entered upon the sand of the Desert.

We strolled about in the sunset light, bidding many a farewell to Cairo, which stood out clear and bright in the evening glow, - its citadel predominant. The green levels between us and the Nile looked flatter in surface and more vivid in colour than ever. Over westwards were the Pyramids, glorious against the orange sky; and near us the palm grove belonging to Bissateen, and the wells where the women came with their water-pots and cords. Close at hand was our camp, with the Arabs in groups round the fires, and camels lying about as if they wanted to be sketched. We were not sorry now to have stopped for the night within sight of Cairo and the Pyramids.

Donkeys First, 1857

Horatius Bonar

We left Cairo on Saturday about eleven, taking our donkeys for a few miles, lest we should make an exhibition of ourselves in the public street in our first attempts at camel-riding. We then went on board 'the ship of the desert'. The motion of the camel is much less unpleasant than I had expected.

Alexandre Dumas, the French writer, wrote of the way to Sinai, where the route of the hajj and the route through Sinai are linked. Dumas noted the whitened track that extended to the horizon, and observed that the line was marked by bones and skeletons. He asked his guide Bechara for an explanation.

Camels, Dromedaries, and Bones, 1835

Alexandre Dumas

"The dromedary," said he, drawing close to me, "is not an unsteady and braggart animal, like the horse; he journeys without halt, food, or drink; nothing on his part reveals disease, fatigue or exhaustion. (He continued): The Arab, who can hear at a great distance the roar of a lion, the neigh of a horse, or the cry of a man, cannot hear, however close, anything but the respiration of the *haghin*, more or less contracted or panting; but never a complaint or groan. When nature is overcome by suffering, when privations have exhausted strength, when life fails in the organs, the dromedary kneels down, extends his neck over the sand, and closes his eyes.

The rider then knows all is over; he dismounts, and without making an effort to raise the animal, for he knows his honesty, and does not suspect him of fraud or laziness, he takes off the saddle, places it on the back of another dromedary, and sets off, leaving the fallen *haghin* behind. When night comes on the jackals and hyenas come, attracted by the smell, and leave nothing of the poor animal but the skeleton.

We are now on the road from Cairo to Mecca: the caravan passes and repasses this road twice a year; and these bones so numerous and so often renewed, which the winds of the Desert never entirely disperse—these bones, which you may follow without a guide, and which will lead you to the Oasis, the wells and fountains where the Arabs seek for water and shade, and which will eventually lead you to the tomb of the prophet, are the bones of dromedaries that have fallen, never to rise again.

Perhaps on looking closer to these remains, you will recognise among them, from time to time, smaller bones, and of a different structure; these are the bones of worn-out travellers, who have here found a resting-place before they reached the end of their journey; these are the bones of true believers, who, consulting their zeal rather than their strength, have been anxious to obey the precept which commands every Moslem once in his life to perform the holy pilgrimage; and who, having been detained by the pleasures or business of life, have undertaken the journey at too advanced an age. Add to these some stupid Turk, some swollen eunuch, who fell asleep when they might have been awake, and broke their necks by a fall: allow a share for the plague, which often decimates half a caravan, and another share for the simoom, which sometimes sweeps away the rest, and you will easily see how these memorials of death are so frequently repeated, as to trace a new road when the old road is effaced, and to point out to the children the path which their fathers have travelled.

A Joyous Start, 1838

Edward Robinson

Our Arabs as they walked by our side, were full of song and glee, at the idea of being once more free from the city and abroad upon their native wastes. To me also it was a new and exciting feeling, to find ourselves thus alone in the midst of the desert, in the true style of oriental travel; carrying with us our house, our provisions and our supply of water for many days; and surrounded by camels and the wild 'sons of the desert', in a region where the eye could find nought to rest upon but desolation. It was a scene which had often taken possession of my youthful imagination; but which I had not dared to hope would ever be realised. Yet all was now present in reality and the journey which had so long been the object of my desires and aims was actually begun.

The roads of the travelers diverged. Those who traversed Sinai to travel between Egypt and Palestine usually took the northern road from Farma to Arish and Rafah. Others who opted either for Sinai itself or were heading to Mecca took the southern road.

Al-Jifar and Its Capital al-Farma, c. 1000

Al-Muqaddasi

Al-Farma on the shore of the Romean Sea [Mediterranean] is the capital of al-Jifar,* and lies about a *farsakh* from the sea. It is a flourishing populous town, over which stands a fortress, and it has fine markets. The town is situated in a salt marsh, so its water is brackish. The area around it provides hunting grounds for quail, and a source of the most excellent fish. A great variety of contrasting things is to be found here, and an abundance of agricultural products. Here, is the point of junction of well-known and well-travelled roads. However, its water is salty, and the flesh of the birds unhealthy to eat. This entire district of al-Jifar is covered with golden sands, and the towns we have mentioned lie here and there within it. The district is traversed by roads, provides dates, has wells, and at a distance of every six miles there is a mart for supplies. Still, the wind sometimes plays upon the sands, the road is covered, and travel in the area is rendered difficult.

Coming from Gaza, 1835

Alexander Kinglake

For several miles beyond Gaza, the land which had been plentifully watered by the rains of the last week, was covered with rich verdure, and thickly jeweled with meadow flowers, so fresh and fragrant, that I began to grow almost uneasy—to fancy that the very desert was receding before me, and that the long-desired adventure of passing its "burning sands," was to end in a mere ride across a field. But as I advanced, the true character of the country began to display itself, with sufficient clearness to dispel my apprehensions, and before the close of my first day's journey, I had the gratification of finding that I was surrounded on all sides by a tract of real sand, and had nothing at all to complain of, except that there peeped forth at intervals a few isolated blades of grass, and many of those stunted shrubs which are the accustomed food of the camel.

Passing through Sinai, 1326

Ibn Battuta

I stayed only one night in Cairo before setting out for Syria.† This was in the middle of Sha'ban of the year [7]26 [A.D.1326]. I then travelled to the town of Balbais; it is a large town with many fruit gardens, but I did not see there anyone whom I should wish to mention. I came next to al-Salihiyah, after which we entered the sands and halted at the post stations on the way through. At each of these stations there is a hostelry which they call a *khan*, where travellers alight

---

* Al-Jifar was historically used to indicate the entire land of Sinai. Today it is used in reference to North Sinai or the land stretching from Rafah in the east to Arish in the west to Qantara to the south. Al-Farma is still used to indicate the northwestern corner of Sinai.

† 'Syria' at this time implied all the lands of the Levant.

with their beasts, and outside each *khan* is a public watering-place and a shop at which the traveller may buy what he requires for himself and his beast. Amongst these stations is a well-known place called Qatya, where *zakat* is collected from the merchants, there goods are examined, and their baggage most rigorously searched. There are government offices here, with officers, clerks and notaries, and its daily revenue is a thousand gold dinars. No one may pass this place in the direction of Syria without a passport from Egypt, nor into the direction of Egypt without a passport from Syria, as a measure of protection for a person's property and of precaution against spies from Iraq. This road is under guarantee of the Bedouins (this is to say, they have been made responsible for guarding it). At nightfall they smooth down the sand so that no mark is left on it, then the governor comes in the morning and examines the sand. If he finds any attack on it he requires the Arabs to fetch the person who made it, and they set out in pursuit of him and never fail to catch him. They then bring him to the governor, who punishes him as he sees fit.

The governor of Qatya showed me hospitality, treated me honourably, and gave free passage to those who were with me. On his staff was the inspector Abd al-Jalil al-Maghribi, who was familiar with the Maghribis and their lands, and whose duty it was to ask of each of them who arrived from what country he came, so that there might be no doubt as to their identity; for the Maghribis are allowed to pass through Qatya without hindrance.

Travelers who took the southern road often had different reasons for travel and often reviewed their purpose in embarking upon this journey, as did the Spaniard Pero Tafur.

To Suez

A Hard Journey, 1437

Pero Tafur

We departed from Cairo and crossed the lifeless desert of Egypt, with much labour and with great peril. The heat was such that I was amazed that any man could withstand it. These deserts, they say, provide the mummies, which are the bodies of those who die there. For with the great dryness which is in those parts, the bodies do not decay, but the radical moisture is consumed, leaving the bodies entire and dried, so that they can be ground up. There is no road in the desert, for the wind effaces it and shifts the sands from one place to another and makes great hills, and people die there, as I have related. They navigate here with the compass as at sea. There is no habitation between Babylonia (Cairo) and Mount Sinai, and the camels carry everything, as well as the travellers themselves.

The journey to Mount Sinai endured for fifteen days. This mountain is very lofty and stands quite alone, about half a league from the Red Sea. On the summit of this mountain there was formerly a monastery, where the body of St Catherine was kept, and they say that one year, when there was great scarcity of bread, the monks, on that account, and also in view of the great labour in climbing those heights, went to Babylonia, leaving the monastery and the holy body unattended. Thereupon the bless St Catherine appeared to them and told them to return, and that they would find provisions and a convenient place to live in and that where they should find a great heap of wheat, there they should build their monastery and house her body. The monks thereupon returned, and found at the foot of the mountain a great heap of wheat, and there, thanking God and the Virgin St Catherine for the blessing they had received, they erected their monastery which is still a most notable place.

Seeing in the Desert, 1820

Sir Frederick Henniker

The desert from Cairo, were it not for the complements that I ought here to pay to my companions, outhorrids that of the Oasis,* and we arrive at Suez without a single moment of interest, excepting an attempt to distinguish some ostriches—our guides said they saw some. The Arabs, who have not the ophthalmia, are remarkably well-sighted in the desert—they are so used to look on sand and stone that they easily distinguish what is not so.

Here the desert is observed by an artist—traveling with other artists—who describes the scenery with an understanding of color, light, and space.

This Desert, 1872

Paul Lenoir

The desert which divides Cairo from Suez is very extraordinary in appearance, in consequence of the wonderful mobility of the sands which compose it. This white, impalpable dust undergoes the strangest transformations, as it follows the caprice of the wind. Now it is heaped up into mountains, anon into swelling domes, and the next day the same sand will be spread out in a flat, monotonous, immense plain. The journey across it is very difficult to travellers, and even to the dromedaries themselves, who can only progress very slowly, as they constantly sink in the sand up to their knees.

Now the first stage out of Egypt is simplified by the railroad, but if commerce, and travellers who are in a hurry, have gained by the change, the real lovers of the East have lost one of the most interesting points of the desert. The sands, extraordinarily white, are strangely affected by the variations in colouring which take place in the sky, during the different sections of the day.

* Henniker had traveled to the oasis of the Western Desert during his journeying in Egypt.

In the morning they are pink, with violet shades; in the afternoon, after the full light of the sun restores their brilliant whiteness, softened by tones of grey and golden, most exquisitely lovely. In the evening, during the brief twilight, these sands reflect the burning beams of the sun at his setting, like metallic plates; then they are no longer mountains of snow, but mountains of fire. How deeply we regretted that we could not study these different aspects, wedged as we were into a carriage for six persons, while our number was eight.

The sand, perpetually in motion, is displaced with startling rapidity. The least stir of the wind produces the effect of the thawing of snow upon the crests of these moving mountains; the sand tumbles down upon itself, and is a gulf and a crater in one. How many caravans has it not swallowed, and is it not still destined to swallow!

Few travelers to Sinai seem to have crossed the path of the hajj caravan, perhaps traveling at a different time of year. The young diplomat William Turner traveled with the caravan for part of the journey.

Joining the Caravan, 1815

William Turner

Wednesday, July 26th: Overcome by fatigue and heat, I began to despair of ever reaching the caravan, and this weariness is always increased by the false reports of the Arabs who state the distance one has to go as one hour, when there are three or four; having no such thing as watches, they have no means of forming an idea what an hour is, but always measure their distances by days and half days.

At ten we came up with the first part of the caravan, which being behind a sand-hill, we could not see until close to it. It consisted of about 1,000 camels, with a guard of eighty Turkish horsemen. It was a motley crowd of Turkish pilgrims and Arab merchants and peasants generally mounted on a camel with its ordinary saddle, but the Turkish women (of whom there were many among the pilgrims) and many of the richer Turks, rode in small square tents of wood covered with linen of different colours, of which two were thrown across the camel to balance each other, and one or even two persons rode in each. These are called howdahs. This is the easiest mode of conveyance on a camel that Arab ingenuity has invented.

At the head of the caravan was a powerful Turk, a minister of Carasman Oglu, of Anatolia, who was going on the hedge, and I pitched my tent close to him, as the place where I should be most free from disturbance. At the place where we tented were a few trees called in Arabick a Sant tree, a sort of Acacia, with very strong prickles, and many plants of wild melons, which are of a yellowish colour and the size of an ordinary orange, but much heavier. My Arabs told me they were poisonous, and indeed I concluded no less from their being left to grow in such quantities untouched.

The Route, 1843

Stephen Olin

March 5: The road through the Desert is commonly very broad—in the more level and favourable parts, often a quarter of a mile wide. It consists of a great number of parallel tracks, each twelve or eighteen inches in width, formed by the tread of the camel. In very stony places, and in the defiles between hills and mountains, the highway of the caravan is much narrower and the number of paths smaller. It is exclusively a natural road, and the only appearance of its owing anything to human industry is seen in an occasional heap of stones, which seem to have been gathered out of this most ancient thoroughfare. This is a very recent improvement, which has been made by the agents of the East India Company to facilitate the new communication overland with India.

Hardly a Desert, 1852

Charles Didier

One hundred miles of desert separate Cairo from Suez. At one time, the desert was an object of dread, as much on account of its complete lack of water as because of the regularity with which caravans were plundered there by the Bedouin. Now, however, it is very civilised: too much so, I would even say, if it is still to merit the name of a desert.

First, the Draconian government of Muhammad Ali completely purged it of robbers who used to infest it; it became as safe as the road from Paris to Versailles, perhaps safer. In the second place, the Transit Administration responsible for transporting the mails and passengers to India across Egypt established a road, a stage-coach, and a total of fifteen post-houses, all supplied with water drawn from the Nile, which costs dear in those parts. The main houses—nos. 4, 8 and 12—are veritable hostelries: yes, reader, hostelries in the midst of the desert. The transformation will be perfected by the completion of the railway currently under construction: following the one from Alexandria to Cairo already in service, this will link the Red Sea to the Mediterranean, whilst we await the channelling imminently to be accomplished through the Isthmus to call old Egypt to her new destinies.

Over the following days Didier and his companion, Richard Burton (who later left him to go to India) met other travelers along the route.

That day and the following ones, we crossed several caravans from the Hijaz, laden with gum Arabic, tamarinds and slaves being brought for sale in the Cairo bazaars, yoked two by two on the baggage, these unfortunates were all very young and more or less inky black in colour. Originating from the borders of Darfur and Abyssinia, the merchants—called *jallabs*—first ship them to Jiddah via Suwakin and the Red Sea, then take on to Egypt only those that they cannot dispose of at a profit in Arabia.

So as to complete our enumeration of the meetings we had during the day, let us mention the express riders of the Transit Company, who tore up the road at full speed. Changing horses in the twinkling of an eye at every post-house, and never travelling from one to the next save at a gallop, they passed on ahead of us, or met us at the speed of lightning. You had scarcely caught sight of them when you saw them no longer.

The Parting of the Roads, 1836

Alexandre Dumas

I resumed my road over the dry bones. At day-break, the line of skeletons (of camels, fallen on the way) glittered on the yellow sand like a line of silver. As the sun ascended above the horizon, the heat became more scorching and intolerable than it had hitherto been. The Arabs advised us not to leave any portion of our persons exposed to the blaze. Still, in spite of their advice and our precautions, it was impossible to guard against the oblique rays of the morning and evening sun; we received several sun-strokes, which immediately raised blisters: the caleined skin rose like a bell, but at the end of a few hours the swelling subsided. I may venture to assert, that while we were travelling in the Desert, I had regularly a new nose every evening.

After a march of three hours, a white point appeared on the horizon. Soon, as we approached, we saw a square, around which is seemed as if some huge serpent, whose coils the eye could not follow, had been partially unrolled. This town, which is about three leagues from Suez, was the residence of a sheikh. It is here that the caravan to Mecca makes a short pause, to part from the travellers who are merely going to Suez. The pilgrims continue their road towards the east; the travellers turn a little to the south, and soon meet the first branch of the Red Sea, whilst the others have still a march of ten or twelve days before they discover the second branch, along whose eastern coasts they hold their course until they reach the holy city. The seeming coils of an immense serpent round the town, were countless donkey-drivers, who came to procure water for the use of the city; for Suez, being on the verge of the Red Sea, has only saline wells and fountains.

Reverend Stephen Olin observed, "Everything connected with this country and our mode of traveling is so unlike all I have before seen, that each hour offers some interesting subject for observation."

Trade and Slavery, 1843

Stephen Olin

We met several caravans of camels today. They were all loaded with Mocha coffee and frankincense, belonging to the Pacha of Egypt. These articles are cultivated for his benefit in the subject provinces of southern Arabia, and transported to Suez by the Red Sea. Thence they are taken by camel across the desert to Cairo, and down the Nile in boats to Alexandria. Some of the best coffee consumed in Egypt is shipped from this port. The frankincense is chiefly exported to Catholic countries, to be used in their masses. I was reminded of the "company of Ishmaelites" who "came from Gilead with their camels, bearing spicery, and balm, and myrrh, going to carry it down to Egypt." Nothing changes here, and the products of the land and the habits of the people are what they were in the days of the patriarchs. Our style of travelling is the same that prevailed at that distant epoch, and a Nubian boy who had been purchased in Cairo by an Austrian gentleman of our party, and was perched upon a loaded camel on his way to a distant and strange country, made the recollection of the Ishamelites who purchased the young Joseph still more natural and vivid.

I ought to say that the Nubian boy was not bought with a view of keeping him in slavery, since he becomes free, of course, in Austria, but as a sort of fancy article, a curiosity of the country, upon the same principle that Turkish dresses and yellow slippers are taken home by persons curious in such things.

Suez—Ancient Clysma

Clysma, 12th century

Peter the Deacon

Before you reach the holy Mount Sinai you come to the fort of Clysma (Suez) on the Red Sea, the place where the children of Israel crossed the sea dryshod. And the tracks of Pharaoh's chariot are permanently marked across the sand . . . right down to the sea-shore at the point where he entered the sea in his efforts to catch the children of Israel.

Clysma is on the shore by the sea, with an enclosed harbor that makes the sea come right inside the fort. Ships from India could come to no other port but this in the Roman territory.

The Red Sea and Suez, 1722

The Prefetto of Egypt

Soon after we had passed by this place, still continuing on the descent, we discovered the Red-sea. and some ships in port, two of which were then actually departing towards Gidda; and having passed much such another place as Hagirut, called Birel Suess, where there is good water for camels, we came at length safe and sound about three quarters after ten in the morning to Suess [Suez], and leaving the gate of the city upon our right hand, we pitched our tents on the outside of the walls, and on the sea-shore, with the city to the south of us, and the sea to the north-east; and remained under our tents during the heat of the day.

The city of Suess is small and inconsiderable, and its walls half in ruins, with three small turrets or moschs. It is situated at the extremity of the Red-sea . . . in which there were then three ships preparing to set sail by the first opportunity, whose companies at present composed the greatest part of the inhabitants of that city. When they are gone the remainder of the inhabitants return towards Cairo, leaving only one or two persons behind to guard the place; and all this on account of the great scarcity of water and provisions, for nothing will grow thereabouts, and there is no water nearer than six or seven hours journey towards the north-east.

Suez as it Was, 1739

Richard Pococke

Dr. Pococke set out from Cairo,* on the 28th of March, 1739, in company with a large caravan, and on the 31st he arrived at Suez, where probably, in ancient times, there was harbour for shipping, though the sea has withdrawn itself perhaps for ages. However, there are two small bays, about a league from the town, where ships lie in deep water, with a bold shore to the westward; and to the E. low lands and shoals.

In this town there are four mosques, and a Greek church; it is governed by a captain, or admiral, subservient to whom there is an immediate governor; and both of these officers are obliged to be upon very good terms with a powerful Arab, who resides in the town, and in fact engrosses all the power, as being able, when he pleases, to cut off their water, which is brought from a place belonging to him, called Naba, lying on the other side of the Red Sea, at the distance of six miles; that of the well of Suez being not only saltish and unwholesome, but more than a league off.

The only trade which Suez carries on is with Jedda, a port near Mecca, on the E. of the Red Sea. The exports thither are coffee, incense, superfine Persian and Indian commodities; the imports from thence are corn and rice. These are brought by clumsily-built Indian vessels. . . .

The Red Sea at Suez is about a mile over; and boats are continually passing to the opposite shore, to bring over water, wood, etc. for surely never was a spot more barren than that whereon the town stands, it producing neither water, corn, trees, nor verdure of any kind.

Suez in Decay, 1816

John Lewis Burckhardt

April 24th. In the time of Niebuhr (1762) Suez was not enclosed; there is now a

* Pococke's recollections are unusually written in the third person from his journals.

wall on the west and the south-west, which is rapidly falling in decay. The town is in a ruinous state; and neither merchants nor artisans live in it. Its population consists only of about a dozen agents, who receive goods from the ports of the Red Sea, and forward them to correspondents at Cairo, together with some shop-keepers who deal chiefly in provisions. The Pasha keeps a garrison of about fifty horsemen, with an officer who commands the town, the neighbouring Arabs, and the shipping in the harbour. At Suez is one of the few harbours in the Red Sea where ships can be repaired, some vessels are constantly seen at the wharf; the repairs are carried on by Greek shipwrights and smiths, in the service of the Pasha, who are let out to the ship-owners by the commanding officer.

The eastern part of the town of Suez is completely in ruins, but near the shore are some well built Khans, and in the inhabited part of the town are several good private houses. The aspect of Suez is that of an Arabian, and not an Egyptian, town, and even in the barren waste, which surrounds it, it resembles Yembo and Djidda; the same motley crowds are met with in the streets, and the greater part of the shop-keepers are from Arabia and Syria. The air is bad, occasioned by the saline nature of the earth, and the extensive low grounds on the north and north-east sides, which are filled with stagnant waters by the tides. The inhabitants endeavour to counteract the influence of this bad atmosphere by drinking brandy freely; the mortality is not diminished by such a remedy, and fevers of a malignant kind prevail during the spring and summer.

A Gathering Place, 1835

Leon de Laborde

Suez, like all towns situated on the borders of the desert, is a general rendezvous for the remote provinces; the inhabitants of which, without assimilating to each other, meet together in all the originality of their distinctive characters. Thus, the Mograbin of Fez, the Syrian, the native of Djidda, Cosseir, and Souakem, are found here side by side, presenting the most striking contrasts of physiognomy and costume. In one particular, these border towns resemble those Italian cities, which attract strangers by reason of the natural beauties and interesting ruins of their environs. The whole population seems to be composed of guides—of ciceroni, who, before they set out on their return home, await the arrival of travellers going in the same direction. They vie with each other in offering their services upon the lowest terms; and the whole town seems little better than a camp prepared to proceed immediately on the march. The latitude of Arabs, the neighbourhood of the desert, the dangers to be encountered, and the character of the inhabitants, impair, perhaps, the general resemblance, by a somewhat graver appearance than Italy presents; but, allowing for the change of scene to Arabia, if we enter into the interests of the Bedouins, and listen to their conversation in the khans and bazaars, we shall find the details exactly the same.

John Lloyd Stephens, like the young diplomat William Turner, encountered the hajj caravan as he passed through Suez during the same time.

The Mecca Caravan, 1835

John Lloyd Stephens

Early in the morning I went out on the balcony, and looking down into the open square, filled with groups of pilgrims, male and female, sleeping on the bare ground, in all manner of attitudes, I saw directly under me a dead Tartar. He had died during the night, his deathbed a single plank, and he was lying in the sheep-skin dress which he wore when living. Two friends from the frozen regions of the north, companions in his long pilgrimage, were sitting on the ground preparing their morning coffee, and my Arabs were sleeping by his side, unconscious that but a few feet from them, during the stillness of the night, an immortal spirit had been called away. I gazed long and steadfastly upon the face of the dead Tartar, and moralized very solemnly—indeed, painfully—upon the imaginary incidents which my fancy summoned up in connection with his fate. Nor was the possibility of my own death, among strangers in a distant land, the least prominent or least saddening portion of my reverie.

Sand and Pilgrims, 1853

Catherine Tobin

Monday, March 11th.—The hurricane—for I can call it by no milder term—has lasted all to-day; but nevertheless we set off at an early hour, and ought to feel most thankful we were enabled to proceed. For safety's sake we walked until quite tired, dreading to mount our awkward towering steeds; and how even the practised Bedouin kept unerringly the proper track, with clouds of sand and flinty gravel blowing in their faces, covering their dark-brown cloaks in flaky waves, I cannot easily imagine. The air was so entirely obscured by sand, we could not always see the heads of our own camels, and the sunlight scarcely penetrated that dense half stifling atmosphere. The wind, although fearfully high, and sometimes fitful, was fortunately not very cold. With extreme difficulty, and after many fruitless trials, two of our tents were pitched this evening, beneath solid limestone walls of the former station-house, belonging to the "Overland Route" Company. Exactly opposite—half a mile to the northward—stands Khan Djeróod, a noted resting-place of the Mecca pilgrims.

Tuesday, March 12th.—This has been a very lovely day, and particularly acceptable after the annoyances we experienced yesterday. Suez—the ancient *Clysma*—may surely vie with almost any other spot on earth for bare sterility and general unattractiveness. The deep blue waters of the Gulf, that speak to us of bygone centuries—of great Deliverance by a Mighty Hand—and the Arabian coast stretching far south, bounding the "terrible wilderness" beyond, add some degree of beauty to the eastern side of this "uncanny" town, where old association lingers still.

"Go forward" are the words we hear. Though nearly Desert bound, Suez may claim a gradually increasing interest as an active bustling seaport; steamers continually come and go; sailing vessels from all parts of the world—laden with pilgrims, or with coffee and other merchandise—constantly arrive, and take their departure. A very handsome large hotel, the property of the Peninsular and Oriental Company, and facing the sea, appears to merit the high reputation it has acquired of being by far the most comfortable establishment of the kind in Egypt.

The Suez Hotel, 1873

Murray's Handbook

The Suez Hotel is situated on the old landing quay. It is a large house with clean rooms, but the attendance and cuisine are capable of great improvement. One of the rooms is fitted up as a chapel, and in it English service is conducted every Sunday.

Babel, 1881

N.P. Kondokoff

We set off from Suez into a rough sea. Happily, during the night, the wind changed, and next day disembarked at Tor, welcomed by all the male members of the family of the vice consul—a Greek—and all his servants. He conducted us to his home where we were received by the feminine section of the family. Arak, coffee, sweetmeats and laborious conversation followed. The master of the house only spoke Arabic, but we managed to exchange some comments formed of Russian, Greek, Arabic and Turkish phrases—each term provoking a general joyous explosion. . . . There were few European residents in Tor: a German doctor from Munich in charge of quarantine and an Italian inspector. Both suffered from ennui and various maladies of the eyes—like most of the other inhabitants.

Onward from Suez by Land, 1861

William Beamont

Leaving Suez about two o'clock, and proceeding round the head of the gulf by a route which is wearisome from its uniformity, we passed imperceptibly, and without knowing it, from Africa into Asia. To mark the boundary where the one continent ends and the other begins, there is not even such an insignificant trench as that which marked out the limits of ancient Rome, and drew upon Remus, who jumped over it, the fatal resentment of his brother. . . .

Across the desert, a dreary plain, without a plant or any work of man upon it, we toiled slowly on for fifteen miles or more without meeting or seeing any living thing, except a crouching camel without an owner, and the carcasses of some others, which the vultures had picked clean, and the blast of the desert had bleached. While we had still some distance to travel, night came on, a bleak north wind swept over the desert, and we had still to find our Arabs with the sumpter camels.*

The Route of the Exodus? 1838

Edward Robinson

The bearing of the preceding details upon one of the most remarkable events of Biblical History, will be obvious; I mean the exodus of the Israelites and their passage through the Red Sea. I propose to bring together in this place all I have to say on this subject; premising such information as we were able to obtain relative to the Land of Goshen, and the probable route of the Israelites on leaving Egypt.

We were quite satisfied from our own observation, that they could not have passed to the Red Sea from any point near Heliopolis or Cairo in three days, the longest interval which the language of the narrative allows. Both the distance and the want of water on all the routes, are fatal to such an hypothesis. We read, that there were six hundred thousand men of the Israelites above twenty years of age, who left Egypt on foot. There must of course have been as many women above twenty years old; and at least an equal number both of males and females under the same age; besides the "mixed multitude" spoken of, and very much cattle. The whole number therefore probably amounted to two and a half millions, and certainly to not less than two millions. Now the usual day's march of the best appointed armies, both in ancient and modern times, is not estimated higher than fourteen English, or twelve geographical miles; and it cannot be supposed that the Israelites, encumbered with women and children and flocks, would be able to accomplish more. But the distance on all these routes being not less than sixty geographical miles, they could not well have travelled it in any case in less than five days.

The difficulty as to water might indeed have been obviated, so far as the Israelites were concerned, by taking with them a supply from the Nile, like the caravans of modern days. But Pharaoh appears to have followed them upon the same track with all his horses and chariots and horseman; and this could not have taken place upon any of the routes between Cairo and the Red Sea. Horses are indeed often taken across at the present day; but then a supply of water must be provided for them, usually about two water-skins for each horse. Six of these water-skins are a load for a camel; so that for every three horses, there must be a camel-load of water. Still they not unfrequently die; and we saw the carcasses of several which had perished during the recent passage of the Haj. Flocks of sheep and goats might pass across; but for neat cattle this would be impossible, without a like supply of water.

* Sumpter camels: those camels which carried the loads.

5
Routines, Hardships, and Pleasures of the Journey

Over the centuries the travelers and pilgrims followed the routines of the journey to Sinai laid down by their guides, the local Bedouin—men of the desert. The isolation of Mount Sinai and later the Convent were little changed from century to century, and thus the experiences of the travelers—the difficulties, wonders, and gratifications—were also very similar from one age to another.

Sweet Fish and Huge Desert, 384

Egeria

This sea has the name 'Red' not because the water is red or muddy. Indeed it is quite as sparkling clear as the Ocean. Its fish are excellent and unusually sweet, and fish of all types from this sea taste as good as the fish of the Italian Sea (the Mediterranean). You have all the sea-food you could want: there are trumpet-shells and oysters of various kinds, white-shells, and several kinds of large snail. And the different things you find along the shore are bigger and prettier than by any other sea. Also there is a great deal of coral on this shore. The Red Sea is a part of the Ocean.

Shur, the desert where they [the children of Israel] went for three days without water* is of an enormous size. No one has ever seen a bigger desert, and no one could guess the quantities of sand. Between the Desert of Shur and Marah there is one staging-point near the sea, and at Marah itself there are some palm trees (very few), and the two springs which holy Moses made sweet.

Sir Flinders Petrie recognized the unchanging nature of the trials of humanity in the Sinai Peninsula between his time and the time of the pharaohs' mining expeditions nearly five thousand years earlier. He was thus able to calculate how the ancient Egyptians would have had to organize their expeditions. Petrie's estimations were confirmed by the ancient records.

In Ancient Times, 1882

Sir Flinders Petrie

The employment of foreigners by the Egyptians shows that much the same relations existed between Egypt and the desert as we find at present. Three expeditions of Amanemhat III were accompanied by "the brother of the prince of the Retennu, Khabet" . . . On two steles (at Serabit) he is shown riding on a donkey, led by a man in front, and with a driver carrying his water-flask behind. He was doubtless employed to manage the Bedawyn and to serve as a hostage for their good conduct. In just the same way, on a lesser scale, the brother of the sheyk was usually with our party, to ensure good terms with the neighbourhood.

We can now form some general picture of the arrangement of one of these great mining expeditions (to Sinai), having the practical conditions of work and life in this region before us, as a background to the details recorded on the monuments. So soon as the inundation (of the Nile) was over in November or December, stores would be accumulated at the head of the Heropolite Gulf, the officials would arrive, and the organisation would be settled.

To get across the desert the full train of 500 asses would be needed, each carrying its own food and water and supplies for one man for three days, down to Gharandel, and enough food for two days more to the spring of the Wady Nasb, where the main halt would be. Then 300 asses would be sent down the Wady Baba to the coast of Burdeys, to bring up the boat supplies.

The maintenance of the camp would be kept up much on these lines. Each man requiring 3 lb. of supplies and each ass (say) 15 lb. daily, this for 500 men

* Exodus, 15.22.

and 500 asses would be nearly 5 tons a day of food. Such would form 50 ass-loads; and as the round journey from the coast to Serabit and back would take five days (allowing for loading and delays), this would mean that 250 asses would keep up the whole food supply from the coast. Water might be put at 4 gallons per head per day; we actually lived on 1 1/2 gallons each, but a larger allowance is more likely. Thus an ass would carry enough for three men; and so, if a single round to water was made each day, then 200 asses would be required to keep up the water-supply. This leaves 50 out of 500 as a margin for sickness and delays. . . .

The preparation of the record of the expedition, on a great stele of local sandstone, was a special care. It must have been begun early in the time, as it entailed some weeks of work. The chief of the party was the main person commemorated; but all the staff are usually named, and after it was finished and erected, probably after the high officials had left, the lower workmen used to scratch in their names on the blank ends and margins. By the time the hot weather came on, all this body of men were on their way back to Egypt, accompanying the bags full of the precious gifts of the "Mistress of Turquoise".

Our Retinue, 1857

Horatius Bonar

As we moved along I surveyed the whole retinue. There was our dragoman, Haji-Ishmael, mounted on one camel, with my two portmanteaus firmly roped to the side of the animal. He was dressed out for the start, with a goodly flowing robe and a head-dress, whose red and yellow stripes glittered brightly in the sun. On another camel were two large square panniers, of palm-branch wicker-work, filled with oranges and lemons, to the amount of at least 600 of the former and 100 of the latter. On another was our 'canteen', that is two immense wooden chests containing our dining apparatus, such as plates, knives, forks, spoons, cups, not omitting candles and *fenusses*, that is lanterns made of linen, apparently saturated with bees-wax or some such substance, which draw out to more than a foot in length when in actual use, but can be contracted or folded together into a very small space for packing. Above this apparatus was placed our kitchen-grate, a long iron box, pierced with a hundred holes in sides and bottom, - its four legs, like signal posts stretched upwards to the sun. Then came another with an immense wicker-cage, which formed the prison house of some 100 fowls, all alive, but quite willing apparently, to go to the stake for us, - as four of them are to be called to do each day at sunset. Balancing these fowls is another cage, with half-a-dozen turkeys, which we are told to be our 'Sunday dinners'. On another our bedding is mounted, on another our tents, on another our charcoal, on another our barrels of Nile-water, on another sacks containing our camp-stools and table, - our bedsteads, and the pins of our tents.

Most carefully was everything packed up before it mounted the camel. A tribe of wanderers knows how to 'pack', as indeed they have no security for any part of their property in moving about save the good packing. They have bags for their money, and sacks for other things.

Toward the end of the eighteenth century the journey to Suez and beyond could be dangerous and even a large caravan might be attacked. Once Muhammad 'Ali was firmly in the seat as Pasha of Egypt from the early 1800s onward, there were almost no accounts of attacks upon even the least well protected of travelers.

With the Caravan, 1792

Carsten Niebuhr

Our caravan had no very formidable aspect. Being in haste to set out from Cairo, before the great caravan, which goes always to Suez, immediately after the departure of the vessels, we had not more than forty camels which were loaded with corn and materials for building. Three of four camels were employed in carrying an anchor. I have already had occasion to remark, that carriages are unknown in Egypt and Arabia.

We could not have been very formidable to any that might have been disposed to attack us. Our camel-drivers, who were but few, carried broken guns and rusty or pointless sabres. A few Sheiks, indeed, to whom the most of our camels belonged, carried complete armour, and rode upon dromedaries. But we could not trust to them for defence; for no Arab will willingly risk his life to save a Turk. It was our part, therefore, to keep in the middle of the caravan, unless we wished to be plundered. In some places, where the danger was least, my comrade and I ventured to go before the main body of the caravan, to rest and enjoy purer air for a little.

Late nineteenth century travelers carried modern equipment with them—cameras, surveying equipment, and the paraphernalia of modern life.

Our Caravan, 1872

Paul Lenoir

To any spectator perched on the mountain heights, our caravan must have presented a very respectable appearance, for our effective force consisted of twenty-seven dromedaries and camels. Our nine riding camels belonged to the stud of the Viceroy; four camels were told off for water transport; three carried the tents and all their fittings; seven were laden with chopped straw and beans for themselves and their brethren—for, though a camel, having laid in a store of water, can go for a week without drinking, he must have one meal a day regularly, however moderate its quantity may be. One of these interesting animals might well have been astonished at the interest we took in him; he was as well entitled to hold up his head as the famous ass who carried the relics, for more than Caesar and his fortunes had been committed to his capacious back. The privileged creature carried our photographic apparatus, and all its bottles and glasses. What care we took of him when he was going down-hill, and through difficult passages!

Our Guides 1, 1820

Sir Frederick Henniker

Our guides, and probably all the Arabs of the desert, live from hand to mouth.—One of them collected dry shrubs, and clearing a bed in the sand, set fire to them, another had taken a measure of flour from his sack, and adding salt and laban (like buttermilk) was forming a flat cake—the third roasted some coffee-beans in an iron shovel, then put them into a wooden mortar, and hammered them to atoms with his bludgeon.—By the time that the cake was made the shrubs were burnt, the place was swept—the cake placed in the hollow, and the embers collected and thrown on it.—There was no quarrel about the bread being sufficiently baked—it was soon brought forth and devoured. The whole time from creating it till it was no more seen might be about ten minutes—The coffee-pot was next produced, and the ashes were raked together to perform the further office of boiling what they had roasted. During this the camels were hallooed home, and came as fast (the call is a continued sound of the letter R.) as their bandages would allow—every animal knew his master's face, and putting his own to it, dropped upon his knees as if to ask for supper. The Arab is as intimate with his camel as the Irishman is with his pig—he feeds and kisses him. While the camels were eating their allotted portion of barley, their masters seated themselves round the fire-place, the coffee-cup was put into circulation, and the ashes finished their services on the bowls of the pipes. It was now dusk, and a long story was still flowing with unabated vigour.

Our Guides 2, 1846

Harriet Martineau

Our escort were all of Bishara's tribe; and some had faces as prepossessing as Bishara's own. They were all armed—with pistols, or match-locks or short swords. A number of spears, stuck point upwards on camels' backs, glittered in the sun. Some of the Arabs wore sandals of fish skin; some were clothed in sheepskins, the woolly side inwards. All had their heads thickly covered, and where possible, with something white, at last in the middle of the days. For the most part they trudged during the eight or nine hours of our daily travel; but sometimes they rode in turn.

Our Guides 3: The Celebrated Hussein, 1846

Lord Lindsay

[A]nd we found there . . . the celebrated Hussein, who accompanied Laborde to Petra ten years ago. We struck a bargain with him to convey us to Sinai, and have since engaged him to accompany us for the rest of our travels in Arabia. "An excellent warrior and hunter," says Laborde, "and renowned for his generous hospitality, he unites in himself all the qualities which render a Bedouin respectable, especially those of so much importance to the traveller, unimpeachable integrity, discretion which always deserves to be confided in, and, what is very rare, genuine fidelity." He is the principal of the three guardians or protectors of the Convent of Mount Sinai, and is known and respected wherever he goes. Laborde made all his arrangements with the other tribes through him, and so shall we.

Hussein and I have become great friends; many a kind pat on the back have I had from him. Our intimacy commenced with a long walk one morning, while he and I took one road and the caravan went the other; we had a great deal of pleasant and most animated conversation; acting, gesticulating, drawing with my stick in the sand, and the judicious use of the very few Arab words I have perforce picked up, were generally sufficient to make myself understood. We out-walked the camels, and sat and chatted a quarter of an hour or twenty minutes under the shadow of a projecting rock.

Our Guides 4, 1857

Horatius Bonar

Notable among the Arabs is Sheikh Suliman, the Sheikh or chief of one of the Sinaitic tribes, who is our guide and guard. He is a tall erect Arab, beyond the middle age, with a happy face of humour and kindness, which he shows every hour, in every possible way. His voice is shrill and cheerful, his step as light as that of a *Wahash*, but he has one or two front teeth knocked out, which mischance, however, does not give him a sinister aspect, for through the vacancy, the free Arab laugh seems to come all the more heartily. He makes a most companionable conductor, though our intercourse is by signs not words, for he knows even less of English than we do of Arabic.

His underdress is a loose white shirt like a nightgown (*Kaftan*), over which goes a brown, covering or sackcloth cloak of camels hair (*Abyah*). He wears a sort of sandals made of skin, and stretched with thongs; they barely protect the souls of his feet. With these he trudges or skips or scrapes along, according to his fancy, his gun (*baroudeh*) on one side and his sword (*jambeh*) on the other.

Our drivers are like their chief, but each of them has quite a face, air and dress of his own, - one a fine Grecian profile, another a pleasant round-featured Scottish visage, another with a shaggy beard, another without a beard, another soft-looking like a female, another fierce as a bandit, another (my own driver and *valet*) tall and vigorous, with an undressed sheepskin hung over his back, which sometimes forms a target for orange-peel and such like. All of them are kind and obliging.

The Bedaween, 1878

Isabella Bird

I find these Bedaween very inoffensive. Hassan is a city Arab, a tall fine-looking man, with the harassed melancholy look which seems habitual to his race. He dresses well in a white garment, with a coloured silk girdle, over which he wears a burnouse, and his turban is of striped yellow silk. He knows hardly any English but attends me well, and things go very smoothly.

Sheyk Barak is a handsome young man, with truly Ishmaelite features and the look of scorn which these desert rangers wear. He makes a courteous salutation morning and evening, and helps me to mount and dismount; as he strides over the sand with his long elastic stride, his 'loins girded' and his matchlock gun slung behind, he looks a true son of the desert—born to a heritage of freedom.

The other Bedaween are swarthy, lean, wiry men, about the middle height, quiet and well-behaved, as, for instance, they never hang about my tent or stare at me. Each man is dressed in a single girdled cotton garment, which has once been white; a whitish turban, and a pair of hide sandals. These men are so lean that if their arms and the calves of their legs were not muscular one would call them emaciated. They never wash—regarding ablutions as a sinful waste of a scarce gift of Allah—and their shining skins have a whitish scale upon them in consequence. Their persons, their clothing, and their gear swarm with vermin, and their chief occupation during the noonday halt is the solemn search for these. Their goat's-hair sacks which are on my camel contain some of their clothing, and my sufferings from the vermin which seize upon me soon after I have mounted are indescribable. The irritation produces fever. These Arabs, though Mohammaddans, never apparently say any prayers—at all events they do not observe the hours of prayer. They have many conditions concerning places in the desert in connection with the heroes of Hebrew history, and have a great reverence of Moses and Aaron. And these are the children of Abraham!

The People of the Peninsula, 1739

Richard Pococke

The country through which we now passed is called Arabia Petrea; it consists of barren mountains, with narrow valleys intersecting them, and sandy plains. The natural inhabitants are wandering Arabs, who live in tents, and remain upon one spot no longer than their water, fuel and fodder for their camels last; then they remove. They know nothing of tillage, nor is there any grass upon the ground; their wealth consists of camels, goats, and sheep; their food is goats milk, dates, and bread made of corn, furnished to them from a good distance. They travel in clans, each under a particular sheik, and are all leagued in amity together. With respect to property, they are the honestest people in the world; and so long as they have victuals, there is no danger of their doing a traveller an injury; on the contrary, if one of them takes you under his care, it is a sacred protection, and they all think themselves obliged to defend you.

The daily pattern of all travelers was similar—even their meals were often the same.

Desert Mornings, 1816

John Lewis Burckhardt

There is nothing which so much compensates for the miseries of travelling in the Arabian deserts, as the pleasure of enjoying every morning the sublime spectacle of the break of day and of the rising of the sun, which is always accompanied, even in the hottest season, with a refreshing breeze. It was an invariable custom with me, at setting out early in the morning, to walk on foot for a few hours in advance of the caravan; and as enjoyments are comparative, I believe that I derived from this practice greater pleasure than any which the arts of the most luxurious capitals can afford.

Many other travelers took John Lewis Burckhardt's advice and also walked out at the start of the day and described with equal enthusiasm their experience.

Our Days, 1868

Francis Conyngham

Now for our days. We rose generally at 6 a.m; breakfast as soon as possible, and in the open air (although the morning air was sharp); then mounted our camels, which were grazing all round us, roaring at being laden; and away we went until about 12, when we usually stopped until about 1, for an hour or so, to have luncheon, consisting of dates, hard-boiled eggs, oranges, cold fowls, etc., during which time our baggage camels went ahead till about 4 p.m., when the sheik chose some place where there were shrubs growing for the camels to graze on. How delightful it was, after going on hour after hour through those dreary wild valleys, to come on our little encampment, consisting of two tents, and one for cooking, in which old Mahomed, the cook, and Bedair, our dragoman, slept.

The Daily Round, 1860

William Beamont

But I must say a word as to the pitching and striking of our tents and the order of our daily march.

When we reach our camping-ground, which is generally at sunset, we select a spot near to some wady where there are a few stray plants for the camels to browse, and where there is either a little hill or a bank to shelter the tents from the wind. Round this place the camels form, and, kneeling down in a circle, are unloaded, and turned loose to shake themselves and pick up such dry and withered stems as the desert yields. The fowls, released from the hen-coop, enjoy a short liberty, and pick up the handfuls of corn that are thrown to them.

Our tent and our cook's tent are next raised, and placed with their backs to the wind, a work which occupies one hour. To catch the air and keep it cool, our zem zemeen always hangs outside the door. Ours being new, discoloured the water and made it astringent, and being not yet reduced to the straits of Darius, who, flying from Arbela, drank of a muddy pool, and declared it the sweetest water he had ever tasted, I could not drink the water of our zem zemeen.

Our fire is then lighted, and our Bedouins, to whom after their long march mere rest is luxury, group themselves round it. As soon as our tent, with its three truckle-beds and a central table, is ready, we enter it, and in another hour dinner is served.

It takes two long hours to strike the tents and pack the baggage before we are able to start in the morning. When the tents are struck the camels again draw round in a circle to be loaded, for which purpose each animal comes down on his belly. Coming down is not natural to any of us; and the tall camel, who grumbles a little when he comes down, a little more when he is loaded, but most of all when he rises under his load, dislikes it very much. In taking down the tents and loading the camels the Bedouins shout and talk so loud that you would think they are going to quarrel and come to blows, but it all ends in noise. They have not learnt the proverb—He who talks, sows; he who hears, reaps, for they are all talkers and no hearers. When the baggage is all packed we mount and move on, the Bedouins alternately talking and singing all the day through.

Harriet Martineau wrote her journal each day after resting, washing, and dressing for dinner. "One's journal," she found, "is a perpetual irritation and mortification. It is such a mockery! When one's whole soul has been full and glowing for hours among marvellous scenes and new experiences, the only result in one's journal is a couple of pages of record which one wants to tear out as soon as written, in indignation at its poverty."

By this stage of the journey travelers grew confident, feeling familiar with the people they traveled with and met, and appreciative of the places they passed along the way. Yet it was also at this time that some of them faced their greatest challenges.

Square Meals in the Desert, 1846

Harriet Martineau

Abasis gave us excellent dinners—good soup, always; mutton and fowls always; and these Arab cooks discover an astonishing variety of ways of cooking mutton. Then, there was macaroni, and potatoes; and always some nice pudding or fruit pie; excellent cheese; and a desert of oranges and capital figs. Then the chibouques (pipes) were brought, - at once the indispensable comfort and chief luxury of Eastern life; - a comfort of whose importance there is no more conception can be found at home than people of the Guinea coast can appreciate our winter-clothing and fires.

The Health of Desert Life, 1868

Francis Conyngham

No words of mine can do justice to the healthfulness of the Desert air, so soft and balmy. Travellers talk much of the freedom of the Desert—and to an extent this is true—but if one reflects, as we did, how completely we were at the mercy of our guides, and that the smallest Arab boy, with a knowledge of the Desert, was superior to us Europeans, and that without their guidance we should be lost in a few hours, I think one's sense of complete independence dwindles down to a sense of dependence on the Sons of the Desert.

A mishap along the way—just after leaving Wadi Feiran—made Conyngham even more aware of their dependence

A serious calamity befell our cook, who being, as I have said before, more of a sailor than a horseman, came to sad grief by parting company with his camel, and I thought at first his back was broken, as he gave a fearful shriek, and lay senseless on the ground. However, we picked him up and did our best for him, but it was no joke having our cook on the sick list, and our dinners were not so good in consequence. We could not help feeling what an awful fix we should be in if one of us had fallen off and broken a limb, and no doctor to set it. It made me shudder to think that it might happen in one moment to my wife, and no help near.

Alexandre Dumas, drawing on the experiences of others, wrote dramatically of the hardships of desert travel.

Delusions in the Desert, 1836

Alexandre Dumas

The sun continued to ascend the horizon, and at length was so completely over our head that the camels threw no shade; I removed from some distance from our *haghin*, to escape the animal's heavy smell; I then lay down on the sand, and covered myself with Bechara's mantle. At the end of ten minutes, I found that the side exposed to the sun could not endure the heat any longer, and I turned on the other. During the two hours that the halt lasted, I did not sleep for a minute; I only shifted sides under my coverlet. I do not know how my companions fared, I could not see them, and it would have been too great a fatigue to ask them how they got on; all I know is, that under my mantle I suffered the pains of a turtle boiled in his shell.

Finally, the nature of our sufferings changed; it was almost a relief; Mohammed came to tell us that it was time to resume our journey; I arose. The sand on which I had lain was as wet as if a bucket of water had been spilled over it. We remounted our dromedaries like helpless and involuntary criminals, not caring wither we were going, but morally convinced that it was necessary to push forward. I only asked if we should find fresh water in the evening. Araballah, who was next to me, replied that we should spend the night close to a well; I did not inquire further.

The evenings and nights of the journey gave the travelers a welcome period of relaxation. Their tents were pitched where fodder for the camels and water were available. Here was the chance to write up an account of the day—diary entries which later became records of the journey.

The End of the Day 1, 1822

John Carne

We sometimes stopped for an hour at mid-day, or more frequently took some bread and a draught of water on the camel's back; but we were repaid for our fatigues, when we halted for the evening, as the sun was sinking in the desert, and, having taken our supper, strolled amidst the solitudes, or spent the hours in conversation till dark. But the bivouac by night was the most striking. When, arriving fatigued long after dark, the two fires were lighted, I have frequently retired to some distance to gaze at the group of Arabs round theirs; it was so entirely in keeping. They were sipping their coffee and talking with expressive action and infinite vivacity; and as they addressed each other, they often bent over the flame which glanced on their white turbans and drapery and dark countenances, and the camels stood behind and stretched their long necks over their masters. Having finished our repast, we wrapped ourselves in our cloaks, and lay down round the fire: and let not that couch be pitied, for it was delightful, as well as romantic, to sink to rest as you looked on that calm and glorious sky, the stars shining with a brilliancy you have no conception of in our climate.

The End of the Day 2, 1878

Isabella Bird

After this halt (at noon), the baggage-camel and the sheyk start early, so that I may find my tent pitched when I arrive at the camping-ground, and I, with Hassan and my driver, follow. Then come five exhausting hours over the blinding burning sand, and oh! how eagerly I watch the driver's lengthening shadow growing, growing, growing till it slants surely twenty feet across the sand, and then in the distance I see my white tent, and soon the day's toils are done.

The End of the Day 3, 1878

Philip Schaff

Then begins the enjoyable part of the day. We throw ourselves upon the iron bedstead, for it is the only place where we can stretch our limbs and rest our backs. In about half an hour the bell rings for dinner, and it tastes as good as an *table d'hote* in Europe. We get soup, two courses of meat, eggs, potatoes, rice and beans, nuts, and an ever-welcome orange for desert, with a cup of tea. But the bread becomes stale, the water insipid, the orange dry, and the chickens and eggs give out as we approach the end of the journey. After dinner, we fill up our journal, study the map, read the Bible and guide-book, and then go to bed. The Bedawin with the camels lie a few yards from the encampment on the ground around a fire and watch our tents. They smoke and chat and quarrel till all fall asleep under the bright stars.

A Luxurious Camp, 1912

Mary Dobson

Owing to the fact that there had been but little civilian camping far afield during and after the War, the tents, beds, blankets, and other camp requisites were all new, and we, who had expected to sleep upon the ground, found ourselves the possessors of the most comfortable camp beds, with soft and luxurious mattresses.

The tents themselves were most gorgeously decorated within, with the usual kaleidoscopic colours used in Egyptian embroidery of this kind; you woke in the morning feeling as if you were in the heart of some gigantic multi-coloured convolvulus, while the suitable Arabic proverbs that decorated the sides cast a dignity over the commonplace of tent life which are so often inclined to become somewhat sordid. But it is hard to grumble over lost packs, or boots cut to pieces by the rocks when "Praise to God" confronts you amid exquisitely curved arabesques, and it is easier to bear a long wait between the courses at a meal when you can spend your time extricating from what looks like a beautiful kind of jigsaw puzzle a promise that you shall "drink of the cup of joy."

Even the kitchen tent was decorated in the same way, and we sometimes wondered whether the cook ever studied his mural decorations; he usually sat in front of his tent with his back to the interior, and a number of pots before him, looking as if he were sunk in deep sorrow; but this may have been due to the anxiety to keep up his reputation as a cook amid desert difficulties. On the road he was always quite jovial and most ready to help in any emergency.

The tent as you entered it at night, made a striking picture; every part of the beautiful colouring of the embroidered walls was illuminated, while the handsome white sheepskin coats of some of the gentlemen, and the Arab abbas or plain English overcoats of others, combined with the bright scarves and wraps of the ladies, gave the effect of some strange Eastern fantasy, in which the West also was taking part.

Encampment at Ain Howara

Desert Evening, 1845

W.H. Bartlett

With the twilight falls the grateful dew, and comes on the refreshing breeze, cooling the heated surface of the wilderness, and restoring the languid frame of the traveller. Wander but a few paces from the encampment, and listen in the profound of the solitude to the low and melancholy sigh of the night wind, which sweeps the light surface of the sand, and drifts it against the canvas wall of the tent; that breeze, laden with the voice of ages, which traverses the old historic desert, and has waved the long grass and stirred the slumbering waters of the ancient fountains where the patriarchs encamped with their flocks. There is rapture in pacing alone with such fancies among the drifted sand-heaps, and listening to that wild music, till night has fallen upon the wilderness, over which millions of stars, rising up resplendently from the very edge of the vast horizon, seem quietly brooding. One may hear, as it were, the solemn pulsation of the universe. . . .

I shall not, however, dwell on the solemnity of such moments. . . .

Man, though his thoughts may roll through space itself, must however, humbling the reflection, ultimately 'drop into himself' and *dine*, with a relish too after a ten hours' ride, as keen and as absorbing as that of the unwieldy brutes around him, that, crunching the prickly shrubs, gaze prone and stupid on the sand.

Walking back to the tent, I catch sight of preparations grateful to a hungry stomach, for the chief meal in the Desert is taken in the evening, and its announcement is looked for with the most intent interest.

On entering I find the transparent lamp lighted, and casting a cheerful glow upon the red curtains of the tent; my portmanteau and camp-stool arranged as a table, with (at starting) a clean tablecloth; for there is as little occasion to sup off your 'dirty towel', as to confine yourself to the *one* shirt of Laborde.* My chief standing dish was that, the memory of which haunted Stephens† with visions of departed joys—to wit, an Irish stew; and I would defy the most fastidious gourmand, were he here, to refrain from falling upon it with eager relish. It is indeed *the* very dish for the *Desert*. Another common *plat*, in addition to an occasional roast lamb or kid, was curried rice and fowl, with lentil soup, the pottage of Esau; followed by stewed apricots, or marmalade, with moistened biscuit, in lieu of bread; after which, tea (oh how refreshing though generally milkless!) in copious draughts, relieved at length the thirst that nothing else would assuage. For this, when a cup too low, a glass or two of punch was now and then substituted.

Such was my ordinary living; it might, as before said, have been more luxurious; but it was well enough, in fact; and it is sufficient to show that the privations of many travellers, for which they draw so pathetically on the reader's compassion; are either affected, like the well-feigned woes of the beggar, or, if real, are at least owing to their own want of proper foresight.

---

* Leon Laborde, a Frenchman, traveled in a simple manner in 1835.

† John Lloyd Stephens, an American, made the journey in 1835.

Camping in the Desert, 1908

Elbert Farman

We found an ideal camping ground for the night on a sandy plateau where there were a number of small thorn trees and many dried desert plants. The camels were relieved of their burdens and allowed to browse. Our tents were hastily pitched and dinner prepared. Dried plants, dead trees and roots, sufficient for a fire during the night, were collected and branches of thorn trees were brought in and cut up finely, with large knives resembling butchers cleavers, for the camels on their return to camp. Our table was spread in the larger tent. There was served a dinner, as sumptuous as could be desired, which we ate with unsurpassed relish, thanks to the wearisome day's journey and the clear, cool, mountain air.

A large camp-fire was built and the camels were brought in and made to crouch in a circle around the fire, with their heads inward, and their legs folded under them after the manner of their race. Each was given a handful of beans brought from Suez and, afterwards, some of the chopped thorn tree branches. The Arabs had partaken of their scanty meal of coarse bread, a few cooked lentils, and the fragments from our table. Their day's work being ended and all preparations made for the night, these simple sons of the desert were seated, Turkish style, on the sand in an inner circle next to the fire.

Some of the more gifted of their number commenced the narration of wild tales resembling those Arabian stories which ever delight childhood. The auditors were certainly interested, for till late into the night I heard their warm applause, the prolonged "Aah! Aah! Aah! Allah! Allah!" The fire was well kept, but weariness finally came and one after another fell asleep. Only toward the morning hours did the hum of voices cease and leave the travellers in their tents, just outside this charmed circle, to the solitude, the fearful stillness of a night on the desert.

These solitudes produce peculiar emotions. They remind one of the old patriarchs, who, in their desert homes, far removed from the scenes of busy multitudes, surrounded only by their families and their flocks, seem, by reason of this isolation from the world, to have held a closer communion with nature and with God.

The Night Hours, 1865

E.H. Palmer

The flickering camp-fires shed a lurid glow over the little knots of swarthy Bedawin as they reposed after the fatigues of the day, and produced a wonderful picturesque and Rembrandt-like effect. The hushed tones of those who had not yet fallen asleep, the whirring of a hand-mill here and there, the half-plaintive, half-surly groaning of the camels—these were the only sounds which disturbed the stillness of the night. I contemplated the scene around me with mingled feeling of delight and awe, I was reclining perchance on the very spot where the Children of Israel had encamped when fleeing from their Egyptian persecutors, and I could not help comparing my situation to some extent with theirs.

I had just left the noisy bustling crowd of Cairo's streets, and had escaped into the freedom of the great lone wilderness, and I too felt that sense of special Divine protection which must have been present to them, for never so much as in the desert does one feel that God is nigh. He it is that enables man to pass in safety through this dreary waste, and whether it be by direct miraculous intervention, as in the case of the Chosen People, or by the scarcely less wonderful agency of reason and foresight, still it is His hand alone that guides him on.

And the Start of the New Day, 1822

John Carne

The sunsets in Egypt are the finest; but to see a sunrise in its glory, you must be in the Desert, - nothing there obscures or obstructs it. You are travelling on chill and silent, and your looks bent towards the East; a variety of glowing hues appear and die away again, and for some time the sky is blue and clear; when the sun suddenly darts above the horizon, and such a splendour is thrown instantly on the wide expanse of sand and rocks, that if you were a Persian adorer, you would certainly break out, like the Imam from the minaret, in praise and blessing.

Many of the nineteenth-century travelers were men of the church and all of them were on a formal or informal pilgrimage in this Old Testament context, aware of how these pieces were linked to their Biblical beliefs.

The Day of Rest, 1860

William Beamont

Today, being Sunday, we did not move from our encampment, which is placed in a cheerful valley, embosomed in hills of moderate height and picturesque forms, amongst which are the Gebel el Gemmel, the mountain of the camel, and Gebel el Kud'r, the hill of the cup, which is so called from resembling such a vessel. We are near, but do not see, the mountain mentioned in the Koran, which is said to have twelve mouths for the twelve tribes. The seclusion of the wady, where the world is shut out, and the mind is thrown back upon itself, well fits it for a place of Sunday rest.

As I walked out of my tent in the middle of the night, the moon and the morning star were both shining brightly in a sky which was intensely blue, while the surrounding hills stood out in distinct and varied outline. The sheah was sending up its rich perfume of unseen incense. Not a breath of wind was abroad, no bird was on the wing, and no tiny insect's voice was heard. I listened intently to catch if I could some sound, but not a breath or a whisper broke the solemn stillness of the hour, and perhaps at this moment there was no human voice breaking the deep silence of these vast unpeopled solitudes from Mecca to Cairo.

In making our bargain with the sheik before we set out, it was agreed that for every Sunday he halted at our request he should receive a small extra number of piastres.

By resting with us yesterday he had earned the first instalment of this pay; but "friendship in the desert wavers like the leaves of the acacia", and how to divide this small prize-money as to which they have no law, was a great trouble to the sheik's tail. Their dispute about it was so loud and wordy that they waked me from a sound sleep; and to get out of hearing, I rose and walked out into the open air, where the beauty of the night and the splendour of the starry sky acted like a sedative, and soon sent me to sleep again.

The Sabbath, 1857

Horatius Bonar

After breakfast and prayers I sat for an hour or two in the tent reading, comparing passages, and noting down texts for friends at home. The heat, however, was great, and the noise of the Bedaween tongues broke the Sabbath-calm; so we went out about twelve to the palm-trees for shady quiet and also for worship. A prostrate palm-log was our first seat; but the shade was insufficient. So we removed to another spot where two bushy palms, forming a sort of angle and waving their long feathers over us, gave us complete shelter. There we worshipped together with the Lord God of Israel, in the place where his people had done so, more than three thousand years ago. We sang the hundredth psalm, "All people that on earth do dwell"; we read the 35th verse of Isaiah, "the wilderness and the solitary place shall be glad for them, and the desert shall rejoice and blossom as the rose"; the subject was our discourse was Isaiah xlviii, 21, "they thirsted not when he led them through the desert." Often did the words of the prophets respecting the days to come recur to us while musing here, - surrounded with some tokens of verdure in the desert. These palms and tamarisks are but the earnest of the promised fruitfulness. God will yet clothe these sands, and rocks, and naked hills.

An ardent believer, it worried Agnes Lewis Smith that her Arab guides did not understand her faith and that if travelers did not themselves speak Arabic then their dragoman might misinterpret their beliefs. She believed the Arabs would respect her more if they understood her beliefs, and explained when she could.

Telling the Christian Story, 1892

Agnes Smith Lewis

A'agi asked me if we had stopped at Ghurundel to photograph, and I replied,

"No, the first day of the week is the Lord's Day. If we were at home we would go to church, but as we cannot do so we must keep it sacred from work."

Protestant travellers who do not speak Arabic can never know how much of their influence is lost through the misrepresentation of their dragoman. How much more these primitive people would respect us if we were not so often ashamed of confessing our faith!

We started at half past seven on foot, Saleem accompanying us to show us the path. I made him thoroughly understand that we had come to this country to see the way in which Neby Musa led the Israelites and that we consider it a figure of how God leads us along the hard paths of our early life. I told him also how we rested on Sunday, because God told Neby Mousa we were to do so, from the top of Sinai, but the day was changed because on the first day of the week our Lord the Messiah rose from the dead, with the promise that we too shall rise to be with him in heaven. To all that Saleem assented. The path led all day betwixt limestone hills. We passed through Wady Useit with its few plundered palm trees, and soon, saw a heap of stones marking the grave of a mare whose owner spurred her to death. Each one of our guides kicked some sand on it with his bare feet, and spat, to show his abhorrence of the deed.

Easter Sunday, 1878

Isabella Bird

Wady esh Sheyk: I have encamped here today with the traditional Sinai within an hour's journey, and Gebel Serbal, the highest mountain in the peninsula opposite the camp rising magnificently above two curtain ranges which form the opposite side of the valley. I arranged with my escort to take a 'Sabbath' today, my seventh day from Ain Musa. . . .

In a Weary Land, 1878

Isabella Bird

All this region (onward from Ain Musa) looks like the level beach of a sea. The Red Sea must have covered it at one time. It is hard sand and gravel, and as easy to walk upon as a gravel walk. When I can walk no farther my camel, with much difficulty and many objurgations, is made to lie down. Hassan stands at one side and the sheikhs on the other, and with Hassan's help I attempt to take a flying leap into the middle of the saddle. Sometimes this is successful the first time, and if it is Hassan puts an arm in front of me and the sheikh puts an arm behind me, and the dreaded moment arrives, which I am more cowardly about each time. The camel, with a jerk that might dislocate one's neck, jumps on his knees, nearly throwing me backwards, then another violent jerk brings him to his haunches, and would throw me over his head but for Hassan's arm, then, the forward movement is arrested by another jerk which sets him on his four legs and leaves me breathless on the lofty elevation of his hump. This process is reversed as one dismounts, and is repeated six times daily! But things are not always so comparatively smooth, for just as I am prepared to spring the brute makes a snarling lunge with his teeth either at me or his driver, or just as I am half up jerks himself up on his four legs, and the whole process has to be gone over again. Yesterday I had just touched the saddle when by a rapid movement he threw me off sidewise, and this morning jerking himself up before I had clutched firm hold of the saddle he threw me over his shoulders and bruised me a good deal.

After being mounted the caravan straggles in single file, Hassan bringing up the rear, my camel being led, and then for four or five hours we crawl over the burning, glaring sand. I now understand what is meant by "As a hireling earnestly desireth the shadow." At 8:30 a.m. the shadow of my driver is fully eight feet long, and as the morning wears by it shortens to something a little over two feet; then I know that noon has come. The camels halt, and if there be a rock which casts a shadow, Hassan lays a blanket in the shade for me, and while the Bedaween smoke and sleep for an hour, I read the Scripture account of the wanderings, and lunch on a cluster of raisins. I am learning a deep sympathy with the Israelites, and their unbelief and murmurings become more intelligible as the days go by. How terrible must have been the trudge through this "waste howling wilderness", how bitter the regrets for the green valley of the Nile, how weary the barren sands, how terrible the burning heat! Better then all do I understand the simile "the shadow of a great rock in a weary land".

Today on the parched plain no rock was found to give shelter in the heat of noon. There was but a big stone about two feet high, under the lee of which the Arabs scraped a big hole into which I crawled, and lay down screened by a blanket laid over my double umbrella. The sand was burning even through my clothing.

6
Coming to Sinai across the Red Sea

Traveling from Suez through Wadi Musa

When travelers left Suez, either by sea or by land, the hardship began. For those who rode to the nearby oasis, three relentless desert days lay ahead of them after they left the refreshing peace of the Well of Moses. This stretch was the most dreary and harsh of the whole journey. The first night at the Fountain of Moses—Ain Musa—was the true beginning of the desert journey. Other travelers crossed the Red Sea further south, passing through the mountains and wadis of Sinai.

The Fountains of Moses, 1722
The Prefetto of Egypt

[W]e rested about two o'clock near certain fountains called Ain el Musa, or the Fountains of Moses, situated among little hills; which I went to, and found the water tolerably good, but with a little saltness; and no sooner does it rise out of the bowels of the earth, but it is lost again in the sand, or, as I may say, is in the day time instantly absorbed by the burning and thirsty sand. At night it seems to flow further than it does by day, as may be seen by the traces it leaves behind; and

I believe if the place were cleansed (it being very full of dirt and mud), the water would be sweeter, and there would be a larger current, for there are three springs which run not far from each other, into which the Arabs suffer the camels to enter when they drink.

From these fountains may be plainly seen a wonderful aperture in the mountains on the other side of the Red Sea, thro' and from which the children of Israel entered the Red Sea, when Pharaoh and his host were drowned; which aperture is situated west-south-west from these Fountains of Moses; and the breadth of the sea hereabouts, where the children of Israel passed it, is about four or five hours journey. But from Suez by land to these fountains would be about seven or eight hours journey.

Ayun Musa

A Beautiful Day, 1822
John Carne

Having passed round the termination of the sea the next morning, we bent our course towards the wilderness of Sinai, and came in a few hours to four or five pools of water, called The Fountains of Moses, but at which it is not probable he could ever have been.

The weather continued beautiful, scarcely a cloud to be seen in the sky, and not a living thing on earth; and this deep solitude and silence, with the uncommon purity of the air, have a strong effect on the imagination. You feel as if you ruled in this vast and inanimate scene, and possess a boat and joyous spirit amidst its savage sands and rocks, and feel the truth of a remark of Lord B's, of a young French renegade, who resided many years in the East, and who said that often, when riding alone in a boundless desert, he has felt a delight that was indescribable.

Harriet Martineau's small party include a Mr. E., director of the Peninsula and Orient Company (P & O), the main shipping line between Egypt and India, and the P & O agent at Suez, a Captain Linguist, who traveled with them from Suez to Wadi Musa. The wind was light and other boats passed them by.

Landing at Wadi Musa, 1846

Harriet Martineau

The view of Suez from the water was finer than I should have supposed possible for such a miserable place; but such an atmosphere adorns everything with the highest charms of colour. The light on the sides of the vessels, on the two minarets, red and dark, contrasted with the pale green above the sandy bottom.

When they landed the rest of the party had gone ahead. Their camels were waiting, but not their food, cook, or guide.

Captain Linguist was delighted to improvise a luncheon for us at his country-house, at the Wells of Moses (Wadi Musa). He showed us his garden, which is well irrigated, and as productive as a garden can be in that place. He showed us the ancient wells, all shrouded in bushy palms; and pointed out indications of moisture which encourage him to search for a fourth well. Of the three which we saw, one is built up with massive and ancient masonry.

We were glad that our kind entertainer had such a recourse as even this place. When weary with the solitude and irksomeness of his position, he comes over here, drives blue devils with a gallop over the sand hills, and plans of improvement about his country-house. The luncheon he gave us was extraordinary enough in its place to deserve mention. Here, among these dreary sands of the Arabian shore, we had butter from Ireland, ale from England, wine from Spain, ham from Germany, bread and mutton from Cairo and Suez, cheese from Holland, and water from Madras! Truly the dwellers on the Red Sea may well be advocates of free trade.—At half-past five P.M. Captain L. helped us to mount, and saw us on our way.

An Evening at Wadi Musa, 1878

Isabella Bird

This is truly delightful. Early this morning the sultry weather changed. The wind was and is north; and the shaded thermometer, which yesterday stood at 91° in the shade, today only reached 72°. Yesterday evening and this morning were spent in making my final preparations, and in getting the food etc reduced to a minimum. At 2:30 p.m. the Sheyk Barak, Hassan, my servant, three gentlemen connected with the P and O Company who have kindly undertaken to see my safely started on my journey tomorrow, and I left Suez in a large Arab sailing boat with all my gear on board.

Blithely it sped over the rippled waters of turquoise blue, its great red sail nearly crimson in the sunlight; blithely the blue waters laved their golden margins—so blithe and beautiful it all was that I forgot the "waste howling wilderness" stretched almost infinitely in all directions. There, on the right, were the hills of Africa, red-and-orange, fiery and blasted-looking; and on the left rose-coloured ranges, with violet shadows on their clefts, all outlines sharp, distance obliterated. It was glorious and the keen life-giving air helped my intense enjoyment of it. Depositing the gentlemen on the Asiatic side, we sailed for nearly two hours down the gulf, and then moored at a rude pier, where a boat was discharging goat-skins full of water, looking like drowned and swollen pigs, and two camels were being loaded with the same.

Leaving Hassan to the slow process of getting the baggage under weigh, I walked the two miles to the Wells of Moses alone.

The first strange sight that I saw was four camels being driven at a lumbering canter down the narrow pier. These were my 'travelling equipage', and I looked at them with dismay. For being so lean and bodiless, they looked as high as elephants, and there was no scaling ladder in the desert!

The Wells of Moses lay straight ahead, visible for many miles by the blackness of their palm and tamarisk groves against the golden sand. It was golden indeed when I landed, but long before the walk was ended it was crimsoned by the sinking sun, and so were the swelling sandhills and the broken ranges beyond them, while the air was very rosy. The bold hills of Africa glowed like incandescent rubies beyond the bright blue water; while Suez, faintly seen at the head of the gulf, suggested human life, The air was intoxicating, and purity itself. Physical life even was 'worth living'. When I was about a mile from Ain Musa, I saw a large Arab caravan, with a number of armed Bedaween, was encamped round the wells, so I sat on a stone and waited for my escort.

The beauty of the sunset increased. I could not help standing up now and then for the almost childish pleasure of seeing my long shadow lie in purple on the crimsoning sand.

Only when you have been in the desert for a few hours and become aware that there is nothing growing, not a leaf or a blade of grass,

Encampment in Wadi Feiran

that you realize how quickly you long for evidence of life. This excitement on coming upon a glimpse of greenery permeates many of the accounts of Sinai.

The Palms of Wadi Musa, 1845

W.H. Bartlett

Since leaving the green Nile we had seen nothing so refreshing as this little oasis; and yet it consisted but in a few patches of wild palm trees and bushes, and one or two gardens, laboriously won from the Desert by force of irrigation from the briny spring, and protected from the sands by reed fences. One of these, surrounded its own white villa, and a most pleasing appearance in such a neighbourhood; we understood it belonged to a gentleman of Suez, who was in the habit of skimming across from time to time in his boat, a brief sail, to inspect the cultivation of his own vegetables. But the most characteristic object was a group of wild palms, nourished by one of those unpalatable springs: in its shade I pitched my tent, and breakfasted while the zemzemins were filled there being no water all the way hence to Marah. The tall and graceful palms of Egypt would hardly acknowledge one of these rugged and stunted specimens of the same beautiful family, with its knotted trunk, untended branches and dingy hue; deriving sustenance from the polluted salt-spring, instead of drinking the glorious Nile, twisted and distorted by its struggle with the sandy desert-blast; yet we hailed it with more delight, and quitted it with more regret, than a region of groves elsewhere.

Most travelers to Sinai walk in the three-thousand-year-old footsteps of Moses and wonder if each place is already known to them from their reading of the Old Testament.

Where Was the Miracle? 1865

E.H. Palmer

The exact spot at which the miracle took place must always remain a matter of mere speculation, but there can be little doubt that at this point, 'Ayun Musa (Moses Well) we are upon the track of the Israelites at the commencement of their desert journey. In the Bible narrative, immediately after the account of the destruction of the Egyptian army and the thrilling song of triumph which 'Miriam the Prophetess' and her maiden's celebrated the Israel's deliverance, it is said: "So Moses brought Israel from the Red Sea; and they went out into the wilderness of Shur." (Exodus xv. 22) The word Shur in Hebrew signifies 'a wall'; and as we stand at Ayun Musa and glance over the desert at the Jebels er Rahah and et Tih which border the gleaming plain, we at once appreciate the fact that these long wall-like escarpments are the chief if not the only prominent characteristics of this portion of the wilderness, and we need not wonder that the Israelites should have named this memorable spot after its most salient feature, the wilderness of Shur, or the wall.

The Arabs, with their usual inconsistency, adopt two sites for the miracle—here, and at the Hammam Far'un, or 'Pharaoh's Hot Bath'—a frowning chalk cliff a little further down the coast. Pharaoh's unquiet spirit is still supposed to haunt the deep, and keep alive the boiling sulphurous spring which started up at his last angry drowning gasp. The sea at this point is called Birket Farun or 'Pharaoh's Lake'. When asked how they can reconcile their accounts of Moses having crossed the sea at both these spots, the simple Bedawin answer, at least they did to me, "What seems remote to us is near to God Most High".

Over the centuries travelers interpreted and re-interpreted the routes they took, linking it to the route of the children of Israel. Mary Dobson's account is clearer than most—and just as convincing.

The Route of the Children, 1912

Mary Dobson

The old childish ideas which made us imagine the people of Israel as toiling over tawny, stinging sand until they reached a high mountain, towering in awful solitude before their astonished eyes—a mountain which was to become the centre of their national life—are as delusive as most of our immature ideas.

Without entering into lengthy discussion as to the route of the liberated Israelites, discussion of which can grow very weary, it is enough to state that after crossing the Red Sea they started from 'Ayun Musa (the Wells of Moses), two miles from the Gulf of Suez, and then came down the coast-strip, passing Wady Amarah (Marah), and entering the limestone range at the end of the Tih by the fertile valley of Gharandel, which is supposed to be Elim. Thence they probably went by the sandstone range to Paran (now called Feiran), where they made their first long stop. Feiran, the most beautiful oasis of the Peninsula, was the scene of their fight with Amalek, Rephidim being by many scholars located there. They finally passed on by the central, winding valley of the Sinai range, the Wady es-Sheikh, to the plain of Raha and Sinai, the Mountain of God. Many of their wanderings were amid steep and inaccessible heights, where even the valleys are often at an elevation of several thousand feet.

By Sea—Suez to Tor

Sailing from Suez, 1852

Charles Didier

On 21 January, at two o'clock, we got under way, and at once hoisted sail; but we scarcely sailed except formally . . . for at four o'clock we anchored at the foot of Mount Abu Anaj for the night. The sea was calm, the wind was favourable, and nothing stood in the way of our voyage. But the Red Sea barques do not sail except by day, furthermore, we were not very far from Birkat Fara'un—Pharaoh's Cistern—the name the Arabs give to the place of the disastrous engulfing—which they believe has ever since been haunted by evil spirits: thus there is not a seaman who would risk crossing this formidable deep at night; indeed, they scarcely dare to do so by daylight, and never without first placating malevolent spirits with superstitious practices.

Around here, everything calls Moses to your mind. . . . Almost opposite to Moses' Fountain Mount Ataquah rises up, on the other shore, a stone giant which, forty centuries ago, witnessed the pack of Egyptians pass by, cavalry at their head in hot pursuit of their foe.

Steaming from Suez, 1912

Mary Dobson

On the arrival of the Khedival steamer (at Suez) the whole of the Camp paraphernalia was put on board and we steamed off, catching, as we progressed, on our left-hand side, through the evening sunset light, a full view of Ayun Musa (the Wells of Moses), where the Israelites probably camped on their journey. We were only on night at sea, and were thus saved several days of waterless desert. This route has only been made practicable since the beginning of the century, as the regular steamers did not stop at Tor, and to go by dhow meant so much uncertainty as to time, and so much discomfort, that the desert route was preferable.

Crossing the Red Sea

In the early years of pilgrimage to Sinai the travelers usually came southward from Jerusalem and then returned to Jerusalem or went westward to Egypt. Later travelers tended to start from Cairo and return to Cairo. However a few travelers who wished first to visit Egypt, went southward on the Nile—possibly as far as the cataracts beyond Aswan into Nubia—and then turned northward again but at Qena left the Nile, crossed the desert to Qosseir on the Red Sea, and sailed from there to the Sinai Peninsula, landing at Tor from where they continued their journey by land. A few travelers took ships at Suez and sailed to Tor, thus avoiding long days across the desert wastes. The Prussian traveler Richard Lepsius traveled in the area east of the Red Sea during March 1845, and then crossed with his party to the Sinai Peninsula.

The Sea and the Sailors, 1845

Richard Lepsius

Yesterday evening it was a perfect calm. It was only during the night that a light wind rose from the north, which we immediately availed ourselves of, for setting sail. With the wind in our favour we might have accomplished the passage across in one night; but now the day is again drawing to a close, and we have not yet reached the port. The ship of burden scarcely stirs, though the long oars have been at length set in motion.

The sailors of this sea are very different from those on the Nile. Their deportment is more reserved, less sly and subservient. Their songs, which commence at the first stroke of the oar, consist of fragmentary first lines, which are sung first by one, and are taken up by another, while the remainder utter short and deep grunting sounds, as an accompaniment, at equal intervals. The Reis, on an elevated seat, rows along with the others. He is a negro, as well as several others among the sailors, but one of handsomest and strongest Moors that I ever saw—a real Othello; when making his athletic movements, he rolls his yellow-white eyes, shows his dazzling teeth, and gives the tone to the song, leading it for a length of time, with a shrill, piercing, but skilful, voice.

On the evening of Good Friday (21 March, 1845) we landed in Tor by moonlight. The harbour is now so much sanded up, that our vessel was obliged to lie off several hundred paces, and we were landed in a boat. We were met on the shore by the old Greek Nicola Janni, who had before received Eirenberg, Leon de Laborde, Ruppel Isenberg, and other well-known travellers; and he had favourable testimonials to produce of the reception they had met with from him. After long negotiations with the insolent Arabs, who, when they discovered we were in a hurry, and that they were indispensable to us, endeavoured in all ways to overreach us, we started early the day before yesterday from Tor, limiting ourselves to what was absolutely necessary for the land journey; and we sent the vessel to wait for us at Cape Abu Zelimeh.

Safe at Tor, 1863

John Gadsby

If ever I knew what it is to be thankful, I do this morning that I am safe at Tor. I was awoke last night, after having quieted the fleas, by a heavy sea banging against us and a row amongst the sailors. It was awful. It was blowing a gale of wind, the boat was dipping in, and being only a foot or two from the water, an extra dip might swamp her. The men were working hard, taking down the large sail. It was done, and well done, and it was well it was done. Had the boat's head got to the wind, we must have gone down, being open at the fore part. As it was, we ran at a furious pace before the wind. It was nearly dark, and the sea hereabouts nearly or quite 30 miles wide. The gale increased. L. got up as well as I, and we never undressed again. There were three of these boats lost only a few weeks ago, and my wonder is how they can live in such a storm. I looked up to the Lord for safety, for I felt there was little in the boat; and while I did so it was suggested to me, "Yes, now you are in trouble you can ask for deliverance." Then came the psalmist's words: "In my *distress* I cried unto the Lord, and he heard me." This gave me confidence. . . . But ours was an appalling situation. Only think of a deep-laden, open boat in such a sea! We were favoured with an excellent steersman. He seemed to know how to meet almost every rolling wave, and every gust of wind. When the moon got up we could see land on the left. We doubled it and were then in quiet water.

We arrived at Tor about 12 o'clock.

They were met by the governor's servant and taken to his house.

Tor was once a place of vast importance, being the highway from India and Arabia, across the Red Sea, to Kossayr and Kenneh; but its principal business appears to be in mother-of-pearl shells, which are fished up in large numbers and sent to Suez . . . or across the desert to Bethlehem, and the Bethlehemites shape them and engrave upon them various figures for all who have visited Bethlehem and Jerusalem have seen.

7

Wide Desert, Deep Wadis, and High Mountains

The journey from Cairo to St. Catherine's Monastery was broken into three main parts: first, the trek across the desert from Cairo to Suez, during which travelers learned about camel riding and desert life; then the three days of harsh desert travel when some must have wished they had never started; finally, the stage when the mountains were in sight and the end—if not in sight—was at least nigh. In later years, by the second half of the nineteenth century, there was even a road of sorts built by the Egyptian government. The first three days out from Ain Musa through Travelers faced not only heat and thirst but also the dreaded khamseen wind. There was no turning back.

Onward from Ain Moosa, 1873

Murray's Handbook

On leaving Ain Moosa the traveller turns his back on civilisation, and enters on the wide desert. And nothing can well be more dreary and monotonous than the first day's journey. At first the plain is a little broken, but after a few miles, at Wady ed Dehseh, a flat desolate expanse is entered on, unrelieved by any feature.

The march is toilsome enough even if the weather be clear and fine; but if, as is frequently the case, a khamseen wind gets up, making the atmosphere oven-like in its heat and oppressiveness, and enveloping everything in a shroud of sand, then indeed the first day's journey is anything but a pleasant and encouraging experience, and the 'flesh-pots' of Egypt will be looked back upon with regret.

The Usual Route to Mount Sinai, 1816

John Lewis Burckhardt

From Ayoun Mousa to the well of Howara we had travelled fifteen hours and a quarter. Referring to this distance, it appears probable that this is the desert of three days mentioned in the Scriptures to have been crossed by the Israelites immediately after their passing of the Red Sea,* and at the end of which they arrived at Marah. In moving with a whole nation, the march may well be supposed to have occupied three days; and the bitter well at Marah, which was sweetened by Moses, corresponds exactly with that of Howara. This is the usual route to Mount Sinai, and was probably therefore that which the Israelites took on their escape from Egypt, provided it be admitted that they crossed the sea near Suez, as Niebuhr, with good reason, conjectures.

The Khamsin, 1862

Arthur Penryn Stanley

Soon Red Sea and all were lost in a sandstorm, which lasted the whole day. Imagine all distant objects entirely lost to view, - the sheets of sand fleeting along the surface of the desert like streams of water; the whole air filled; though invisibly, with a tempest of sand, driving in your face like sleet. Imagine the caravan toiling against this, - the Bedouins, - each with his shawl thrown completely over his head, half of the riders sitting backwards, the camels, meantime, thus virtually left without guidance, though from time to time throwing their long necks sideways to avoid the blast, yet moving straight onward with a painful sense of duty truly edifying to behold. . . . Through the tempest, this roaring and driving tempest, that sometimes made me think that this must be the real meaning of 'a howling wilderness', we rode on the whole day.

Desert Day and Desert Night and Morning, 1894

Pierre Loti

Friday 23 February: All day, travelled in the immensity of arid sands, following the vague traces that are made from the force of centuries of the passing, though rare, of men and beasts, and are the roads of the desert. Far off, the monotonous horizon quivers. The sands are scattered with greyish stones; all is grey, rose-grey or

---

* Exodus xv 23.

yellow-grey. Occasionally a pale green plant, with a hardly perceptible black flower—and the long necks of the camels bend as they try to graze.

The horizon quivers with heat. One hopes—now and then—for the shadow of a cloud—in the infinite sky or on the infinity of the sand. But there is none. They are gone, any little shadows of the clouds—refreshing only stones or old bleached bones.

Saturday 24 February: Until two in the morning, the wind tormented our little camp—so isolated in the midst of empty space—without let up. Our tents flapped like veils; in the darkness one's couch was shaken as in a storm at sea. On the edge of the camp, the camels called out together like bears in a menagerie. In spite of oneself, one was aware of how little there was between oneself and the pillage of the night and against all the uncertainties of the desert.

When day came, the wind dropped, stopped. Then, coming out of the tent one saw: the sun mounting, in an absolutely pure atmosphere, nothing to remind one of yesterday evening—everything was returned to their true appearance and proportions: the camels, the sand, the meagre plants—all is sharp and fixed as under a clear, crude light. And far off, and below, is a sheet of lapis, which is the Red Sea—and the mountains of Egypt are still there.

To Wadi Ghurandel

The Third Halting Place, 1873

Murray's Handbook

[W]e reach Wady Ghurundel, a broad well-defined valley, at this point about 600 yards wide, and running between chalky cliffs 60 to 80 feet high. There is plenty of desert herbage, and small clusters of stunted palms are frequent. In this valley grows plentifully ghurkud, a plant with a small red berry, which some suppose to have been the 'tree' used by Moses to sweeten the waters at Marah. This plant, however, has no such properties.

The Springs of Wady Ghurundel form usually the third halting place of the traveller, as here the stock of water can be renewed, and the camels refresh themselves after 2 days march from Ain Moosa. In spring time the supply of water is abundant, and bursts forth in several places, but it is insipid and not over clean. In the cliffs on the left above the springs, are some old tombs.

Where Are We? 1762

Carsten Niebuhr

The country through which we passed is famous as the scene of the emigration of the Jews under Moses. We were therefore desirous of learning, from the Arabs, the names of all the places, and of all the mountains, especially on our way. Mr von Haven who could not resolve to make himself familiar with the Bedouins, could obtain nothing but vague and uncivil answers from them. I

Spring in Wadi Ghurundel

again sought to gain the confidence and friendship of one of the Arabs, by making him some presents, and causing him to ride sometimes behind me on my camel. From him I received honest and distinct answers. To the objects which I pointed out to him, he gave the same names coming and going. I likewise measured the distances of places, by counting the steps of the camel, and comparing the number with the time in which they were travelled, by my watch. By means of a compass, I distinguished, likewise, the directions of the road. None of the Arabs understood the nature of this instrument. It is plainly, therefore, an idle tale that they follow the direction of the compass, on travelling through the desert.

William Turner, a young diplomat, on a lengthy tour of the Near East, felt a certain responsibility to record the facts of his journeys.

Maps and Experience, 1815
William Turner

Garandel is far from the sea, Niebuhr's map has laid it down correctly. I climbed partly up the mountains round, which are composed of brown soft rock, that is every where crumbling down; I was sorry that my thermometer went no higher than 111°, as I was thus unable to judge the temperature of the atmosphere in the sun, and of that of the burning sand, on which it was very painful to us to set our naked feet. Having heard much of the accuracy of the Arabs in marking the position of places in the Desert, I tried one of them by asking where Mount Sinai was, and on comparing his account with my compass and Niebuhr's map, I found he was exact to a point.

Plants and Insects, 1816
John Lewis Burckhardt

The Wadi Gharandel contains date trees, tamarisks, acacias of different species, and the thorny shrub Gharkad, the *Peganum retusum* of Forskal,* which is extremely common in this peninsula, and is also met with in the sands of the Delta on the coast of the Mediterranean. Its small red berry, of the size of the grain of the pomegranate, is very juicy and refreshing, much resembling a ripe gooseberry in taste, but not so sweet. The Gharkad, which from the colour of its fruit is also called by the Arabs Homra, delights in a sandy soil, and reaches its maturity in the height of summer when the ground is parched up, exciting an agreeable surprise in the traveller, at finding so juicy a berry produced in the driest soil and season. The bottom of the valley of Gharendel swarms with ticks, which are extremely distressing both to men and beasts, and on this account the caravans usually encamp on the sides of the hills which border the valley.

Toward the Coast and Tor

Reaching the Sea, 1906
Baedeker's *Palestine and Syria*

We follow the valley descending towards the sea, now called the *Wâdi Tayyibeh*, with numerous windings, several springs of bad water, and a few stunted palms. The valley is enclosed amphitheatrically by barren slopes of whitish-yellow sand and by rocks. A striking appearance is presented by the *Jebel Tayyibeh*, situated near the sea, and consisting of oblique strata of different colours; the lowest of these is golden yellow, surmounted in turn by red, rusty black, and yellow layers. After 1 hr. the valley expands, and we approach the open sea, washing the banks on a sandy plain of *El-Mehâir*. After a walk of 1 hr. along the coast we reach the Râs Abu Zenîmeh, which still bears the tomb of the saint, and affords a beautiful and sheltered camping-ground. At this spot some authorities locate the *Reedy Sea* of

---

* A member of Niebuhr's Danish expedition.

the Bible (Numb. xxxiii. 10). In ancient times the roads, by which ore and stone was brought from the mines of the Wâdi Maghâra and Sarbût el-Khâdem for farther conveyance by water, converged here.

By the Sea, 1857

Horatius Bonar

At eight we started. Our way led along the shore. Not a ripple on the sea, not a cloud in the flaming firmament! The coast-cliffs were wild and precipitous, - seamed and scarred, - split into spikes, and wasted into cones, as if by the joint action of rain and lightning. The road lies over a broad platform of flat rock. In rounding one of the points we touched the water, so that the tide-ripples, for there were no others, washed round our camels' feet. I had bathed in the morning moonlight; but my companions, more wisely preferring sunlight, now took to the sea, with some two or three of our younger Bedaween, who enjoyed the sport of swimming and splashing amazingly. Soon we began to turn inwards in a south-easterly direction, and to turn away from the sea.

Thomas Shaw, like many other travelers, could assume in his reader a knowledge of the Bible which would be rare today. Fortunately for the modern reader, Shaw gives frequent biblical references. Here, he moves on from the desert of Marah toward Tor.

Elim and the Seventy Palm Trees, 1721

Thomas Shaw

There is nothing further remarkable, 'till we see the Israelites encamped at Elim (Exodus xv. 27; Numbers xxxxiii, 9) upon the northern skirts of the desert of Sin, two leagues* from Tor, and near thirty from Corondel. I saw no more than nine of the twelve wells that are mentioned by Moses; the other three being filled up by those drifts of sand, which are common in Arabia. Yet this loss is amply made up by the great increase in the palm trees; the seventy having propagated themselves into more than two thousand. Under the shade of these trees, is the Hammam Mousa, or bath of Moses, particularly so called, which the inhabitants of Tor have in great esteem and veneration; acquainting us, that it was here, where the household of Moses was encamped.

We have a distinct view of Mount Sinai from Elim; the wilderness, as it is still called, of Sin lying betwixt them. We travelled these plains in nine hours; being all the way diverted with the fight of a variety of lizards and vipers, that are here in great numbers. We were afterwards twelve hours in passing the many windings and difficult ways, which lie betwixt these desert and those of Sinai.

* A league is about three miles or five kilometers.

And Ne'er a Drop to Drink, 1878

Isabella Bird

Turning off the shortest route, and passing below some magnificent cliffs of crystalline limestone, we came down upon the sea. The foam-crested sparkling blue waters dashed blithely on the shore, and I revelled in the cool spray on my face, delicious after the long blazing day. There we encamped by the sea, between black and white cliffs and deep blue water, and all night long the waves murmured along the silent shore. The sun set in glory bathing the desert in fiery light, and I strolled in the evening along the shell-strewn shore, reading Numbers xxxiii, feeling sure that the Israelites came down the Wady Taiyibeh to the sea which had befriended them so well, and the hills of Africa, behind which lay the 'House of Bondage', purpling in the sinking sun, for this Dean Stanley makes no doubt is the site of the 'encampment by the sea'.

Toward the Mountains

But soon Isabella Bird was in trouble again. Her caravan ran short of water and for a day she had no more than a teacupful of rancid sludge and a few sips begged from passing Bedouins. She was exhausted and dehydrated. Her guide showed her how to put pebbles in her mouth to stem the thirst.

My Tongue Rattled in My Mouth, 1878

Isabella Bird

Then there were voices, and Hassan, speaking thick, uttered one word, "Water!" I took the bandage from my eyes, and saw that we were in a valley. In front palms waved, and there was greenness on the earth. I thought I was again being mocked by the mirage, but the blessed reality was confirmed the next moment, when I saw in the distance Sheykh Barak running towards me with a pitcher of water in his hand. I seized it, and in unreasoning haste drank an enormous quantity, when Hassan forced the cooler from me and drank the remainder, poor fellow! The thirst still raised but there was hope, for in the long valley which we had entered I recognised the Wady Feiran, the great oasis of the Sinaitic Desert. The Arabs lifted me very gently from my camel and laid me on a blanket under a palm tree.

Hassan brought me a cup of goat's milk, warm and healing, and putting a water-cooler beside me, warned me to take the water only by sips. It was pure and ice-cold; it was abundant; and reason having returned, I drank it rationally. Three thousand fruit-bearing palms, and perhaps two thousand young ones, grow in the grand oasis. Barley was springing, flocks were nibbling herbage which, though scanty, was green; there was a murmur of water, and as I feel asleep that murmur became transformed into the sound of "the river of the water of life", and the rustle of the palm fronds overhead into the whisper of the foliage of that tree "whose leaves are for the healing of nations".

Mountains Ahead, 1853

Catherine Tobin

Tuesday, March 26th.—At every step of this day's journey the heights and valleys have increased in grandeur. Wide sandy plains exhibit now and then a mound or jagged rock detached, and standing picturesquely, far separated from the general mass. In beautifully defined perspective, twelve distinct mountain ridges all at one time appeared. Besides, we always seemed entirely enclosed within a formidable rocky barrier; and yet, the passage from one wady to another is so very gradual, it is quite impossible to ascertain where each of them begins or terminates. We rested in the hollow of a beetling cliff; and then pursued our way, hour after hour, along a winding glen—between high granite ranges, unequalled in the splendour of their general effect by any mountains I have ever seen. So real was our enjoyment of the scenery, we became almost unmindful of the excessive heat; which was occasionally tempered by a gentle breeze. Our course has varied from due north to north-west. The chosen camping-place—in Wâdy Machuse—to-night, is still more picturesque than that of yesterday; stupendous cliffs rise boldly all around, and shut us in, without any apparent opening.

The Mount Sinai Group, 1906

Baedeker's *Palestine and Syria*

This huge range, composed of primæval gneiss and granite, or, in more precise geological terminology, of colourless quartz, flesh-coloured felspar, green hornblende, and black slate, rising in majestic and precipitous masses and furrowed by vertical clefts, extends from Serbâl to the Om Shomar to the Râs Mohammed. Since the time of their formation these crystalline masses have undergone no geological change, but have reared their summits above the ocean from the beginning of time, unaffected by the transitions of the Silurian or Devonian, the Permian, Triassic, or chalk periods. At the base only do these venerable mountains show any trace of alteration. Thus the Red Sea has on one side thrown a girdle of coral around mount Sinai, and so in recent times produced a coast district; while towards the N. the sea, during the chalk period, has formed the limestone plateau of the desert of Tîh (5900 ft. above the sea-level), which stretches across the whole of Sinai to Mount Lebanon. The crystalline masses of the Sinai chain, which extend from N. to S. for a distance of about 40 M., exhibit no great variety. The whole range forms a central nucleus traversed by diorites and porphyries.

Where We Passed, 1912

Mary Dobson

The very pebbles we often trod underfoot—jasper, agate, and crystal of various kinds—were so sparklingly attractive that we longed to carry away innumerable specimens, and were only deterred from doing so by the difficulty of porterage.

The Pasha of Egypt, Abbas Pasha, commissioned a new road built through the Sinai Peninsula—a road which spread the modern world of the nineteenth century into lands which had until them avoided the progress of the age.

The Road through Sinai, 1852

Charles Didier

From Tor to the Monastery of Mount Sinai is twenty-five leagues; that is to say, camels take twenty-five hours to make the journey. The road that I was inaugurating—seeing that I was one of the earliest travellers, if not the first, to travel along it—runs in a direction a little east of north: it almost imperceptibly leaves the shore as it approaches Mount Sinai. If, instead of going round the huge wall of granite, one could cross it in a straight line, the route would be vastly shortened. But that is not possible. The road is distinct from the terrain it crosses only by reason of its solidity, which allows the camels to walk along it more quickly than on the sand, where their feet sink in, despite their width. Furthermore, the road, unlike the Suez one, has neither post-houses nor stage-coaches, and used by nobody. At no time throughout the day did we meet anybody.

They did however come across a group of people of the Tuwara, the Bedouin of Tor, and there was some discussion about payments. Eventually they passed onward and camped that night.

The sun rises late in these abysses. When it did make its appearance, I was struck by the grandeur of the spectacle that it illumined. The night before, on arrival, I had glimpsed nothing of the shadow of it through the darkness. Wadi Hibran is no more than a narrow defile cut as though by a pick between Mount Serbal on one side and, on the other, a range of the same formation belonging to the same system, which runs in the same direction. So far as can be seen, these two chains appear to be but one, and their compact massing seems to be mounting a challenge to all Nature's destructive force. When and how were the two sides separated? What powerful irresistible agent brought about this violent rupture, and clove so deep a gash into the granite? Was it water? Was it fire? Either hypotheses is just as likely as the other.

Perhaps more than any other traveler to Sinai, John Kinnear felt true compassion for the Israelites of the Old Testament who, it is told, passed through this land three thousand years earlier.

Into the Mountains and Wadis, 1839

John Kinnear

We had now left the more open part of the Desert, and our route lay among narrow sandy valleys, between rugged precipitous crags of calcareous rock, mixed with beds of gravel and indurated sand. You can hardly imagine a more savage scene. The crags rose sometimes perpendicularly, like enormous walls, their summits riven and shattered into the most wild and fantastic forms; occasionally the valleys opened out wider, and high isolated masses of rock rose abruptly from the sand, curiously turreted and embattled, and having their naked sides worn and undermined by the drifting sand, as if they had been subjected to the action of a torrent. Nature has often been represented as smiling: here she might be said to wear a ghastly and frantic grin. No living thing was to be seen, except the little grey lizards that darted across our path, or lay basking in the burning sunshine on the stones: the air was hot and motionless, and the glare from the white rocks and sand became painful to the eyes. For the first time I began to feel the thirst rather distressing, and the water, being heated by the sun, and having already acquired a nauseous taste from the skins, afforded little refreshment.

How little do we think, in reading the history of Israel's wanderings in the wilderness, of the trials and temptations to which they were exposed! Our minds are too apt to dwell on their rebellion and want of faith; their forgetfulness of the mighty signs and wonders which had so recently been wrought for their deliverance; their want of trust in His power and wisdom who, with a mighty hand and an outstretched arm, had brought them forth out of their house of bondage; and perhaps we may at times feel that their murmurings against the Lord and against Moses were something so extraordinary and unreasonable, that we never could have been guilty of the like, under the same circumstances. But how much must all that they had to endure of mere physical privations have been enhanced, and made more overwhelming, by the almost irresistible despondency which oppresses the mind, amid this fearful silence and solitude! It is impossible to look around on the ghastly and almost unearthly desolation of this "great and terrible wilderness" without feeling that their trials were far greater than we had ever before imagined; without feeling sympathy with their sufferings, and pity for their frailty.

After a painful day's march, we encamped at the entrance to Wady Homr, where we were fortunate enough to find some rain-water among the rocks, a little better than what we had in the skins.

Traveling from Tor, James Hamilton reported construction on the road described by few other travelers.

Lightning, Roads, Engineers, and Soldiers, 1857

James Hamilton

From Tor a long sandy flat, called El A'our, stretches to the foot of the majestic range of mountains, right well named the Black. The rugged peaks of Mount Serbal occupy the centre of the group; to the right rises Omm Shommar, and between them lies the Wady Shommar, and between them lies the defile of Wady Hebron, which leads up to Sinai.

Five hours it took us to reach the hills, which seemed at Tor scarcely half an hour distant. The sky had clouded over early in the morning, and at mid-day the summits of the mountains were hidden in dark vapours; at length heavy rain began to fall in the plain, and then forked lightnings were seen playing in vivid flashes around the rocks, and issuing in every direction from their black barren sides, and thunders, repeated in a hundred echoes, rolled loud and terrible overhead.

Such was the moment when Sinai should be seen; and we could only regret that we had not been one day earlier, to have witnessed this war of the elements in the rocky defiles of the mountain itself. The rain ceased, and in less than half an hour the thirsty sand was again dry, but the plain and the mountainsides were still chequered with the shadows of the heavy white clouds which rested in the air.

At the entrance of the pass, a short way up which the new road is completed, we passed through a camp of soldiers, the so-called engineers, who are employed in making it. The well-filled hospital, and the officers' and the common soldiers' tents, formed a long street, through which we rode with stopped nostrils, glad to escape the pestilential smells hanging around. An hour further up the valley we encamped near a beautiful natural bath, formed in the granite by the streamlet 'Ain Hebron, called by the natives the Christians' Pool, Birket el Nosrany.

James Hamilton's party pressed on through to Wadi Es-Slaf where they camped for the night.

At the further end of the plain commences the second ascent, Nagb-el-deir—the pass of the convent. It is as steep, and in places more difficult than the Nagh Hebran. Along its course may be seen, here and there, the remains of a paved road, which tradition ascribes to the pious munificence of the Empress Helena, but which was more probably the work of the monks, who in the sixth and seventh centuries were collected in and about Mount Sinai to the number of many thousands.

The scenery here is most terribly grand; no description could do justice to its general effects. The bare rocks rise on every side in long succession fantastically coloured, - grey, red, blue, bright yellow, and bronze, - sometimes strangely marked with white lines of quartz, or black bands of basalt; huge blocks, worn into fantastic shapes, and round which the laden beasts wind their way with difficulty, interrupt the narrow track which successive ages have worn along the face of the precipice, or hanging overhead threaten to overwhelm the traveller in their fall.

Beneath lies a veritable chaos, through which now trickles a slender thread of water, where in winter rushes down a boiling torrent. The time-polished faces of the rocks send back each sound in a hundred echoes, and at some points of the pass the report of a gun reverberates like a roll of thunder. A few vultures soaring overhead, longingly eyeing our wearied camels, were the only living animals to be seen.

Reaching the summit we stand at once on the edge of a table, which is bounded on three sides by the mountains of Sinai. This is Wady Er-Racha—the plain of repose—about three miles broad. At its furthest limit arises the group, which contains Sinai and Horeb, and between this and the hill called of St Episteme runs the pass, on the sloping side of which is seen a fortress-like mass, whose heaviness is relieved by a few projecting towers and a minaret. This is the Hostelry, established under the name of St Catharine, or of the Transfiguration.

Like others before and after him, Friar Felix of Ulm thought the route followed through the mountains and wadys of the peninsula might be chosen at the will of their guides rather than from the necessity of going that way.

Toward the Wished-for Spot, 1483

Felix Fabri

After a long journey through that valley, we came to the end of the valley, and passed out into a spacious plain, to the other side whereof came down the roots of the mountains, among which was the holy Mount Sinai. We journeyed across this plain towards the mountains which were over against us, and entered a valley wherein we made tedious circuits round about, now to this side and now to that, according to the windings of that crooked valley. We were led aside a long way out of the direct path to the holy mountain, and we passed by valleys which seemed to lead straight to it; for Mount Sinai stood directly to the south of us, but as the mountains barred our way, we went along the winding valleys now toward the east, a little way later toward the north, and sometimes toward the west, which vexed us much, because sometimes we saw Mount Sinai standing quite behind us. About noon we came to a place where the valley makes another turn toward the south, and here we left the high mountains behind us, and saw the peak of Sinai more clearly as it towered above all the other mountain-tops. Indeed, in this wilderness of Sinai there is a wondrous region of exceeding lofty and sharp-peaked mountains.

After we had journeyed for a little way with joy towards the holy mount, we left the valley which leads southward, and which seemed to lead straight up to its foot, and, following our guides, turned aside up a valley leading to the northward, turning our backs to Mount Sinai for a second time, whereat we went on our way murmuring and greatly disturbed. It was said among the pilgrims that our Arab camel-drivers were purposely leading us by roundabout paths through the wilderness, and trying to weary us out, that we might give them money to go by the shorter road. Indeed, they had turned aside out of the valleys which seemed to lead towards the wished-for spot, and went into valleys which lead the opposite way, wherefore those pilgrims who suspected they were being tricked and led purposely out of their way grumbled and cursed Calinus and the guides.

On the other hand some of the pilgrims said this was the right way, and that there was no trick about the matter, and these reproached the grumblers for cursing, and hereupon two knights quarrelled with one another, and began to disparage one another with abuse and foul language, upbraiding and cursing one another. These two became so angry that they dismounted from their asses, drew their swords, and made many passes at each other with the points. Howbeit, as both knights were well skilled in fence, each one parried the other's thrusts with his own sword. When the other pilgrims saw this, they ran up and strove to part them; but no one dared to come near to them for fear of his own skin, since both of them were exceeding furious, and wielded their swords recklessly. The Arabs who were with us also ran up, and albeit they were naked, yet they fearlessly put themselves between, stooping down beneath their swords. By this means the duel was brought to an end, since they could no longer thrust at one another without hurting an innocent Arab.

The Written Valley

Wadi Mukatteb—The Written Valley, 1873

Murray's Handbook

Leaving the point where the Wady Igne joins the Seih Sidreh, we continue along the latter till its junction with the Wady Mukkateb (the 'Written Valley'), a broad shallow watercourse, with terraced cliffs, piled up at the base with crumbling blocks and fragments. It derives its name from the so-called Sinaitic inscriptions with which its rocks abound. Those inscriptions are to be found in more less abundance all the way from Wady Igne to the head of Wady Mukkateb, but the great number of them occur in clusters in the space of about a mile at the lower end of this wady. At one time supposed to be of great antiquity, they are now proved to be the work of Christian hermits and pilgrims of certainly not earlier than the 3rd century.

The Bishop of Clogher, who translated and published the account of the "Prefetto of Egypt" in 1722, offered a large prize to any man of letters who would undertake to copy the inscriptions in Wadi Mukatteb.

Forty years later Carsten Niebuhr was less sure of the importance to the study of language of these inscriptions.

Of the Mountain of Inscriptions, 1762

Carsten Niebuhr

But the marvellous part of this discovery by degrees disappeared; and the sanguine hopes which had been built upon, vanished. Several travellers had before observed, upon the way to Mount Sinai, some rocks inscribed with strange characters: even in the third century, these inscriptions had been mentioned by a Greek author. Monomys had formerly copied some of them; Pococke and Montague had copied others, and had communicated them to several men of letters. They were judged to be neither Jewish nor Arabic, from the appearance of some coarse pieces of sculpture that accompanied them. Some considered them as a mixture of Coptic and Arabic characters. At last, a person, who was very well versed in Oriental literature, conjectured that they might be Phoenician: an opinion which is more probable, as the Phoenicians had, at a very remote period, settlements upon the eastern coast of the Arabic Gulf.

As little were the learned agreed concerning the purport of those inscriptions, and the information that they might afford. Those who examined them the most accurately, concluded, from their position, and the manner in which they were engraven, that they related nothing more than the names of travellers, and the date of their journies. In the same place are still to be seen a vast number of ill-engraven inscriptions, in Greek and Arabic, of the names of persons who have sought, by this means, to transmit the memory of their existence to future times.

After examining the situations and the engraving of these inscriptions, I incline to the opinion of those who think them executed at idle hours by travellers, who were satisfied with cutting the unpolished rock with any pointed instrument; adding to their names, and the date of their journies, some rude figures, which bespeak the hand of people but little skilled in the arts. When such inscriptions are executed with the design of transmitting to posterity the memory of such events as might afford instructive lessons, greater care is generally taken in the preparation of the stones, and the inscriptions are engraven with more regularity, as I shall have occasion to observe, when I come to the ruins of Persopolis.

By Whom Were They Written? 1853

Catherine Tobin

We wandered about the Mohkatteb for at least an hour. Many of the inscriptions are marvellously preserved, if they were *verily* traced by the wandering Israelites: but if not, by whom *were* they written? They *may* be relics of the early Christians, as some travellers suppose; and this was my own first impression; but I have since heard such powerful arguments in favour of their greater antiquity, that I must patiently await the decision of more competent judges. I had, perhaps too hastily, formed my opinion upon the appearance of these sandstone rocks themselves; whose surface, time and the action of the elements have worn, in some parts, into large holes and fissures. Pieces of curiously variegated granite lay scattered about. We descended towards the Wadee Feiran over uneven and rocky ground; the blue peak of Mount Serbal towered high above those of its neighbours; and more beautiful than ever was the after glow of sunset. A couple of friendly Sheikhs visited our camp that evening: they helped to form a very merry party, round a blazing fire, in front of the tents. The weather was so exceedingly warm that we could not bear the covering of a quilt at night.

An Early Interpretation, 1863 and A.D. 535

John Gadsby

I must mention the fact, however, which I learn from Beamont, that one Cosmas who travelled about 535 A.D., considered the inscriptions, or some of them, to be the work of the ancient Israelites, and says that certain Jews who had read them explained them to him as nothing the journey of such a tribe in such a year and month. Mr. Beamont then gives a translation of Cosmas' remarks:

"When the Israelites had received the law in written characters from God, and were just beginning to practise the art of writing, God turned the desert into an undisturbed school, wherein during forty years he permitted them to carve letters; hence at all their resting places in the wilderness of Sinai you may see all the fragments which have been detached from the rocks inscribed with carved Hebrew letters, a fact which I can testify from having visited the spot; and certain Jews read these inscriptions and explained them to me as signifying the journey of such a one of such a tribe, in this year and this month, just as many in our own days are wont to have records of their sojoinder in inns. The Israelites, however, as having recently learnt the art of writing, delighted in its exercise, and multiplied the number of inscriptions, so that all those sites are full of carved Hebrew letters, which remain even to the present day an argument against the unbeliever, I ween. The truth of my statement will be plain to any man who will either personally inspect the locality or make inquiries."

The Wadi Mukkateb, 1877

Samuel Manning

(Inscriptions) are not peculiar to this valley, but are found in many other parts of the Sinaitic range. They always occur in the lines of route along which caravans of traders or bands of pilgrims are likely to have passed, and are inscribed in the soft sandstone rock which forms the fringe of the harder granite in the centre of the peninsula. The sculptures are grotesque representations of birds, camels, asses, horses, ibexes, and other animals. The inscriptions are sometimes in Greek, Latin or Hebrew, but more commonly in a character unlike that of any known language.

Loiterers' Graffitti, 1854

R.W. Stewart

[T]here are innumerable inscriptions, often accompanied by rough representations of animals. A certain number of these writings are in Latin, Greek and Arabic, where the cross at times appears, and a great many are in an unknown tongue, some letters of which look like Hebrew. The simple and credulous traveller Cosmas (a merchant of Alexandria who had become a monk and visited the Peninsula early in the sixth century) was inclined to believe his Jewish travelling companions when they told him that the inscriptions in this wady dated back to the day of the Israelitish wanderings, and that they noted the arrival and departure of different tribes. Professor Palmer (E.H. Palmer), however, declared that the work was merely done by idle loungers, and the modern opinion is that they date from early Christian centuries, and that the unknown tongue is a lost Aramean dialect.

The explanation of the aforesaid loungers (whom you would not expect according to present conditions to find in such a place) is that in early Christian days Feiran was an important centre, with its own see and bishop; some idea of its magnitude may be gathered from the remains of stone buildings, which still may be seen on the hill of El Maharrad, where are also hermitages and graves, and *nawamis* or small circular stone erections with an entrance on one side.

Feiran then being practically a city is mentioned as large and prosperous as late as the fourth century; there must have been much coming and going, and travellers seized the opportunity, just as they do nowadays, to perpetuate their memory; the inscriptions in the Wady Mukatteb are the result.

W.H. Bartlett, who had read widely before his journey, and had met the German traveler Richard Lepsius, sometimes struggled with his guides who preferred to press on rather than explore places closely. Lepsius had told him where he might see hieroglyphic tablets. His guides denied it: "Not one of them had ever heard of it in the entire peninsula!" Still, Bartlett pressed his case.

Written Valley to Oasis, 1845

W.H. Bartlett

Arriving at the mouth of a side valley, which appeared to me to answer the position in the Map, I came to a halt, in the midst of a scene of loud uproar, the servants abusing the Arabs, and Komeh being, with some difficulty, prevented from beating our incapable sheik, who kept on reiterating with true Arab pertinacity, "Maghara ma fish." (There is no Maghara!)

By good luck, in this remote place, a solitary Arab was descried passing down the wadi and was hailed. Yes, he knew the place, and he would conduct us to the place all the travelers went to see. At last the Arab led them into a cave, but there was nothing to see. Then, as he had just despaired. . . .

[L]o! perched up within a hundred yards of the very spot we had gained at the risk of our necks, yet concealed from thence by some rocky projections, behold the large sculptured tablets, with numerous figures, grinning down at us, as it were like Efrits (demons), and asking whether we would like to come up again and have a look at them.

By the time they reached the tablets their last drop of water was gone and it was now noon. Without a sheltering umbrella, he could not draw them.

It seemed wonderful, and almost incredible, to find here, in so distant a spot, high up on the side of the mountain, sculptured records of so remote antiquity, and by the precision, and even spirit, of their style, testifying to the high civilisation of Egypt, at a period when the utmost limits of the historical, recedes into the fabulous and mysterious obscurity of unrecorded time.

The principal tablet . . . represents the conquest of the surrounding country by an early Egyptian king, whose name appears on a cartouche, or oval; the word 'Tau', hieroglyphically written by the hand, bird, and crowns on each side of the principal actor, signifying mountain lands, and the conqueror's title, Lord of Battles, given (or gifted) with life for ever, appearing in the other emblems.

Is it not almost too marvellous for belief that these tablets existed before the Exodus of the Israelites, when Moses, with all his host, actually passed, beyond question, down the valley towards Wady Fieran and Sinai?

They proceeded toward Wadi Mokatteb, the 'Written Valley.' Bartlett contrasted the carving with that he had just seen.

This drawing will convey a correct idea both of the characters and of the rude attempt to portray camels, and other animals—perfectly childish efforts, and widely different from the finished works of Egyptian art that we had just been inspecting.

Careless Writing, 1878

Isabella Bird

In the Wady Sidreh, where the grey granite gives way to coloured sandstone, I saw the first inscription, and, turning up another valley, visited the Egyptian hieroglyphics, which are reputed to be among the oldest in the world anterior to the exodus.

"The Written Valley" is however the next one—Mokatteb—and with this I was disappointed. There is no look of solid, earnest labour about the inscriptions. They are mostly scrawled carelessly and slightly on a sandstone which is very easily worked. They are untidy and illiterate-looking. Their height is not great, and they are nearly always on rocks easy of access. The carelessness and apparent haste in which they have been scratched is in contrast with the solid carefulness of the ancient Egyptian hieroglyphics which are their neighbours.

They are a heterogeneous medley of Greek, Arabic, Latin, and other characters, and names missed up with crosses, the cross sometimes placed between the Greek Alpha and Omega, and with childish and grotesque representations of animals. I think that the ibis occurs most frequently, but it is the ibis caricatured, butting other animals with enormously exaggerated horns. Besides the ibis are donkeys, horses, dogs, and there is a man riding on a horse or ass, sitting very near its tail and carrying a cross. The Greek word *Polloi* occurs, I think, several times. Many of the inscriptions, according to Professor Palmer are in a dialect of the Aramaic tongue. I think that the consensus of learned opinion is that they are of a date not earlier than the fourth century, and that they are the work of Christian hermits and pilgrims. There is very little about them which is interesting to me, while I could not but look with profound reverence on the Egyptian tablets of the ancient Maghara. The turquoise mines, of which they record the discovery and the workings, have not been worked by the Egyptians for 3,000 years!

Not All That It Seems, 1914

Oliver Brockbank

April 1st—Started at 6:20 a.m., and after an hour or so reached Wady Mokatteb, and snapped some of the ancient Nabatean inscriptions which abound on the rocks. Possibly here was Rephidim, where Amalek attacked the Children of Israel, and where, with the Lord's help, Joshua won his first great victory. We were now approaching the fertile Wady Fieran, and on every hand

Tablet in Wadi Magharal

we could see tracks of animals on the sand. Mr Hensman and I began to emulate boy scouts, and soon became proficient in distinguishing snake and game tracks. Amidst great excitement we found the track of a gazelle, which was evidently being chased by a hyena. We followed it for over a mile, to find a Bedouin dog driving a goat for its master towards the pastures and springs of Wady Feiran!

Oases and City

The Grandest Wadi, 1873

Murray's Handbook

The road now descends from the summit level, and enters a wide boulder-strewn valley towards the Wady Feiran, the grandest of all the Sinaitic wadies. About a mile up the valley . . . are some stone circles and cairns, probably sepulchral monuments of a very early date. . . .

The Wady Feiran now opens out into a succession of long open reaches, with Jebel Serbal and its neighbouring peaks filling up the background. . . . The rich colouring of the sandstone rocks is now exchanged for the somewhat more sober hues, but more varied outlines of granite, gneiss, etc. As we advance further the bed of the wady narrows, and the scenery becomes grander at every step.

The ruins of Feiran

The grandeur and desolation of the scenery now becomes almost overpowering, and the eye rests with pleasure on the little oasis of El Hesweh, to be followed not long after by the welcome sight of the great palm-grove of Feiran, a rich mass of dark-green foliage winding eastward through the hills. A rugged valley, Wady Aleyat, at whose head stand Jebel Serbal, here comes in from the south-east; and in the centre of the open space caused by their junction stands a hillock crowned with ruins. In this pleasant oasis the traveller will pitch his tent with delight, and, if he can, devote at least one, and better two days to an examination of the surrounding district.

A Good Staging Post, 384

Egeria

Next, two mountains come into sight on the left, and, before you reach them, there is a place where the Lord rained manna* on the children of Israel. They are lofty mountains, and very steep. On one side of the mountains the valley is perfectly flat and like a colonnade about two hundred yards wide, with the steep high mountains on either side. But where the mountains open out the valley is six miles wide and a good deal longer.

* Exodus 16:14.

All around the mountains caves have been carved out, and, if you just took the trouble to put up some curtains, they would make marvellous bedrooms. Each bedroom is inscribed with Hebrew letters. At the far end of the valley there is good water in plenty, but it is not the equal of Elim. This is called the Desert of Paran, and it was from here that Moses sent out spies to explore the land. It is protected by mountains on both sides, but it has no fields or vineyards, and there is nothing there but water and some palm trees.

Approach to Wadi Feiran, 1845

W.H. Bartlett

But a sudden change awaited us; about noon, at a turn of the road, the scene that burst upon us was more like the dream of a poet, than any reality in this arid wilderness. The cliffs on either side still towered, bare and perpendicular, to an immense height.

Disaster in the Wadi, 1877

Samuel Manning

Leaving the Wady Mokatteh by a boulder-strewn valley, we enter the Wady Feiran, the most beautiful and fertile of all the wadis in the peninsula—perhaps the only one to which these epithets can properly be applied. A few years ago it was devastated by a frightful inundation caused by storms of unusual violence in the mountains, which turned the wady into a torrent ten feet in depth. Thirty Bedouin were drowned, hundreds of sheep and goats perished, and upwards of a thousand palm trees were washed away. Many years must pass before the traces of this destructive deluge have disappeared.

The Color of the Place, 1938

H.V. Morton

We crossed the plain and turned eastward into the entrance of a mountain gorge that rises gradually between towering heights. This was the beginning of the Wadi Feiran, which runs for about thirty miles into the mountains and drains the whole of the Serbal Range. Walls of rose-red and mauve granite rose up sheer into the sky, where they hung with bare and jagged peaks, shining against the blue; and side by side with them were mountains of pale amber and sulphur-red, streaked with plum-coloured veins of porphyry and black bands of diorite. All the beauty which we normally associate with the colours of grass, heather and flowers were poured recklessly over a fantastic wealth of geological formations. Never for one moment did the eye become weary of this wilderness. There was some new beauty to be seen along every yard of the way. As if Nature were not content with the natural colours of the rocks, the light filled each hollow and cranny and the long downward gashes of the mountains with blues so pale and delicate that I was reminded of the pale blue of the Connemara hills, and blues so deep and definite that I compared them to the darkness of the hills of Skye. How different is this Desert of Sinai from the terrible monotony of the Libyan Desert, with its meaningless contours and its stone-scattered plains, which take the very heart out of one.

Artists in the Fertile Wadi, 1872

Paul Lenoir

Arable land announced itself by shrubs and tufts like those which had already charmed our eyes by their silvery foliage and elegant forms; then the shrubs gave way to trees, and palms pushed their proud tufted heads through the apertures in the rocks. This oasis is the only fertile wadi in the peninsula of Sinai. As we got further into it, we found a veritable forest of superb palm trees, with a delicious stream running through it. The village, composed of earthen huts, was hidden by these wild palms, whose branches, having been allowed to grow from the entire trunk of the tree, swept the ground.

We were much struck by the novel aspect of the primitive palm tree; it completed the wild character of this strange locality. The little low houses were sometimes below the level of the beaten track, for in this gorge the keenest cold succeeds to the suffocating heat which we were then experiencing. The less vivid colouring of the mountains rendered the background of the magnificent picture more natural. We had never seen anything more picturesque. We all wanted to set to work on 'studies' without an hour's delay; and a halt of several days was voted unanimously, a halt which we occupied in conscientious and delightful hard work.

Every day we bathed in the limpid waters of the stream. One fine morning we were paddling about like ducks, when a caravan turned into the wadi. It was that of an English lady, accompanied by her son and his tutor. We promptly hid ourselves in hollows of the rocks when we caught sight of the new-comers; but in the evening the two caravans exchanged visits. The English lady gave us delicious tea, but we could not entertain her by any means so handsomely, so that we were obliged to resort to our photographs with special eagerness. The lady, who was travelling rapidly, was to set out the next day for Sinai. She had just a month in which to 'do' Syria and Asia Minor, and get back to London *via* St Petersburg.

The City of Pharan, 1873

Murray's Handbook

The ruins of Feiran itself are those of the old Episcopal city of Pharan. The old convent and church stand on the top of the hillock, at the junction of the wadies. The principal walls of the convent still remain, built in flat stones and mud, with sun-dried bricks at the top. The church is at the northern end, and, from the number of capitals, broken shafts, and other remains found within its walls, appears to have been a building of some importance. On a low neck of land which connects the hillock with the wady are the remains of the town, surrounded by a wall which is seven foot high; parts of it remain, the composite of mud and small stones being here faced with large unhewn boulders. Both within and without the walls are the remains of buildings, and to the west in a 'jorf' or bank of alluvium, is the cemetery; the tombs are partly cut perpendicularly in the face of the rock, and partly built with large stones, and the entrances are closed by large slabs of stone, or built up with mud and stones. These tombs are often used by the Bedaween.

On the right bank of the Wady Feiran is a deserted village, which probably formed part of the old city, but which bears traces of having been occupied at a later period by a settled Arab population.

Isabella Bird—one of the most intrepid of Victorian lady travelers—was determined to see the ruins of Pharan, although she had been so ill only the night before. She clearly used her* Murray's Handbook *when she wrote of her visit.

Visiting the Ruins, 1878

Isabella Bird

The Bedaween feasted on the kid which I had given them, and we all had abundance of good water. They had brought firewood from Feiran, and when the darkness came the red light from their fire lighted up the neighbouring mountains and made me think of the Pillar of Fire which had, probably near this spot, lighted these same mountain sides. Contrary to my usual practice I sat at my tent-door till midnight.

Nearly all recent scholarship, however divided and uncertain as to most of the localities of the Israelitish wanderings, is agreed that Israel passed to Sinai by the Wady Feiran, making a long halt by its waters. It is probable that the battle of Rephedim was fought near this spot, that the little hill of Gebel-el-Tahooneh was the mount from which Moses witnessed that great fight between Israel and Amalek, that the altar was built there, and that to Feiran Jethro came to visit Moses, and was compelled to acknowledge that Jehovah was god above all gods. These events all stood out that night as though they were facts of our own time.

Early the next morning, before the sun was fully risen, and while the camels and the Bedaween were still lying around the embers of the bivouac fire, I climbed up the little hill of El-Maharrad at the junction of the wadys to visit the ruins of the old Episcopal city of Pharan—most mournful ruins in a solitary place.

The convent and church, in a state of undraped ruin, are on the top of the hill. Capitals, broken shafts, and carved stones lie about in profusion, and these and the size of the walls show it to have been a building of much importance. The principal walls of the convent also remain. These are partly adobe and partly flat stones and mud. The neck of land which connects the hillock with the wady is the site of the town of Pharan, formerly a walled city. The remains have the appearance of a very picturesque fortification. Parts of the walls are of unhewn boulders, and are about seven feet high and four feet thick, the middle being composed of rubble.

To the west, in a bank of alluvium, is the cemetery. Many of the tombs are cut in the face of the rock, and their entrances are closed by big slabs of stone. Others are built up with mud and stones. The tombs are very numerous, and are still used by the wandering Bedouin.

On the opposite hillock, which I also went up, there are uncouth ruins of a chapel, pillars of red sandstone of a square shape, and the form of the apse still remains. In 600, Antonius Martyr says that a chapel stood on the spot from which Moses viewed the battle of Rephidim. This chapel was turned into a mosque afterwards.

The whole flight of rude steps which leads up to it from Wady Feiran is marked by the ruins of small chapels, many of which are built over the cells or tombs of hermits. In truth, this now solitary and desolate region must once, owing to its sanctity, have had a considerable population. Besides several monastic establishments, of which the ruins remain in the neighbourhood of Gebel Serbal, the sides of a considerable part of the Wady Feiran are honeycombed by the cells of anchorites, who are described as having sat "like a lot of rabbits in the mouths of their holes."

Leaving My Name, 1845

W.H. Bartlett

October 11: It was with positive reluctance that I prepared to leave the palms of Wady Feiran; but a long journey was before me, and travelling in the Desert is slow work at best. About noon we were ready, and after inscribing my name on the limestone altar by the side of the stream, in grateful token of the great enjoyment I had derived from my stay, I saw my tent descend, and solitude gathering over the spot lately animated by my temporary home, then proceeded slowly on foot up the valley towards Mount Sinai. Palm groves continue for half an hour's walk in this direction, and the whole passage, till they cease, is like a region of enchantment; an old convent, in ruins, juts out on a spur of rock, in the midst of the vegetation, just where the sublime summit of the Serbal peeps over the precipitous walls of the valley, which here forms a narrow grassy glade, between two avenues of palms, and is kept moist and green by the spring, which, issuing from the base of a small cliff, trickles across the little area. Among thickets and gardens are seen the Bedouin women, who suspend the rude cradles of their children from the boughs, while others are playing among flocks of sheep and goats; a scene fancifully beautiful as the fabled golden age.

Detour to Mount Serbal and Serabit

A Parallel Road, 1835

Leon de Laborde

We rode on for eight hours in order to reach the baths of Pharaoh, which are situated at the foot of a mountain of the same name. They presented no object for the pencil, and after examining them we rejoined the camels, which we had sent on before us through Wady Wisset, a valley, or rather the bed of a torrent, parallel to Wady Garandel. Wady Wisset is a precipitous defile, devoid of vegetation; the rocks which form its sides are sometimes of freestone tinted with red colour, sometimes of chalk of a dazzling whiteness. The traveller is particularly struck by the rude appearance of these rocks, and by the fantastic features of so narrow a passage through these lofty mountains, the first which he has to penetrate. At every turn of this curious passage the aspect of the rocks becomes bolder and more picturesque.

After having traversed this defile for an hour and a half, we reached a more open part of the valley; then leaving Wady Wisset on the left, we entered the valley of Issaitu, in which some palm trees are to be found. A little farther on we halted for the night, the country around us being arid and desolate in the extreme.

We quitted our encampment at half past six in the morning, and soon after began rapidly to ascend, until we entered Wady Sal, which, though not extensive, particularly delighted the eye by its verdure, presenting a strong contrast to the fatiguing monotony we had hitherto encountered. We passed the tomb of a Sheick; and at nine, descended towards Wady Taibe. Twelve hours of a wearisome march led us to Wady Nasb, at the foot of a lofty rock of sand stone, by which all pilgrims and travellers usually pass on their way to the convent of Sinai.

During these journeys in the desert, where the impressions one receives as one rides along are seldom communicated to others, and remain almost dormant within the mind itself, nothing is more delightful than to meet with the traces of a former traveller, in a place otherwise of no importance. The rock under which we slept at Wady Nasb was the same that afforded shelter to Niebuhr, Seetzen, and Burckhardt. The recollection of this circumstance gave a social character to the spot, and seemed to increase for the moment the number of our companions. A half-formed sketch, slightly drawn on the face of the rock, a few names scratched here and there, scarcely legible, gave life, as it were, to the desert around us, so seldom exhibiting any signs of the scattered population by which it is inhabited.

Niebuhr remained for a while at this place, and his companion, Bauerfeind, made a view of the rock, which he called Wady Ussaitu. While our people were preparing supper, I also sketched this solitude. The mountains of Tih, and the bustle of our caravan, added some features to a scene by no means picturesque of itself, but which, nevertheless, may possess some interest for a traveller, who, like myself, comes to seek a night's repose beneath the shade of this hospitable precipice.

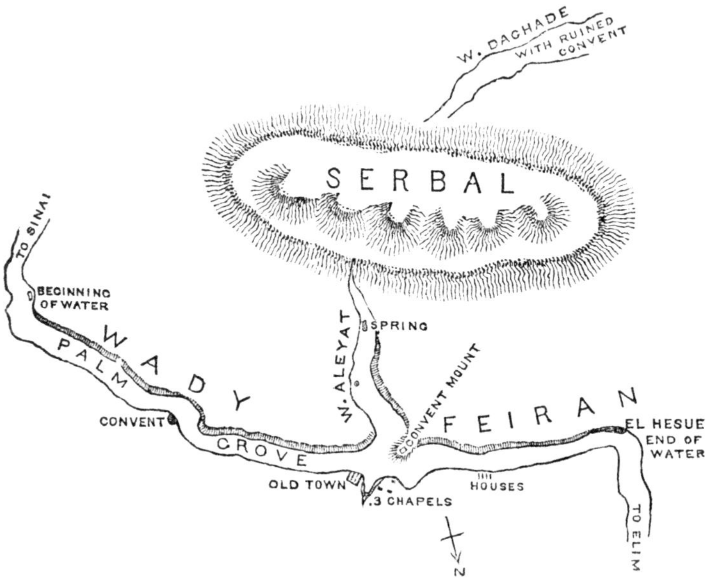

Mount Serbal, 1854

R.W. Stewart

Serbal does not disappoint one on a near approach to it. Majestic as he seems when you survey his serrated crust towering above all his compeers for days before you reach the base, his presence is still more noble as seen from Wadi Aleiat.

There are no outworks or fences, no shoulders or projecting spurs, to detract from his stature or hide his summit, until you have achieved half the ascent; his precipitous sides rise sheer and clear from the rough valley along which we were toiling, like a large three decker from the sea. I perceived at once the force of that description which is given of the Mount of God, "the Mount which might be touched!" Someone has most happily described Serbal as "a series of inverted stalactites". Between each of the peaks there is a ravine, so steep and narrow, that the ascent through it seems impossible; but to that which separates the easternmost and highest peak of the mountain from the rest, the guide led me, intimating by signs and words, that up its almost perpendicular face we were to make our way. Burckhardt, however, mentions another road, containing flights of steps, which wound round its eastern shoulder, till it reached the summit, as that used by the monks and pilgrims in former days. I have no doubt that his statement is correct as we fell in with it about a quarter of an hour from the top.

Ascent of Mount Serbal 1, 1864

Arthur Penryn Stanley

From Wady Feiran some hardy travellers turned aside to spend a hard day ascending Jebel Serbal—to some the most striking mountain of the peninsula, rising to a height of 4,000 feet above the valley. This was not, warned Murray's Handbook, an activity "to be undertaken by any but good walkers and climbers."

It is one of the finest forms I have ever seen. It is a vast mass of peaks, which, in most points of view, may be reduced to five, the number adopted by the Bedouins. These five peaks, all of granite, rise so precipitously, so column-like, from the broken ground which forms the root of the mountain, as at first sight to appear inaccessible. But they are divided by steep ravines, filled with fragments of fallen granite. Up the central ravine, Wady Abu-Hamad (Valley of the father of wild figs, so called from half a dozen in its course), we mounted. It was toilsome but not difficult, and in about three hours we reached a ridge between the third and fourth peaks. Here we rested; close by us were traces of a large leopard. A little beyond was a pool of water surrounded by an old enclosure.

Three quarters of an hour more brought us over smooth blocks of granite to the top of the third or central peak, the steep ascent being broken by innumerable shrubs like sage or thyme, which grew to the very summit: and at last, helped by loose stones arranged by human hands (whether yesterday or two thousand years ago), and through a narrow pass of about twenty feet, to the eminences of which this peak is formed.

The highest of these is a huge block of granite; on this, as on the back of some petrified tortoise, you stand and overlook the whole Peninsula of Sinai. The Red Sea, with the Egyptian hills opposite, and the wide waste of the ka'a on the south, the village and grove of Tor just marked as a dark line on the shore; on the east the vast cluster of what is commonly called Sinai, with the peaks of St Catherine; and, towering high above all, the less famous, but most magnificent of all, the Mont Blanc of those parts, the unknown and unvisited Um Shaumer.

Every feature of the extraordinary conformation lies before you; the wadys coursing and winding in every direction; the long crescent of the Wady es-Sheykh; the infinite number of mountains like a model; their colours all as clearly displayed as in Russegger's geological map, which we had in our hands at the moment: the dark granite, the brown and stone, the yellow Desert, the dots of vegetation along the Wady Feiran, and the one green spot of the great palm-grove of Rephidim. On the northern and somewhat lower eminence are the visible remains of a building, which, like the stairs of stones mentioned before, may be of any date from Moses to Burckhardt.*

The Ascent of Mount Serbal 2, 1914

Oliver Brockbank

My Arab guide (a dervish) came for me at 4 a.m. The sun had not yet risen, and

---

* Burckhardt was there in 1816.

for the first half hour or so we had to climb with the aid of an electric torch. The track for the first hour lay along the Wady Aleyat, and just as we reached the upper end of it, and a little oasis at the foot of the ascent of Mount Serbal, day dawned and the sunlight gilded the five rugged peaks of granite which towered above us. My dervish guide stopped for a few minutes to pray towards Mecca, and then we commenced the long, steep climb. Fortunately for another hour we were still in the shadow, so that the early part of our climb was done in comfort. On many of the rocks at the beginning of the mountain we could see inscriptions and crude carvings of ibex, camels, birds and men.

About 6:30 a.m., we reached the foot of the great Couloir, and before us rose a very steep climb up slippery granite rocks. My guide therefore hid our lunch amongst the rocks to await our return, and, pacing it far too quickly for my comfort, climbed on. The mountain was almost destitute of vegetation, but on the lower slopes, we disturbed two large coveys of partridges—fine handsome birds with pretty plumage. The last half hour, above the Couloir, was even steeper and more dangerous, and my thin, smooth-soled boots slipped badly on the granite slopes. Just below the summit I saw some more inscriptions on the rocks, and the ruins of a building of some kind.

At 8:45 a.m., we reached the top of El Medauwa—the highest of the five peaks of Mount Serbal. The views in every direction were glorious, including the Gulfs of Suez and Akaba, the Sinai group of mountains, and, in the far distance to the north, the Araba and Mount Hor.

I found the descent much more dangerous than the ascent, for my boots constantly played me tricks, and my dervish guide forged on far ahead. For times I shot down the rocks and fell, once very heavily, but as my guide carried my camera no great damage was done.

Murray's Handbook ***suggested two routes to the convent from Suez. The majority of travelers, took Route (a); a few, including E.H. Palmer, took Route (b) via Serabit al-Khadim. In the heart of the rugged Sinai Peninsula, is a rock-cut Twelfth Dynasty sanctuary to Hathor with inscriptions of pharaohs Hatshepsut and Tuthmosis. Nearby an ancient track leads to the turquoise mines of Magara.***

The Route Via Serabit el Khadim, 1865

E.H. Palmer

On the broad plateau of sandstone mountain stands a little group of ruins containing a number of upright flat stones, with rounded tops, exactly similar in form to the conventional gravestones of a London cemetery. On closer inspection these, as well as the stones of which the walls were once composed, are found to be covered with hieroglyphics, and the ruins are in reality those of a temple (or rather temples, for there are two distinct buildings) erected for the convenience of the Egyptians who worked in the numerous mines around. The upper end contains the sanctuary, which is excavated out of the natural rock.

Our baggage camels had been sent on ahead while we turned aside to visit Serabit el Khadim; and as it was necessary for us to reach the encampment before dark, we had not much time for moralising on the quaint aspect of this relic of an elaborate civilisation amongst the savage wilds of Sinai, nor for speculating upon the condition of that little knot of worshippers who mayhap were bowing down to Apis while the great Pilgrim Father passed, led onward by the cloud by day and the fire by night. After a hurried glance, therefore, we descended the mountain and rode along through a narrow defile between sandstone cliffs called Nagb Suwig, encamping a little further on, in Wady Bark. The sun had already set before we came up to the tents, and I was thus enabled to enjoy the pleasure of a new sensation—that of a hungry man who sees a distant fire and knows it is his dinner which is being cooked. Alas! there is no romance that will stand the test of appetite.

Reaching Serabit required the traveler to toil through deep sand to a rocky ravine, leave the riding-camel and walk for an hour up the wadi and up a rough incline. Seven hundred feet above the wadi are the ruins. C.W. Wilson provided the description for the **Handbook.**

Clambering to Serabit, 1873

Murray's Handbook

The view is very striking and extensive, but a more immediate cause for admiration will be found in the ruins which lie around. These consist of two temples of different dates; the earlier merely a rock-hewn chamber with an open vestibule in front; the later a large building, connected with the former, but not in the same straight line with it. Both appear to have been reconstructed.

In the centre of the rock-hewn chamber a square pillar of solid rock has been left to support the roof; both this and the walls of the chamber were formerly covered with hieroglyphics and coloured. At the end of the chamber are two recesses; one of which, formerly provided with a door, leads to a small space roofed over with large flat slabs; near this is another rock-hewn chamber, and in front of the two stretches an open court, the walls of which are covered with sculptured scenes. In this court are some *stele,* which appear to have been removed from their original position.

The later temple consists of a large square court, with fragments of pillars and Athor-headed capitals, and of a long building divided into numerous small chambers. At the end nearest the rock-hewn temple is a large gateway. The walls are covered with tablets and inscriptions, and the whole must have been very fine when perfect; at present it is one mass of ruin.

Round the temples are long heaps of stone, the remains probably of enclosing walls. The whole is much buried in sand, and C.W. Wilson thinks that excavating would bring a good many things to light. The little digging done by the Ordnance Survey (of which Wilson was a member) resulted in the finding of a small gold ornament, a few scarabaei, broken necklaces, fragments of pottery, etc. The number of *stela* is remarkable.

No Copying! 1762

Carsten Niebuhr

The Arabs suffered us to examine those curiosities at our leisure, and to note down upon the spot, some particulars relevant to them. But, when I began to copy some of the hieroglyphics, they gathered all about me, and told me, that the Schiech of the mountain would not permit this to be done. That pretended Sheich was an Arab of their acquaintance, whom they had agreed to honour with the title, and invest with the power, of purpose to draw money of us. The lord of Jibebel-el-Mokatteb, who had waited our approach upon the top of the hill, came up upon this and told us that he would not for a hundred crowns suffer us to copy the least thing, or permit Christians to carry away any treasures that were hidden in his territories. The Arabs believe, or pretend to believe, that the Europeans are in possession of secrets by which they can make any hidden treasure arise out of the earth, and can convey it away through the air, if they are only permitted to copy any inscription indicating its situation. Upon this fancy, they raised a claim of either sharing with us in the treasures which might be found, or receiving an hundred crowns for their permission for us to search for them.

Niebuhr later returned with one of the expeditions' own Arabs and copied hieroglyphics "as well executed as any I have seen in Egypt."

The Tombs of Serabit, 1835

Leon de Laborde

We resumed our journey before dawn, in order that we might have time to survey the antiquities of Sarbout el Cadem. After having proceeded for about two hours through rocky valleys, we entered on a small plain bearing that appellation. On the left, the mountains separated from each other by several ravines, were inferior in height to those which rose upon our right, and which being precipitous and terminating in a lofty peak, appeared like the enormous walls of some gigantic fortification. Just at the commencement of the plain there is a large cavern in the rocks, within which we found a fine cascade, walled in on each side by fragments that had fallen from the top. Some tamarisks, acacias, and green shrubs, which grew by these waters, served to mitigate the severe aspect imparted to the whole mountain by the sombre colour of the rocks.

A precipitous, difficult, and dangerous pathway conducted us to the southern summit of the mountain. We were obliged to use our hands as well as our feet in effecting our ascent, which was no easy manner to accomplish, as the rocks sometimes gave way, and fell with a loud crash into the ravine below. On reaching the top we found a firmer footway along a narrow ridge of the mountain, which was straitened on one side by a large basin, filled with water, during the rainy season, and on the other by a sort of entrenchment of rocks, which towered above the valley.

The passage then became considerably wider, and we reached the funeral monuments, which rise like so many apparitions in the midst of this strange and gloomy wilderness. The first appearance of these tombs astonished us; consisting as they did of stones standing up, carved in the Egyptian style, and placed amidst solitude and silence, without any connection whatever with the neighbouring desert.

When we proceeded through these ruins, and carefully examined the remains of the tombs which still exist, we felt more and more surprised discovering out of Egypt, thus isolated, and remote from all haunts of men, that indefatigable taste for the construction of memorials; that unexampled perseverance in labour, which quarried out materials, polished, sculptured, and painted them, and endowed them with all the peculiar national and religious characteristics of that still mysterious country.

Whose Words Are These? 1838

Edward Robinson

Not the least singularity about these monuments is the wonderful preservation of the inscriptions upon this soft sandstone, exposed as they have been to the air and weather during the lapse of so many ages. On some of the stones they are quite perfect; on others both the inscription and the stone itself have been worn away deeply by the tooth of time. . . .

What then could have been the intent of these temples and these memorial stones in the midst of solitude and silence in this lone and distant desert, with which they would seem to have no possible connection? This is a point wrapped in the darkness of time, which the hand of modern science has not yet unveiled.

An ingenious hypothesis was mentioned to me by an English nobleman.* viz. that this was perhaps a sacred place of pilgrimage for the ancient Egyptians, just as the mountain near Mecca is to the Muhammadans at the present day; and to it the Egyptian kings made each a pilgrimage and erected a column with his name. A slight historical ground for such a hypothesis, may perhaps be found in the fact, that Moses demanded permission for the Israelites to go three days journey into the desert in order to sacrifice,† - a demand that seems to have caused no surprise to the Egyptians, as if it were something to which they were themselves accustomed. Still all this can be nothing more than conjecture. Yet this lone spot, although inexplicable, is deeply interesting; it leads the beholder back into

* Lord Prudhoe, later Duke of Northumberland.

† Exodus viii, 27, 28.

the gray mists of high antiquity; and fills him with wonder and awe as he surveys here, far from the abode of life, the labours of men unknown for an object alike unknown.

The Monuments and Story of Serabit, 1882

Sir Flinders Petrie

The beginning of the monuments of Sinai is in the 1st dynasty, about 5300 BC. The seventh king of that dynasty is here written at Semerkhet; and this is doubtless the true form of the name, though it is usually inverted in Egypt to Mersekha. On a smooth natural face of the upper sandstone rock, at 394 ft. above the valley-floor, the scene of this king has been engraved, by sinking the ground and leaving the figures in relief. The surface of the figures are left of the natural fractured face of the stone, without any rounding or dressing. The stone does not appear in the least weathered since it was cut, except in the title, and part of the figure of the general; the original face does not seem to have lost even a single coat of sand-grains. The position is rather difficult to reach, and requires some climbing towards the end. . . .

It will be seen that there are three figures of the king. First as king of Upper Egypt, with his *ka*-name, or name of the hawk, with the crown of Lower Egypt; second as king of Lower Egypt, unnamed; and third as king of Upper Egypt, with the hawk-name, uncrowned, smiting a chief of the Bedawyn, whom he has seized. The face of the Bedawy, roughly indicated here, is very like that of the present chief of the same district, Abu Ghaneym. . . . The general of the expedition is figured also here, a little in advance of the group of the king, and on the same scale.

Hussein, Laborde's dragoman and companion on his journeys, became famous in the region, accompanying other travelers over the years.

Searching for Turquoise, 1835

Leon de Laborde

Hussein attended me during my labours, and in order to find occupation for the time that to him appeared tedious in the midst of heaps of rubbish which he deemed insignificant, he searched amongst the ruins for turquoise stones, which are found here in great abundance, being brought to the surface by the rains. He gave me five of these stones, which were of considerable size, parting with them without the slightest reluctance.

The Arabs of the present day attach no value to the turquoise, though in former ages it was much sought after in the East, the most extraordinary medicinal qualities having been ascribed to it. Tiefaschi, in his treatise on precious stones, thus speaks of it: "Sadi gives us to understand that it was highly esteemed in Persia. A person spending a few days upon this mountain, where he will be exposed to no danger, and which is not more than six days; journey from Cairo, might take a large collection of turquoises, which, though not to be ranked among the best of precious stones, nevertheless possess a great value."

The 'Mazhur,' 1882

Sir Flinders Petrie

Turning to modern times, the most curious personality connected with Sinai is that of Major Macdonald. After visiting the place in 1845, he returned and settled here with his wife in 1854, to search for turquoise. His house was built on the east of the 'Fort' hill, and many Bedawyn came to work for him, and settled nearby, learning to build stone huts from his example. The walls of his settlement yet remain, and Abu Ghaeym still uses the principal building. . . . He (Major Macdonald) lived, vainly trying to succeed in turquoise mining, until 1866. Then he left, and lived at Serabit for a year, after which he retreated to Cairo, where he died in 1870. Sheik Abu Ghaneym remembers him well, and is always ready to talk about 'Mazhur' and his boy 'Willem'. That memory is the main pivot of Aby Ghaneym's boyish recollections, and the ways and doings of 'Mazhur' are always appealed to as an authority. He at least set the best example of mining explorer, for he was always diligent in taking paper squeezes of the inscriptions, to search out fresh ones, and to preserve all that he could find. The great collection of squeezes at the British Museum is mainly due to his care.

Another Route

Murray's Handbook ***informed travelers that it was conjectured that the bulk of the Israelite host passed through Wadi al-Sheikh, a longer but easier route to Sinai. The wadi has important significance to Muslims as well.***

Wadi esh-Sheikh, 1816

John Lewis Burckhardt

In the afternoon we crossed the mountain by a by-path, fell again into the Wady el-Sheikh, and at the end of eight hours from our setting out in the morning reached the tomb of Sheikh Szaleh, from which the whole valley takes its name. The coffin of the Sheikh is deposited in a small stone rude building; and is surrounded by a thin partition of wood, hung with green cloth, upon which several prayers are embroidered. On the walls are suspended silk tassels, handkerchiefs, ostrich eggs, camel halters, bridles etc, the offerings of the Bedouins who visit this tomb.

I could not learn exactly the history of this Sheikh Szaleh: some said that he was the forefather of the tribe of Szowaleha; others, the great Moslem prophet Szaleh, sent to the tribe of Thamoud, and who is mentioned in the Koran; and others, again, that he was a local saint, which I believe to be the truth. Among the Bedouin this tomb is the most revered spot in the peninsula, next to the mountains of Moses; they make frequent vows to kill a sheep in honour of this Sheikh should a wished-for event take place; and if this happens, the votary repairs to the tomb with his family and friends, and there passes a day of conviviality, Once in every year all the tribes of the Towara repair hither in pilgrimage, and remain encamped in the valley round the tomb for three days. Many sheep are then killed, camel races are run, and the whole night is passed in dancing and singing. The men and women are dressed in their best attire. The festival, which is the greatest amongst these people, usually takes place in the latter part of June, when the Nile begins to rise in Egypt, and the plague subsides; and a caravan leaves Sinai immediately afterwards for Cairo. It is just at this period too that the dates ripen in the valleys of the lower chain of Sinai, and the pilgrimage to Sheikh Szaleh thus becomes the most remarkable period in the Bedouin year.

Marks of Thanksgiving, 1839

John Kinnear

It is a continued ascent until you reach the open valley, and there has been a regular path along the side of the mountain, formed of large blocks of granite, but now much destroyed by the winter torrents. A small stream runs in the bottom of the defile, frequently interrupted, and diverted from its course, by huge masses of granite which have fallen from the mountains on either side. The path winds along similar masses of rock, some of such enormous size, that one wonders how they could have been arrested in their headlong descent before reaching the bottom of the ravine.

On some of the most conspicuous of these rocks smaller stones are placed, sometimes one stone above another, which it is the custom of pilgrims to set up as they pass. This is intended to express, and is generally accompanied by some verbal expression of, thanksgiving for their safe arrival at the end of their journey; and is evidently a remnant of the very ancient custom, of which many instances are recorded in the Old Testament. To remove any of these stones is considered very improper, and sure to bring some misfortune on the person who does so.

The Valley of the Saint, 1864

Arthur Penryn Stanley

The other sanctuary of the Desert must be mentioned. The Bedouin tribes, as has been said, have lost their ancient reverence for the traces of the Prophet, and every traveller has observed on their godless life. It is very rare indeed that any sign of religious worship can be found amongst them. Few have any knowledge of the prescribed prayers of the Mussulman; still fewer practise them. But there is one exception. In the eastern extremity of the great crescent-shaped valley which embraces the whole cluster of Sinai, is the tomb of the Sheykh, from which the wady derives its name—the "Wady es-Sheykh", the "Valley of the Saint". In a tenement of the humblest kind is Sheykh Saleh's grave. Who he was, when he lived, is entirely unknown. Possibly he may have been the founder of the tribe of that name which still exists in the Peninsula; possibly the ancient prophet mentioned in the Koran as preaching the faith of Islam before the birth of Mahomet. The present belief would seem to be, that he was one of the circle of companions of the prophet, which, according to defiance of all chronological laws in the minds of uneducated Mussulmans, included Saleh, Moses, David, and Christ, as well as Abu Bekr, Omar and Ali. This tomb is to the modern Bedouins the sanctuary of the Peninsula. As they approach it they exhibit signs of devotion never seen elsewhere; and once a year all the tribes of the Desert assemble round it, and celebrate with races and dances, a Bedouin likeness of the funeral games round the tomb of Patreoelus. Sacrifices of sheep and camels, with sprinkling of blood on the walls of this homely chapel, are described as accompanying this sepulchral feast.

> ***Palmer was an Arabic scholar and understood the tales shared by the Bedouin along the way. Fifty years later the uncertainty about who the sheikh was continued, but the reverence for him was as great as it had been in Burckhardt's day.***

A Legend of the Journey, 1865

E.H. Palmer

Early on the following morning we passed two heaps of stones called Mangaz Hisan Abu Zena, 'Abu Zena's Horse Leap', concerning which the following legend was recounted to me by an old Bedawi of the 'Awarimeh tribe:

> "As an Arab named Abu Zena was riding a mare that was with foal, and, notwithstanding her critical condition, was urging her along at a cruel speed. When she came to this spot he dug his spurs into her sides, whereupon the mare made a tremendous leap and fell down dead. Abu Zena, in wonder at the immense length of the stride which his horse had taken, marked the distance with two stones, and related the incident afterwards to his friends.

The matter soon became noised abroad, and every Arab who passed that way with a comrade would discuss the marvellous leap and mark out the distance with a stone as Abu Zena himself had done, and thus the stone heaps grew. Admiration for the mare's performance soon increased with the pagan Arabs of that time, and she became at last an object of veneration, and was worshipped as a deity, offerings of corn being brought to the spot.

But when they forsook idolatry for the worship of the true God, they came to look upon their former gods as devils, and turned their pagan observances into an expression of aversion for the demon whom they supposed to haunt the accursed spot. Thus instead of the usual offering of corn, they would throw stones upon the heaps, and, kicking a little dust upon it with their feet, cry out, "Eat *that*, and get thee gone!"

This custom is still kept up, and every one of our Arabs as they passed the spot picked up a stone to cast at the heap, and, kicking the dust over it contemptuously, cried: "*Agsa 'Allig*," "Begone, and feed!"

8
Episodes and Encounters on the Journey

The experiences of travelers as they moved towards Mount Sinai were often similar from one year to the next and from one generation to another. They were governed by the terrain and by the culture and customs of the inhabitants of the peninsula. Travelers recorded similar encounters with the Bedouins of Sinai, who were, until well into the twentieth century, hardly touched by the whirl of modernity in the world beyond their land. Often the travelers saw in the land and the life of the people a link to the Old Testament tales they knew so well.

My Companions, 1845
W.H. Bartlett

My companions the Bedouins now became objects of great interest to me. I had almost overlooked them when crouching in a circle near the hotel in Cairo, speaking with bated breath and glancing uneasily to and fro with their restless black eyes; now abroad in their own wilderness, they are totally different in manner and bearing. They are mostly fine athletic fellows, graceful and even noble in their movements; a result derived from constant exercise and the sense of untrammelled freedom; spare and sinewy, both from the sobriety of their habits and the dry heat which parches up also superfluous flesh, and under which the traveller himself speedily undergoes something of that condensation of muscle which at home could only be produced by systematic training. Their complexion has a duskiness like that gypsies in our own country, and of those races who are exposed to all the chances and hardships of out-of-door life; and this peculiar tint serves to bring out, with the greater effect, the keen blackness of their flashing eyes, and the brilliant whiteness of their uniformly white teeth. One cannot doubt, in looking at them, that they are of keen, quick intellect and lively passions; but the fixed habits of ages have confined their ideas to a narrow range, from which they cannot escape. Within this circle of ideas they incessantly revolve and display a subtlety and a refinement of cunning which, in a civilised state, would work marvels. They are as sagacious in tracking a particular footmark of man or beast through the sand, even in it is said, the confused and trampled track of a caravan as a North American savage in following the trail of his foe through the tangled forest. In proportion to the paucity of their rational ideas is their love of the imaginative and the marvellous poems embodying the wars and loves of their desert existence; and they have a no less keen sense of the ludicrous, and love of practical jokes.

Umbarak, the chief of our little caravan, was a remarkable fine fellow, and on all occasions most obliging, as were indeed the rest. Small gratuities of coffee and eatable, which Komeh dispensed with great tact, kept them in constant good humour; they were always ready to assist in pitching the tent and gathering wood for our fire.

Passing Life, 1816

John Lewis Burckhardt

I always commenced the day with a long walk; nothing can be more enjoyable, - the desert, half gravel, half sand, crunches under the feet like snow, - sometimes bounded by low hills, sometimes it stretches out into an interminable plain, but always of the same unvaried hue. We passed skeletons of camels repeatedly, and scattered bones bleached to the whiteness of snow; and, one morning, prowling about near our encampment, I found an open grave and a skull grinning up into my face within it—the relic, doubtless, of some hapless pilgrim. Melancholy memorials these! but all was not death there; a frog, a species of grey lizard, some quails and vultures, were symptoms of animal—and various thorny shrubs, a few wild flowers, and a strongly scented plant (a species of wild camomile we thought it), called by the Arabs *behharran*—of vegetable life; nor should I forget a solitary tree, long conspicuous on the horizon with the apparent dignity of a palm, but which dwindled, long before we reached it, into a stunted thorn, covered with rags streaming in the wind, hung there by every pilgrim as he passes *en chemin* for Mecca. The half-eaten carcass of a camel lay beneath it, and the vultures that had been garbaging on it flew heavily away at our approach.

A Fight, 1835

John Lloyd Stephens

My days in the desert did not pass as quickly as I hurry through them here. They wore away, not slowly alone, but sometimes heavily; and, to help them in their progress, I sometimes descended to very commonplace amusements.

On one occasion I remember meeting a party of friendly Bedouins, and, sitting down with them to pipes and coffee, I noticed a fine lad of nineteen or twenty, about the size of one of my party, and pitted mine against him for a wrestling match. The old Bedouins took the precaution to remove their knives and swords, and it was well they did, for the two lads throttled each other like young furies; and when mine received a pretty severe prostration on the sand, he first attempted to regain his sword, and, failing in that, sprang again upon his adversary with such ferocity that I was glad to have the young devils taken apart, and still more glad to know that they were going to travel different roads.

Meetings along the Way, 1846

Lord Lindsay

Following the windings of the valley, alternately through sun and shade, under lofty rocks and umbrageous date trees, whispering in the breeze, and shedding the most delicious coolness, we heard from time to time the chirping of birds, the barking of dogs, and the merry voices of children—generally unseen, though occasionally we caught a passing glimpse of them, and of their dusky mothers and sisters, under the thick foliage embowering their huts and tents. We exchanged cordial *salaams* and *bissalams* with some of the natives that we met on the road, particularly with one ancient white-bearded patriarch. Our guides too were constantly meeting their acquaintance, receiving their welcome, and striking wrists with them; their greetings struck me as remarkably low-voiced, though cordial as between brothers.

Meeting German Journeymen, 1845

Richard Lepsius

We here [at the harbour of Abu Zalimeh where Lepsius had sent their boat to wait for them], to our no small surprise, found four German journeymen: two of them Prussians, from the district of the Neisse, in Silesia.

They had started from Cairo with the intention of visiting Sinai, and reached Suez safely; had there waited in vain for a ship, and at length, like genuine modern Crusaders, started alone to attain their bold object. They had been told (hardly in good German) that the way was short, and could not be missed, and that there was no want of water. Possessed with this happy belief, their pilgrim's bottle filled to the brim, they entered the wilderness. But the footsteps of the children of Israel had long since disappeared, and no pillar of smoke went before them. The third day they lost their way, their bread was consumed, they had missed the wells, had several times been stopped by Arabs, and only escaped being robbed because they possessed nothing worth robbing; and thus they certainly would have been starved in the wilderness, had they not looked down from the mountains and beheld our vessel on the coast many hours distant, and fortunately reached it before our arrival.

On my inquiring about their trades, to perfect which, they had had undertaken this journey to the East, and also whether they hoped to find employment with the monks on Mount Sinai, as they had no money with them, it appeared that one was a carpenter, who was in hope of making himself very useful there; I was, alas, compelled to inform him, that he would have to compete with a lay-brother in that department; the other was a shoemaker, the third a stocking weaver, and the fourth, after some hesitation, confessed that he was a women's tailor.

Nothing remained but to take these strange people along with us in the vessel, although they were regarded with a jealous eye by the sailors, as we began to feel some scarcity in the supply of water. I landed them at Tor, and arranged that someone should accompany them thence to the convent.

A Timeless Meeting, 1865

E.H. Palmer

Our entrance into the Desert of Sinai was marked by a singularly appropriate incident, and we had a piece of the Bible translated for us into every-day life as it was in the time of the Patriarchs.

We had reached the neighbourhood of our Sheikh 'Eid, and his wife and two children, accompanied by an aged male relative, came out to meet him. 'Eid saluted the old man, embraced him, and kissed him on either cheek, and the pair then, with right hands clasped, repeated over and over again the words *Taiyibin*? "Are you well?" with the answer *Al hamda lillah taiyibin*, "Thank God, well!"

As I watched the scene. I could not help calling to mind the words of Exodus (xviii. 5–7): "And Jethro, Moses' father in law, came with his sons and his wife unto Moses in the wilderness, where he had encamped before the mount of God: And he said unto Moses, I thy father in law Jethros am come unto thee with thy wife and her two sons with her. And Moses went out to meet his father in law, and did obeisance, and kissed him, and they asked each other of their welfare; and they came into the tent."

Dining With the Bedouin, 1860

William Beamont

In about three hours we were abreast of a party of the Towara Arabs encamped under a score of black goatskin tents. They were some distance from us, and our dragoman visited them, and brought back a pressing invitation from one of their number, who had once travelled with a member of our party, that we would visit their encampment. Such an instance of desert hospitality was not to be refused, and riding to the camp, we were most kindly received in the public tent, which in the desert supplies the place of a town-hall, where a divan was extemporised for the occasion, and where, when the sheik perceived that our legs, less limber and pliable than theirs, were not so easily doubled under us, he ordered in some camel-saddles and placed them for us to recline upon.

In a very short time a dozen or more olive-skinned sons of the desert, amongst whom were two old men, neither of whom knew his age, though one of them said he was a grandfather, assembled and sat down outside the tent. The young man, the author of the invitation, had handsome aristocratic features, large expressive eyes, and beautiful white teeth, and all the others (except two Negroes who had a sinister look and ugly unsheathed knives in their girdles, and were a disagreeable contrast to the rest) were handsome and well-favoured.

We were no sooner seated than a basin and ewer were brought in, and water was poured on our hands to wash in the oriental style; a quantity of coffee-beans were then placed in a shallow pan and roasted over the fire, after which they were put into a mortar and bruised with a wooden pestle; a coffee-kettle filled with water was then set on the fire, and when it boiled the coffee was put in, and after boiling a little, was poured into small cups and handed to us. Presently *mafruka* bread, crumbled and mixed with butter was brought in and set before us in a 'lordly dish', a huge bowl cut from the solid trunk of a large tree called attal; and three smaller bowls, each containing a thin cake of Arab bread and the choice portions of a kid, were brought in and set before us. The kid had been killed since our arrival, a trace of the same custom which prevailed so long ago (Genesis xviii, 7). Using the cake as a spoon to gather up the *mafruka*, we ate the kid's flesh, which was tender and good, as well as we could, remembering meanwhile the poet's advice:

> You must genteely with your fingers raise;
> And, as in eating there's a certain grace,
> Beware with greasy hands lest you besmear your face.

When dinner was over, which was not until our hospitable hosts had pressed us again and again to eat more, coffee was served again, and this time with the addition of tobacco and pipes; after which water was again brought in, and we again washed our hands. The repast over, our entertainers gathered round the dish and ate the fragments of the feast, the old one being served first.

Meeting Pilgrims, 1860

William Beamont

Dec. 13 Our ride today has been a dreary journey across the open and wide-spreading wady Sudr, with its Gebel in view the whole day, and this evening our tents are pitched abreast of it. The Russian pilgrims are encamped near; and so little do our escort know of other people or creeds, that our Berber cook would fain persuade us that these pilgrims were a party of Jews from Tiberius. We could distinctly hear them talking and singing, and if we had visited them we might have had tea from the *samovar* which I saw in their equipage.

Meeting a Missionary, 1892

Agnes Smith Lewis

Our tents were pitched at the foot of the Nugb Hawa, and there to our great delight we met Dr. Grote, the Anglo-German missionary to the Bedaween, who had been spending the three months of winter in the convent, and had made a good deal of use of the time in exploring its Greek library. He had no tent, but slept on an airbed just on the sand, and ate with his Bedawee escort. He reported that most of the Towarah are simply starving, and very thankful for the doles of bread they get from the convent.

Visiting a Hermit in Wadi Feiran, 1938

H.V. Morton

We continued for four hours or so in this exquisite fantasy of rock, climbing all the time, picking our way between scattered boulders and rushing the soft sandy portions of the track, so that we might avoid becoming stuck. Small birds with a curious swooping flight were the only living things we saw until, many miles up the wadi, we came on camel foals eating thorns, and we knew that, somewhere in a crook of the hills, or behind the giant boulders, was a Bedouin tent lying like a black bat spreadeagled on the ground.

At the climax of the gorge we came to the only oasis in the whole of southern Sinai, the Oasis of Feiran, the "Pearl of Sinai"; but in any other part of the world it would pass as a pleasant, shady spot with a few trees, a bit of grass, and a stream. In this wilderness the Oasis is a paradise, and, after four of five hours of stark mountains, it was good to see green avenues beneath palm trees, and to hear the sound of goat-bells and the thin tinkle of water.

The only inhabitants are a few Bedouin and one Greek monk, Father Isaiah, who lives in the capacity of watch-dog and gardener in a house belonging to the Monastery of Mount Sinai. Mr Vallinis (Morton's guide) had told me about the old man, who grows vegetables for the monastery. I thought it would be courteous to pass the time of day with him, and we pulled up at the mud wall surrounding his dwelling, and hammered on the door which had a small wooden cross nailed to it.

Through a crack in the door we saw a white-bearded Greek monk, half patriarch and half bandit, come in a crouching defensive attitude down the garden path, wearing a dirty cassock over a pair of khaki trousers and grasping a gun. His long grey hair as pinned up in a tight bun at the back, and on the top was the high black hat of a Greek priest.

"Who is it?" he called from the other side of the gate.

"Thieves and robbers," promptly replied Mr Vallinis, who never lost an opportunity of chaffing another Greek.

There was a long silence. Looking up, we saw the solemn face of the old monk gazing down at us from the top of the wall. He lowered his gun.

"You should not joke about such things," he said. "It is wickedness. Have you any tobacco? I have been smoking dry weeds for many months. Come inside . . .

A Pilgrimage of Birds, 1854 and 14th century

R.W. Stewart

In the oases the tiny wagtails strutted up and down with their usual dandified air without uttering any sound; a dainty black and white creature with a clear robin-like note and a friendly disposition (usually alone) watched us inquisitively, while sandpipers seemed to collect in flocks. The ubiquitous sparrow, having apparently adapted himself to his surroundings by a slight lengthening of his tail and a greener tingeing of his coat, held his own cheerfully wherever habitation was possible for him, as indeed he does all the world over.

Sir John Mandeville, that delightful romancer of the fourteenth century, who seems to rejoice in the extraordinary and bizarre, notes that rooks and other fowls fly about the Convent of St Catherine in great numbers "as they should make pilgrimages in their manner, and ilk ane of them brings in their nebbe (beak) instead of offering, a branch of olive, and leaves them there, and on that wise there is great plenty of olives left to the sustenance of the house."

The Grave of an Englishman, 1857

Horatius Bonar

As we wound slowly through the defile, black peaks came up on the left, and huge yellow precipices overhung our right. Farther on we were met by a long line of terraces and peaks, - white, black, red and yellow. At half-past ten we turned into the Wadi Feiran, which at its commencement is not unlike Wady Mukatteb, in its general aspect. On the left the hills were black, on the right yellow. The sun was without a cloud and the heat intense. Just at this spot our dragoman came up to us to point out the grave of "the English minister"—Mr Ewbank of Liverpool, who had died here above a year ago. Our dragoman had met his widow at Howarah returning homewards, leaving her husband's dust behind her in the wilderness. The grave was on the side of a mound of sand or rough soil, such as abound here. No tree, no flower! No stone nor epitaph. No mourner to sit down and weep. How solitary did it seem; - and how sad to die and be buried here! An oppressive sense of loneliness seemed to come over us as we looked at the unmarked tomb, and then turned our camels' heads to journey slowly onwards.

What should hinder that our grave might be as lonely as this? The desert was all around us. Friends were three thousand miles away. Our own life was but a vapour. Yet He who is "the resurrection and the life" is in this desert as truly as our own loved land. He has his eye upon the dust of his saints here as well as in our own churchyard, where the united in life are joined together in death. Only Arab dust may hitherto have rested here; but the first resurrection will find its objects in many strange spot and amid unexpected company. . . .

9
Arriving at the Convent

At last, after a week on camel-back, at first trailing through the desert and then through the more gentle wadys which led into the harsh mountains, came the day of arrival at the Convent of St. Catherine, the end of the journey and the start of a new experience.

The End of the World, 1820
Sir Frederick Henniker

Early in the morning we pursued our course, and at sun-set arrived at a green valley, whence we had the pleasure of descrying the wished-for convent. It has the appearance of a fortress, and is situated at the extremity of a cul de sac formed by overhanging rocks. If I had to represent the end of the world, I would model it from Mount Sinai.

During the day's journey we did not see a human being, nor even the vestige of man, save that, on the edge of a precipice, the figure of the cross proclaimed the zeal and labour of some adventurous Christian. In vegetable nature I saw nothing remarkable except a species of sorrel, which my guides brought me as a *galantaria*. The streamlet compensated for all deficiencies, and a person travelling in the East finds a murmuring rivulet as agreeable in reality as poetry. The dullness of the scene was forgotten in the amusement of shooting. We found

Convent of St. Catherine

many coveys of partridges; some the red-legged of the Grecian isles, others brown and differing but little from the English, and a third species speckled like the quail.*

The New Road to the Convent, 1857

James Hamilton

The road-making was easy work enough in the plain, but here, on entering the pass, the difficulties had begun. A carriageway has to be carried through rocks, which resist obstinately even the gunpowder's blast; and the sharp glass-like edges of the granite soon wear away the workmen's shoes, and cripple their feet. From this cause, from sickness produced by bad diet, and accidents, there are generally one hundred of the eleven hundred men in hospital. The men are paid fourpence a day extra pay, and, strange to say, they really get it, but still they hate the task, and regard it as the work of galley-slaves.

---

* Henniker a great sportsman, added this footnote: "In Egypt and Nubia we find the pink partridge, the pin-tailed brown, and pin-tailed sand coloured. Of forty-four different species of birds, of which I stuffed samples, six were partridges, I had intended a present to the British and other Museums, but the skins are mostly destroyed."

They frequently desert, but the chances of escape for men are small; if they die not of hunger in the desert, they are pretty surely captured by the Bedouin, who on delivering them up receive 100 piastres' reward per head. To sharpen the officer's surveillance, a portion of his pay is deducted each day a man is absent from his company. To give an idea of the expense of this undertaking, I may state, that 2 lbs (pounds) of gunpowder are required to blast every cubic yard of rock, and 24 days' labour of one man to bore the mines, or, in other words, eight shillings of cheap labour and four shillings of powder. The distance to the foot of Gebel Musa is 72 miles, of which the twenty miles completed are the easiest. . . . The whim will probably cost more than the railway from Alexandria to Cairo.

Ask the Monks to Help Us, 1838

Edward Robinson

As we approached the mountain our head Arab, Beshârah [his guide], became evidently quite excited. he prayed that our pilgrimage might be accepted, and bring rain; and with great earnestness besought, that when we ascended the mountain, we would open a certain window in a chapel there, towards the South, which he said would certainly cause rain to fall. He also entreated almost with tears, that we would induce the monks to have compassion on the people, and say prayers as they ought to do for rain. When told that God alone could send rain, and they should look to him for it, he replied: "Yes, but the monks have the book of prayer for it; do persuade them to use it as they ought." There was an earnestness in his manner which was very affecting, but cannot be described. Just after crossing Wady esh-Sheikh, we passed at the mouth of Wady Shu'eib, a burial-ground much venerated by the Arabs. Here Beshârah repeated a few words of prayer; the first time we had known him or any of our Arabs pray since leaving Cairo.

The Convent in History, 1816

John Lewis Burckhardt

The convent formerly resembled in its establishment that of the Holy Sepulchre in Jerusalem, which contains churches of various sects of Christians. Every principal sect, except the Calvinists and Protestants, had its churches in the convent of Sinai. I was shown the chapels belonging to the Syrians, Armenians, Copts and Latins (Catholics), but they have long been abandoned by their owners; the church of the Latins fell into ruins at the close of the seventeenth century, and has not been rebuilt. But what is more remains there than the existence of so many churches, is that close by the great church stands a Mahometan mosque, spacious enough to contain two hundred people at prayers. The monks told me it was built in the sixteenth century, to prevent the destruction of the convent.

Their tradition, however, is contradicted by some of the old Arabic records kept by the prior, in which I read a circumstantial account how, in the year of the Hedjra 783, some straggling Turkish Hadjis, who had been cut off from the caravan, were brought by the Bedouins to the convent; and being found to be well educated, and originally from Upper Egypt, were retained here, and a salary settled on them and their descendants, on condition of their becoming the servants of the mosque. The conquest of Egypt by Selim did not take place till A.H. 895.

The mosque in the convent of Sinai appears therefore to have existed long before the time of Selim. The descendants of these Hadjis, now poor Bedouins, are called Ratheny, they still continue to be the servants of the mosque, which they clean on Thursday evenings, and light the lamps; one of them is called the Imam. The mosque is sometimes visited by Muslim pilgrims, but it is only upon the presence of some Mussulman of consequence that the call to prayers is made from the Minarat.

In the convent are two deep and copious wells of spring water: one of them is called the well of Moses, because it is said he first drank of its water.

Another was the work, as the monks say, of an English Lord, it bears the date 1760. There is also a reservoir for the reception of rain water.

Arriving, 1835

Alexandre Dumas

We mounted our dromedaries and in about half an hour we entered the Oasis of St Catherine, which leads to the foot of Sinai. The road is steep, difficult and precipitous; but we were approaching the end of our journey, and this notion smoothed the road, embellished the landscape, and levelled the acclivities. The sun itself, though scorching, seemed milder and more easy to endure than on the preceding evening. Still this rough road lasted two hours, and in spite of our moral courage, we were beginning to feel physical fatigue; when, on turning an enormous rock, which hid the horizon, we found ourselves at the foot of the mountain of St Catherine, rising like a queen above its neighbours. To the left rose the magnificent peak of Sinai; and on its eastern slope, at about a third of the height, appeared the convent, a strong fortress, built in the shape of an irregular quadrangle; whilst, on the north side, an immense garden goes down the last hill which joins the mountain to the valley; it is surrounded by walls, not so lofty as those of the convent, but still sufficient to resist a sudden attack. Its graceful trees have a refreshing aspect to eyes unaccustomed to verdure.

The entry to the convent was memorable in itself—not just because it was the climax of the journey, but also because it brought both anxiety and drama. The monks wound a huge windlass to lift travelers up into the interior. A party of French architects and photographers arrived from a more difficult route than that followed by most travelers.

Mountains and Convent, 1872

Paul Lenoir

Wadi-Solaf, or the Gorge of the Wind, was the last station we had to reach, but it was hard work. We had to dismount, and our dromedaries suffered much in the downward climb, through the rents in the mountains. One issuing from the wadi, the spectacle which awaited us recompensed for the difficulties of the road. In front of us, Mount Sinai itself rose into space, and its imposing profile stood out against the background formed by the mountains which surrounded it. Djebel Catharine, which is reached first, amazed us by its colossal size. The mountain is held by *savants* of a new school to be the real Sinai of the Holy Scriptures. On the right, at an extraordinary elevation, we observed some white buildings, the remains of the palace which Abbas Pasha took it into his head to rear in so inaccessible a region.

At last, after many ups and downs, we crossed a field of some yellow herb, which resembled cane in its flexibility and strength. Our beasts would have devoured it eagerly, but we were in haste to conclude this stage of our journey, and we had to restrain them by vigorous application of the *courbache*. In turning the foot of Djebl Catharine, we found ourselves in the valley which extends to the foot of Horeb, and Sinai. The convent, perched on the escarped side of the holy mountain, looked like a small fortress, and the gardens rejoiced our eyes with their novel gaiety, in this arid land of terrible memories.

We pitched our camp in sight of the convent, and, after we had hastily arranged our dress, we set off to visit its hospitable inmates.

The travel writer Isabella Bird went to Sinai as a pilgrim, and this is made abundantly clear in her constant references to the Bible on her final approach to St. Catherine's Monastery.

Pilgrim to Sinai, 1878

Isabella Bird

The sun was westering fast, and the mountain shadows lay violet-tinted on the yellowish granite when we emerged from the pass. Far ahead, familiar as if I had seen them all my life, yet strange with an unspeakable strangeness, were the gigantic cliffs which form the front of Sinai. So familiar were they that when Hassan said, "Gebel Musa," he only put my thought into words. A short descent brought us to a gravelly wady, which soon widens into an ascending plain; and when we reached its highest altitude, 5,140 feet above the sea, the whole plain of Er Rahah, with the grand mountains of the Sinaitic group standing as sentinels round "the mount of God", were revealed in all their majesty.

I dismounted; I should have liked to take the shoes from my feet, or do any other thing which could express profound reverence, the ground seemed holy. This—this "Mount Sinai in Arabia", is what I came out into the wilderness to see, but how far it exceeds all my expectations I cannot say. As I reverently trod the last two miles of the journey, the view became more and more magnificent, as Sinai itself (as I thought) disentangled its vast columnar mass from the surrounding mountains, and stood out alone against the cool blue sky. To my fancy it seemed as if all the entanglements of splintered and pinnacled mountains fell away from it, leaving it alone in the sky and in the wilderness.

My sensations in travelling to the shrines of Nikko (Japan, where Isabella Bird had been earlier on the same journey) up the cryptomeria avenue forty miles long were feebly prophetic of what I felt yesterday as I passed up the Wady ed Deyr, an avenue of mountains of black, red and yellow granite, blocked up by Gebel Musa. Then came evening, with its coolness and tenderness, its deeper blues, its violet purples, its vermilion and gold, and its long solemn shadows; and in the midst of this transcendent beauty and grandeur I saw in the deep ravine, the other end of which is blocked up by a great black mountain, the fortress convent of St Catherine.

This, like all else, far exceeds my expectations, and is in complete harmony with its surroundings. I have not yet been inside the convent, but my impression of it as it lay in the mellow light, nestling under the awful front of Sinai, is of an immense irregular building or congeries of buildings of great height and massiveness, less the builder's work than an outgrowth of the rock, dead walls fifty feet high in some parts following the irregularities of the rock, with round and square flanking towers loop-holed for defence; churches and chapels, if not mosques, a fortress rather than a monastery, with shelving terraced gardens, and tall cypress-trees, and blossoming almonds, and monks in Greek monastic dress walking in the garden in twos or threes, holy men, I hoped, in a holy place; fortress and convent with all their intricacies and picturequeness, the growth of fourteen centuries, with a certain degree of harmony preserved throughout.

The Camels Arrive, 1854

R.W. Stewart

Our tired beasts, having knelt for us to descend, rose again and stood immovable, silent and patient, for once, at a halt; their red neck-trappings showed clear through the gathering darkness; they were thin and shaggy beasts of the desert, but at this moment they were clothed with the glamour of the situation. We forgot, as we looked at them, their wayward and perverse antics on the march; they seemed to us, as they stood there, like some picture of the camels of the wise men who followed the star in the east. We, too, were on a starry quest, and this was part of it.

Our Arrival, 1906

Emily Hornby

Thursday, March 2nd, 12th day in the Desert. Arrival at the Convent of Sinai. This has indeed been a day. I started at 7:10 on my camel, M. and F.* had started walking.

* Her sisters.

but I thought I should have a better view from my camel. Almost directly Abdul said "Sufsafeh," and I looked, but saw no peak, only a wall of rock. I thought I must have mistaken him, but he went on saying it. We crossed a bare plain, a bitterly cold wind blowing, I had to hide my hands in woollen gloves under my rug. We passed some black Arab tents for the first time, saw Abba's house quite plainly on a mountain.*

I overtook M. and F.; they also had been much excited to find Sufsafeh was so very close, it is a wall of rock, with several points, and now Abdul pointed out Sinai. (The top of Gebel Musa (Sinai) is not visible, it is behind a pointed crag overhanging the Convent.) We are to go from one point to the other, though they seem to be quite separate. We now saw cypresses and almond trees, and a white building. I had expected to mount quite a stiff pass, but it was hardly anything. Suddenly Abdul made the camel kneel down and I got off. We walked a very little way along a high causeway (the wall of the garden) with almond trees and cypresses below, turned to the right, and were at the Convent door, in a high wall. Abdul and I and the camel alone, nothing to be seen of the others. It was nine o'clock.

We knocked for a long time, at last a monk opened the door, and I was taken through some courts and up some steps, and put into a nice little room, with a divan all round, and pictures on the walls. Another monk appeared, and I explained in Italian that I was one of three, and I thought the others must be sketching the convent, and they told me to wait there till the others came. I waited ages, looked at all the pictures, one of scenes from the life of St Catherine, portraits of several Archbishops, one of the Sultan, and one of the German Royal Family. Then I looked out . . . I saw a very nice cat down below, and I went down and tried to caress it, but it would not let me touch it. I went up again and waited, and another monk came with whom I had a great deal of conversation. His name was Cyril. I gave him a visiting card and explained where I lived, near London, on the River Thames, that 'Manor' meant a 'chateau' (we conversed in French), then as he seemed not to know the days of the week, I got out my Greek vocabulary and showed him 'Monday' in it and said we wanted to stay until then, and he found out for himself that today was 'Thursday'.

Cyril took her around the church.

There is a lovely marble pavement, great slabs of porphyry. Rows of pictures, a large one of our Saviour, and behind, the chapel containing the tomb of St Catherine, but only her head and hands are in it, it is not known where the rest of her body is. There is a most beautiful mosaic of the Transfiguration. Then I was

* The palace of Abbas Pasha.

taken into the chapel of the Burning Bush, and had to take off my boots. I quoted the words, "Take off thy shoes from thy feet etc." There was a little altar with three lights burning on it. We came out on the other side, and they brought my boots round to me.

Arriving, 1938

H.V. Morton

Without warning the monastery came into view round the shoulder of a hill.

It lay in a valley enclosed by immense dark mountains, whose feet were in shadow, whose summits were in starlight. Towering ridges and peaks dwarfed the monastery, making it seem like a child's toy on the floor of a room. There were scores of cypress trees, pointing their dark fingers in the twilight, and there was a timid burst of green in the garden, lying against the thirsty wall of the mountains.

Mr Vallinis switched on the headlights and shattered the silence of the valley with the hideous scream of a klaxon horn, to warn the monks of our arrival. Before the horrid noise had flung itself from side to side of the gorge, first one black figure, then another, then two or three, appeared on the battlements, all gazing down at us and pointing.

They wore black gowns and black stove-pipe hats. We could see their black beards as they turned excitedly to one another before disappearing to open the great door.

Burckhardt reached the convent from Suez in early May 1816, but continued on to Akaba after only three days. His main record of life in the convent and its environs was made on his return two weeks later.

Returning to the Convent, 1816

John Lewis Burckhardt

May 18th. We left the tent before dawn, and proceeded along a Wady and then NW up an ascent, whose summit we reached in two hours. From thence a fine view opened upon a broad Wady called Sebaye, and towards the mountain of Tyh. We crossed Wady Sebaye, and then ascended the mountain which commands the convent on the south side, and descending again, reached the convent at the end of three hours and a half.

The convent of Mount Sinai is situated in a valley so narrow, that one part of the building stands on the western mountain, while a space of twenty paces only is left between its walls and the eastern mountain. The valley is open to the north, from whence approaches the road from Cairo; to the south, close behind the convent, it is shut up by a third mountain, less steep than the others, over which passes the road to Sherm.

The convent is an irregular quadrangle, of about one hundred and thirty paces, enclosed by high and solid walls built with blocks of granite, and fortified by several small towers. While the French were in Egypt, a part of the east wall which had fallen down was completely rebuilt by order of General Kleber, who sent workmen here for that purpose. The upper part of the walls in the interior is built of a mixture of granite-sand and gravel, cemented together by mud, which has acquired great hardness.

Our Arabs and the Israelites, 1822

John Carne

This night, our place of halting was in a very wild valley, enclosed by naked and precipitous mountains, on whose sides the moonlight fell vividly. In the midst of the glen below, the Arabs and their camels formed an animated group. The dress of these people is picturesque, being of a course white colour, and consisting of a turban, a tunic, sash, a *shiluah*, or loose pantaloon, that reaches just below the knee, like the Highland kilt, and sandals.

We sent Jouma and Michel on before to the convent of Sinai, to give notice of our approach. Long before sunrise the following day, we set out, and stopped in a most romantic valley; and the morning being chill, we collected a large quantity of shrubs for fire, and made our breakfast.

The Israelites, during their wanderings of forty years in these deserts, must have lived but insipidly, even with manna and quails, having nothing but water to drink, after a cold night's encampment, or amidst the burning heats of the day. You feel careless what you eat in such a region, but to be de-barred coffee, tea or now and then a little lime-juice, would be misery; without the former, it is certain Arabs could not endure existence; they are satisfied with a little coarse bread or unleavened cake twice a day, but coffee is more than manna to them.

A few hours more, and we got sight of the mountains round Sinai. Their appearance was magnificent; when we drew nearer and emerged out of a deep pass, the scenery was infinitely striking, and on the right extended a vast range of mountains as far as the eye could reach, from the vicinity of Sinai down to Tor. They were perfectly bare, but of grand and singular form.

We had hoped to reach the convent by day-light, but the moon had risen some time, when we entered the mouth of a narrow pass, where our conductors advised us to dismount. A gentle but perpetual ascent led on, mile after mile, up this mournful valley, whose aspect was terrific, yet ever varying. It was not above two hundred yards in width, and the mountains rose to an immense height on either side. The road wound at their feet along the edge of a precipice, and midst masses of rock that had fallen from above. It was a toilsome path, generally over stones, placed like steps, probably by the Arabs: and the moonlight was of little service to us in this steep valley, as it only rested on the frowning summits above. Where is Mount Sinai? was the enquiry of everyone. The Arabs pointed before to Gebel Musa, the Mount of Moses, as it is called; but we could not distinguish it. Again, and again, point after point was turned, and we saw but the same stern scenery. But what had the softness and beauty of Nature to do here? Mount Sinai required an approach like this, where all seemed to proclaim the land of miracles, and to have been visited by the terrors of the Lord. The scenes, as you gazed around, had an unearthly character, suited to the sound of the fearful trumpet that was once heard there. We entered at last on the more open valley, about half a mile wide, and drew near this famous mountain. Sinai is not as lofty as some of the mountains round it, and in its form there is nothing graceful or peculiar to distinguish it from others.

Near midnight we reached the Convent of St Catherine, at the foot of the mountain, and surrounded by a high wall, to guard it against the Arabs. Jouma was lying fast asleep at its foot, wrapped in his cloak, beside the embers of his fire, but he instantly arose and welcomed us.

Just as we reached the walls of the convent, an Arab, richly dressed, passed close to us, and gave a salute, which we returned; he went up to Taleb, and, after exchanging a few words, continued his journey. We skirted the interminable walls of the convent, meeting at every step wretched Bedouins, ragged and naked, attracted by the neighbouring monastery, and living on the charity of the monks, as the poor at the gates of churches in Catholic countries live on the alms of the congregations.At length, the walls of the convent succeeded those of the garden; after incredible fatigue, we were attaining the haven which Christian devotion had preserved for those who travel over this ocean of sand, and amid its rocks of granite. It was our Promised Land, and I doubt if the Israelites were more anxious about theirs.

The Great Door Is Closed, 1722

The Prefetto of Egypt

And foreasmuch the great door is always walled up, to prevent the incursions of Arabs, immediately after the entrance of a new archbishop, which happened this very year, every other person who is desirous of going in to the convent, must be drawn up with a rope to a great window, thirty feet high from the ground, in that part of the wall which looks to the north-east. And when one is got into the convent, there is nothing of curiosity to be seen, all the buildings and edifices, especially those which concern the friars or the religions, and the smaller chapels, being built of rough bricks, in great confusion and irregularity, without either symmetry or order, making here and there crooked dark passages, with several ascents and descents; only the building of the great church of the Transfiguration of our Saviour Jesus Christ may be considered as worthy of our observation.

The arrival at the convent could be an anxious time. Would the monks accept one's papers and take one in? This was not always the case.

Parleying to Enter, 1857

James Hamilton

On entering the Wady Er-Racha, the edifice appeared close at hand, but it was more than an hour before we reached it. Banners floated from the walls, for this day was one of the two hundred annual festivals of the monks. Outside the convent were stationed some soldiers, and here for the first and only time during our six months' tour were we asked for our passports. We were next detained beneath the walls of the fortress, and held a parley with our ghostly hosts, who apostrophised us from a window some twenty feet above; the window being furnished with the invariable crane and windlass of Greek convents. They were chagrined, the holy fathers, and puzzled at our travelling without a dragoman. After a time we were directed to a low door at the back of the building; this opened into a small court, from whence passing through two gates strongly plated with iron, we found ourselves within its precincts. Next by a precipitant flight of wooden steps we were ushered into a balcony, on which opened the rooms provided for guests. After a short time the brother Dispenser brought us excellent araki—convent-manufacture—dates and coffee.

Our Claim Accepted, 1853

Catherine Tobin

As we approached Mount Sinai, granite rocks of stupendous height seemed to close in upon us; although Gebel Mousa itself is not visible until one arrives within a short distance from its base. On our right we saw some Arab tents—the women, as usual, running away as we drew near; and not very far from thence we came to two wells of water; at one of which we were accosted by the *Basha*, as he is called—Turkish government agent—who with no small difficulty wrote down our names in a book.

A broad pathway—made by the monks of Sinai—leads, by a gradual ascent, to the *fortress convent*; a gloomy looking building—with its massive turreted walls, loopholes, and bristling cannon. Voices were heard, and faces peered through a door—perhaps thirty feet from the ground—which is masked by a wooden projection. The letter we had brought from the Greek bishop at Cairo—for this convent belongs to the Greek church—was forthwith produced, drawn up by a windlass, and carried to the Superior. Without this introduction, a traveller cannot be received here on any pretence whatever. Only two nights previous to our arrival, and man and his dromedary, and a single attendant, joined our encampment for a few hours. He was returning from Mount Sinai to

Cairo; having been refused admittance into the convent, because he had neglected to provide himself with the required document; and notwithstanding that one of the monks was his own brother!

Our claim to hospitality accepted, we were not raised aloft, as we rather *hoped*—according to the *every day* mode of ingress and egress—but were led to the back of the building; and entered, by a very low postern, into the midst of a perfect *chaos* of uncouth erections! Walls, churches, houses, stood huddled together in confusion! We were paraded through dark passages and badly paved courts; up and down awkward stone staircases and wooden ladders; until at *long last*, we reached the 'Strangers' Corridor'; where we found apartments much more spacious, clean and comfortable, than we had anticipated. Each of them was furnished with a broad divan, covered with gaily printed calico, and well supplied with cushions; a few plain chairs; and a common deal table, with a brass lamp upon it—which had three burners, like those from Pompeii, and of which so many are used in Italy at the present day. To these our own mattresses, sheets, pillows, quilts, and carpets, were speedily added; so that we had no reason to feel otherwise than quite satisfied with our quarters. The walls of the room were whitewashed; and the floors, like that of the balcony upon which they opened, were paved with flag-stones.

Up into the Convent, 1839

John Kinnear

The sun had set before we reached the middle of the valley; and I have seldom seen anything grander than the appearance of these great granite mountains, with their ragged peaks glittering in the moonlight. As we entered the narrow valley in which the convent stands, lights were seen moving about the building; and when we rode up to the walls, a grey-bearded figure appeared, with a torch, at a small window high above our heads; and, after reconnoitring us for a few moments, withdrew without speaking a word. Presently another window opened, several monks appeared with lights, and a rope was let down for our letters. After a minute or two, during which our friends above appeared to be in deep consultation, the rope was again let down for ourselves.

The ascent is somewhat nervous, I assure you; for the whole apparatus consists of a rope with a loop at the end of it - rather ominous - . . . Your whole safety depends on your holding the rope firmly with your hands, and you find constant employment for your feet, in keeping yourself from coming in collision with the rough projections of the wall. Then the old monks walk so slowly round their windlass above, that you think you are to be left all night dangling in the air; and, when you are fairly wound up, you find yourself hanging one or two feet from the window, without the possibility of getting in, till the monk get hold of the rope and land you like a bale of goods . . . many were the loud peels of laughter during my ascent, from my friends who remained below to enjoy the scene.

To enter the convent throughout the centuries it was necessary to have a letter of recommendation from the Greek convent in Cairo—as the Reverend Fisk had done in 1846 and James Hamilton and Lady Catherine Tobin more than a decade later. This requirement was fulfilled by Joan Plowden, who arrived there in 1937.

Where Is Your Letter? 1937

Joan Plowden

Twelve days in the desert had imbued in me a distaste for renewed contact with my fellow men. My cheerful, inconsequential, and 90 per cent unintelligible Arab entourage made absolutely no demands on my attention. Mentally I had had twelve days' rest-cure but now some kind of effort would undoubtedly be called for: I must be interested and courteous; must polish and present to the world that receptive side of man's nature that diligently registers information; instead of merely reflecting and absorbing I must now actively adjust myself to the unfamiliar; Instead of turning over old vague memories I must conscientiously acquire the new material for new experiences. I must play the part of an ardent sightseer.

Also I ached all over, Tel walked falteringly, the caravan moved listlessly and raggedly, too tired to close up the ranks and approach as a unit.

We must have presented a draggled appearance indeed to the monks gathered on the ramparts; perhaps we even looked a little bit like pilgrims.

The Convent was still some distance away; we rode slowly up the ravine of the Wadi ed Deir, which narrowed till little but the track was on level ground; on our right was the gaunt sweep of Jebel Musa, on our left we were hemmed in by the massive slopes of Jebel el Deir.

And now we were passing along beneath the walls of the Convent gardens, and all among the filigree of blossoming fruit-trees stood up the dark uncompromising spear-heads of cypresses. They strike such an incongruous and withal singular appearance, standing singly like sentinels or in conspiratorial groups around the bleached old pile of Justinian's fortress-convent.

Ranged now beneath those steeply towering walls we waited expectantly, knowing we had been seen—there were voices—a gate clanged—two monks emerged and gave us a formal welcome.

Musa reined across to me [on his camel]: "They want the letter. Where is the letter?"

There were questions, puzzled discussions, head shakings, then amazed ejaculations. I sat aloof very weary, unreasonably criticising an education that had instilled the bones of English, medieval charters, and classical Greek—long forgotten—and had disregarded modern Greek and Arabic.

Musa's English always became chaotic in moments of stress but at last I caught the import: the missing letter was the letter of recommendation that every visitor to the Convent must bring from Cairo—and the monks could not grasp that I had not come from Cairo but from London.

There were further questions: Where are the others? Where is the car? How can the lady have come alone on a camel?

Without authority I might not enter the convent.

One monk took the camels and the men to the watering place. Joan Plowden looked for a place she might pitch a tent—the surroundings were bleak and strewn with camel-droppings.

Then Musa reappeared with a third monk, an older man, and explained that the little omission of the letter would be overlooked and that I might enter the Convent and rest and get warm while the caravan was set up.

Morton asked to be shown as far round the wall of the convent as one could go. He was led, through a few narrow, stone tunnels, onto sentry walks with a grand view below.

The Windlass Still Works, 1938

H.V. Morton

We came to a dark chamber in which stands a windlass of such gigantic size that it must require the combined strength of the monks to push it round.

This is the machine that was used to pull visitors up in a boatswain's cradle from the year 1600 until the British occupation of Egypt (1882). It is still worked, said Brother Gabriel, when anything heavy has to be introduced into the monastery, or for anything too large to be carried round the narrow lanes. While we were looking at it, two lay brothers arrived with a sack of what appeared to be brown stones, but, having been in Coptic monasteries, I recognised it as that hard bread which must be soaked before it can be eaten. They opened the pent-house door and arranged a rope over the pulley. Looking down, I saw a number of Bedouin standing at the foot of the wall and gazing anxiously up at us.

"They have come for their bread," explained Brother Gabriel, "we give it to them every morning."

Before 1600 travelers had entered through the great gate of the convent.

Made Welcome 1, 1483

Felix Fabri

We hurried away from that place after the camels and asses toward the convent. When we reached the wide terrace before the convent gate, we found many Arabs sitting there armed after their fashion. These men had been driven out of the wilderness by hunger, and forced to go up to the convent for a morsel of biscuit. When we saw them we were sore afraid, fearing to be plagued by them before the convent gate. Many Arabs also went up with us, who had joined our company in the wilderness.

We therefore unloaded our beasts, made all our luggage into one heap, and stood round about it, lest the robbers in whose presence we were should steal anything from us. When the brethren heard of our coming, and of our presence there, some of them came out and kindly bade us welcome. They also helped us to carry all our baggage inside to the guest-house.*

In the guest-house there were many empty cells, among which we divided ourselves according to our several companies†. Moreover near these cells there was a chapel of the Latin rite with an altar; and here, as noon was not yet past, one of the pilgrims read Mass to us, to which we devoutly listened.‡ After Mass we bought firewood to cook with from the monks, and cooked and ate some of the food which we had brought from the Holy Land. After this we laid ourselves down to rest, and when our rest was over we went into St Catherine's Church, saw her tomb, and the Oratory of St Mary at Bush§ and visited other holy places, which I shall describe in their place. After we had done this we stayed within the monastery and its grounds, and did not go outside the walls that day.

A few days later the pilgrims planned to climb Mount Sinai, but were deterred.

Towards evening came one of the Arab chiefs, a captain of the robbers of the desert, with many of his armed followers.ç He came into the convent and

* It would appear from this that in the late fifteenth century travelers were not winched up into the monastery, but entered by a gate.

† Fabri was traveling in a large company of pilgrims.

‡ The Latin rite or Catholic rite and this Catholic chapel is not mentioned by later travelers.

§ The Chapel of the Burning Bush.

ç It would be another three and a half centuries before pilgrims reported such unrest and threats from the Arabs, when in 1822 John Carne and his companions were abducted and held hostage.

encamped with his men by our dwellings, where they watched our going out and coming in, for they had come on our account, that they might extort unjust dues from us. This was a terrible cross to us, and cast a shadow over all our joy, for we could not pass from our dwelling to St Catherine's Church save through the midst of our plunderers.

There were stairs down which we went for our convenience into the courtyard, and from the courtyard into St Catherine's Church; but the Arabs lay in the courtyard day and night and most narrowly watched us as we went up and down the stairs, neither could we go to the well for water save through the midst of them. They did nothing to us, either good or evil, neither did they cry out at us, but nevertheless their waiting there was grievous to us. When supper time drew near, we cooked food for our supper and also for next day's dinner, as we had been wont to do in the wilderness, because on the morrow we should not have had time to spare for cooking dinner, as will be shown.

Welcomed In, 1860

William Beamont

We were no sooner in the convent than we were welcomed by a lay brother, and conducted to the guest hall, a large and spacious chamber with a divan on three sides, and two windows, one looking into the convent court, and the other into an outer enclosure at a distance below, where our Arabs and camels bivouacked.

Our lay brother, after regretting on our account that we had arrived on a fast day, set before us a tray of conserves, some absinthe in small glasses, and a decanter of sparkling water, such as we had not seen since leaving Cairo. The dinner to which this was but a prelude arrived in due time, and consisted of rice, olives, white cheese called Bidneh, and a bottle of the best St. Emilien [sic] wine, followed by coffee; a table in the wilderness not difficult to fast upon, and for which he must be a thankless traveller who would not pay his grateful thanks.

In front of the guests' apartment, there runs a wooden gallery, which (after passing the monks' lodgings, the kitchen where the names and dates of the visits of various dragomen are scored up, and various other buildings of different ages, distinguished neither for their architecture nor their arrangement) leads up a stairway of two flights to the ground-floor, on which is the church, the only part of the convent that has not been renewed, and is a really handsome building.

Welcomed at the Gate, 1865

E.H. Palmer

Presently there issues forth from the gate at the side an old gentleman, reverend though fuddled in mien, dignified though unsteady in gait, - with a patriarchal beard, and the most medieval of serge costumes, who, if such attention be not dexterously avoided, will fall upon your neck and greet you with a paternal kiss.

This is Brother Jacobus, the oeconomos, or bursar, of the convent, once a flourish Smyrna merchant, but now, either because he is tired of the world, or, more probably, because the world is tired of him, brought here to end his days in the Convent of Mount Sinai.

"I was an unbeliever," he said to me one day, "until I came and saw what a holy place this is. For, when the earthquake shakes the mountains round, it never moves a thing within the convent walls; and that convinced me."

As an earthquake has not taken place here within the memory of man, this test of the sanctity of the establishment can hardly be called a crucial one.

It was by this worthy that the members of the Sinai Expedition were ushered into the Convent of St Katherine.

Oliver Brockbank and his companion were welcomed into the monastery and entertained by the Economos, Prior Anthimos.

Made Very Welcome, 1914

Oliver Brockbank

A native servant soon appeared with Turkish coffee, and three innocent little glasses containing a clear colourless liquid. I asked the Economos what it was, and he replied, "A preparation made from dates, peculiar to Sinai, and very famous."

I gulped mine down, and to my dismay found it to be strong date gin, or arak, which almost burnt my throat, and upset my temperance equilibrium. It was an abominable liqueur, tasting of aniseed.

Made Welcome 2, 1938

H.V. Morton

It is only in comparatively recent times that the monks have grown sufficiently confident to have a door.

At last we heard them at the locks and bars; at last the gate opened; and we were soon shaking hands with a number of pallid young men, for it was the younger monks who had rushed down to greet us. Their long hair was bunched beneath rimless birettas, and their pale cheeks were fringed with incipient beards like the down of black swans. The two cars were left under the monastery walls, guarded by the monastery Bedouins. Mr Vallinis (our guide) shouldered his gun and we walked across a courtyard in the starlight, into a space crowded with whitewashed buildings.

We passed through a narrow alley from which cavernous archways led here and there. One side was in starlight, the other in deepest shadow. Above us white towers and roofs, all on different levels, and clustering together, rose into the serenity of the night. Standing behind a door was a cannon on a wooden gun-carriage; a white cat sprang out of a shadow and crossed our path. The silence was unbroken except for the sound of our steps on the stones. I could smell incense and knew that we were passing the church, Justinian's church; then we ascended steps into an open space. Turning to the left, we ascended a long wooden staircase to an outside gallery which reminded me of the New Inn at Gloucester. The monk who was leading us tapped on a door, and I found myself in a small room full of yellow lamplight, in which the Archbishop of Sinai was sitting behind a knee-hole desk.

An Inscription at the Gate, 1892

R.W. Wilson

Above the low door through which the Convent is now entered are two marble tablets which, though not earlier themselves than the thirteenth or fourteenth century, bear, in Greek and Arabic respectively, what is perhaps a copy of the original inscription of Justinian on an older and entirely illegible tablet nearby. It is as follows:-

The holy convent of Mount Sinai where God spoke to Moses was built from the foundation by Justinian the lowly king of the Romans, dependent on God, and hoping in the promise of his Lord, in eternal remembrance of himself and of his consort Theodora. It was completed in the 30th year of his reign, and he placed a chief in the same one of the name of Dulas in the year 6021 since Adam, 521 since Christ.

A Holy Place, 1823

Joseph Wolff

Nov. 6: We arrived in the evening in the convent of St Catherine, on Mount Sinai, called Jibbel Musa, the mount of Moses. We were drawn up by a cord through the window. We all kneeled down and prayed. I did not think I should have been so much overpowered by the thought "the place whereon I stand is holy ground". I am now on the very spot where, it is generally believed, Moses did keep the flock of his father-in-law, upon the mountains of God, even Horeb; in that wilderness, where he encamped at the mount of God, where the angel of the Lord appeared unto him in a flame of fire, out of the midst of a bush: where he looked, and, behold, the bush burned with fire, and the bush was not consumed: where Moses turned aside to see this great sight, why the bush had not burned. I was much overpowered by the thought that I was on that very spot, where the Lord called Moses out of the midst of the bush, and said, "Moses, Moses!", and he said, "Here I am. . . ."

10
The Convent and Convent Life

The Convent of St. Catherine

Life in the convent changed little over the centuries. Thus the earlier travelers found it similar to life in other monasteries where they had stayed. Beyond the boundaries of Sinai, life was greatly changed during the nineteenth century. Coming into the convent seemed like moving backward in time. Additionally, whereas the early travelers were either Orthodox or Catholic, gradually from the seventeenth century on, Protestant travelers began to make their way to Sinai. To them the rituals of the Greek church and the life of the monks sometimes seemed strange. This was the second visit of Adnes Smith Lewis and her sister.

The Place, 1892
Agnes Smith Lewis

Sinai is really a block of mountains 8550 feet in height. About 1600 feet from the top it branches upwards into three peaks, Jebel Catarina, Jebel Musa, which is considered by the monks to be the traditional Mount of the Law, and the Râs Sufsafah, or Mount of the Willow.

The scenery in these lonely valleys is almost too grand for description. Whether we gazed on the majestic rugged cliffs around us in the fierce glare of daylight as they stood out sharp against the intense blue of the sky, or watched the shadows creeping upwards on their worn sides when the sun had dipped behind Jebel Musa, one hour before his actual setting, and saw the vivid contrast of their summits bathed in golden radiance, as if the glory of Him Whose robe is the light touched them, or whether we stood in the garden in the clear moonlight, looking at the sheer towering cliffs and the tall waving cypresses, or at the carpet of fallen almond blossoms at our feet, with a glimmer on it as of snow, we felt how suitable the whole place is for the communion of man with his Maker.

We reached the Convent at 11.30, and were received by Father Eumenios, the new Economos, in Galaktéon's old room, which had been converted into the Ekonomîa, or steward's room. There we had coffee, and afterwards lunch, and waited till our tents arrived. Galaktéon's office as Prior had not been filled up; the Archbishop being permanent Abbot, and having now been in residence for more than a year, there was no need for a second in command.

Interior and Backdrop, 1865

E.H. Palmer

The whole effect of the interior of the convent is peaceful and picturesque, and the background is simply magnificent. On the left is Jebel ed Deir, with its rugged, pathless sides, and upon a ledge, where the green markings on the smooth surface of the rocks indicate the presence of water, there springs up from a heap of stones (the ruined convent of St Episteme) a solitary cypress; anywhere else this would look an imposing tree, but here it seems a mere dark-green thread against the glowing grey of the mountain-side. On the right rises the shoulder of the Jebel Musa block, stern and gigantic as its neighbour, and in the opening between these wondrous walls the green round summit of Jebel Moneijah stands out in bold relief against the sky.

A Town of Stone, 1634

Basil Gogara

Near to the mountain of Sinai is a town of stone, in it are forty monasteries—and they are all empty. Only one, that of the martyr St Catherine, is inhabited. Here lives the bishop of Mount Sinai. There are three hundred brothers in the convent, and they live by paying the Arabs for a licence. They feed the Arabs with the food of the convent, - each day five hundred are fed, lest these people take up arms against the convent.

The Convent and the Dwellings Therein, 1872

Paul Lenoir

The convent of Mount Sinai is the strangest imaginable assemblage of buildings.

Every style may be traced in it: from Byzantine architecture to the most modern epochs of Arab art. Colossal outer walls, flanked by towers and counterforts, give the convent the aspect of a great fortress, quadrangular in form, though conforming to the bend of the mountain against which it is reared, as though it had attempted to scale Mount Sinai, and remained suspended in space like the eyrie of an eagle. It is a little city, an immense strong castle which could sustain more than one attack, more than one siege, on the part of the Arab tribes who covert its treasures. Such is the effect produced by these medieval buildings, where long lives pass in silence, and whose inmates never come forth from them, except to make war. Judging by the height of the towers and their counterforts, they must be very rarely scaled, and for some time we could not guess the position of the drawbridge or entrance of this impregnable fortress.

At length we found it out. It is a kind of flap-door of basket-work worked by a pulley, by means of which the monks communicate with the outer world. The aperture, masked by a wooden shutter, is level with the extreme height of the wall, and excludes every supposition of surprise. The rope which serves to hoist up packages and travellers is worked by a capstan, to which the monks harness themselves to lift their wood, which is brought to them by the Arabs in exchange for certain alms. On a fixed day, a distribution of bread and rice is made to all the poor of the neighbouring tribes. We were present at this curious ceremony, when bread literally fell down to them from heaven, out of the high-pitched tower. We had hoped to make an aerial trip, and enter the convent by this singular aperture, but we arrived too late. The modern mania for embellishment has reached even to Sinai, and the monks have allowed themselves a real door in the newest and worst taste. This new entry, which was 'inaugurated' by us, was not so much to our fancy as the basket, a privileged mode of entrance now reserved for sacks of rice and flour, and forbidden to us, even in our capacity of artists, by the rules of the convent. This was our first mortification, but we speedily forgot it in the novelty and interest of our visit.

We began at the beginning, by paying our respects to the superior. He was in the library, and we were received by a reverend father with a fine, but sickly face, who conducted us to the reception room. In order to reach this apartment, we had to ascend several inclined planes, to mount steep staircases, to pass through dark and winding passages, and to reach a second series of constructions, which, being on another level, seemed like a second little town built on the top of the first.

A vast courtyard, ornamented by three superb cypresses, formed the centre of this second layer of habitations. Out of this court we went, turning in various directions until we came to a wooden stair, which we climbed, and which was no better than a worm-eaten and slippery ladder. At the end we found ourselves on the principal balcony opening on to the interior courtyard. Our polite guide then led us into a low-roofed room with two windows, one opening on the yard, the other on the garden. While we waited for the superior, who our guide went to fetch, we carefully inspected the furniture of this strange room, in which religious emblems, crucifixes, portraits of the popes, sacred pictures, Greek inscriptions, and the oddest conceivable ex votos were mixed up with piles of boots, zouave pipes, tobacco bags, and match-boxes adorned with portraits of actresses belonging to the boulevard theatres.

The superior appeared, the presentation took place, and we were welcomed with the most gracious gestures. Our dragoman did all the talking; we had merely to smile acquiescence, and thus had leisure to observe our entertainers closely. The superior was probably sixty years old; his features were fine, strongly marked, and fittingly framed by his snow-white, luxuriant hair; his white beard hung down to his waist, resting like a huge snow-flake upon the thick folds of his black habit, which covered him from head to foot. Like the priests of the Greek church, he wore a sort of mitre of black felt, with a long veil attached to it, which, when thrown back, protected his neck and shoulders from the sun.

The superior presented to us the other monks, the more important among them having joined us in the reception room. More dialogues in gesture, more smiles. They were mostly old men, and their faces expressed supreme gentleness; all their equipment consisted of a large rosary and a book of Psalms written in Greek and Arabic. The hospitable reception of pilgrims and travellers is not the only occupation of these good monks; they are also engaged in deep study of the rare works and incomparable manuscripts contained in the convent library.

Welcomed In, 1722

The Prefetto of Egypt

When we first came into the convent, we were received by the fathers and brothers of the convent with the greatest affection and regard, and especially by the arch-bishop Jaanikins, who was the superior and president of the place; and who gave us a very elegant supper, and assigned us very convenient apartments, consisting of five chambers, in a part of the convent that was newly built: and also for our better accommodation, indulged us with the liberty of going when we pleased into the garden; which is not permitted even to the monks. And we having there pitched a tent, dined and supped in it every day while we stayed.

The Monastery's Protectors, 2004

Michael Haag

From Justinian's time St Catherine's Monastery has enjoyed the special protection and patronage of rulers. The monastery possesses what it claims is a copy of a document from Mohammed granting security; later the Crusaders took St Catherine's into their care, as did the Ottoman sultans, the Russian czars (who saw themselves as the inheritors of Byzantium) and Napoleon during his Egyptian expedition. Since 1782 the monastery has enjoyed autonomy within the Greek Orthodox Church and today its archbishop is normally resident in Cairo. Though it is sometimes said that St Catherine's is the oldest continuously inhabited monastery in the world, in fact it was sacked in the 10th century and abandoned for some time in the 15th century when relations with the Mamelukes (who ruled Egypt) were bad. Generally, however, it has been respected both as a refuge for wayfarers—including those making the haj—and as a protector of shrines holy to the religions of the Book. So it is not surprising that opposite the narthex of the church is what was a hospice built in the 6th century for pilgrims, but converted to a mosque in 1106. The free-standing minaret was added in the 12th century. From here you can look up at the northwest corner of the church and see the bell tower, built by a monk in 1871, its bells gifts of the czar of Russia.

Churches, Chapels, and Mosque

This Is the Convent, 1820

Sir Frederick Henniker

We now proceeded to survey the convent—a square area, enclosed by a lofty wall; in this are jumbled together a number of rooms, erected at various times, and on uneven surfaces, here are likewise a church, a mosque and a library; and among the most necessary articles is a well.

The monks are frequently quarrelled with by the Arabs; and, consequently afraid to stir out. The wall prevents intruders, and the appearance of two small guns, one of which is wood, contribute materially to their protection. The mosque, strange as it appears adjoining to a church, is necessary to the existence of this Christian foundation—it sanctifies the place in the eyes of the Mussulman, and professes to acknowledge his superiority; it is even allowed for one person to enter it on the Turkish Sabbath.

The Great Church and Small Chapels, 1722

The Prefetto of Egypt

When you come into the great church there are on the south side three chapels; the first that of St John the Evangelist, the second of St Simon the Stylite, and the third of St Cosma and Damianus. And on the other side towards the north, there are also three more viz. first of St Andipe, secondly of the Saints Constantine and Helena, and the third of St Mariana. The whole church is covered with lead.

Besides this church and these chapels, there are seventeen other little churches or chapels situated here and there in the convent: 1. that of St Peter and St Paul, which is tolerably large and roomy; 2. St George; 3. St Stephen; 4. St Michael the Archangel; 5. St Basil, Gregory and Chrysostome; 6. Demetrius the martyr; 7. St Nicholas; 8. St Moses and Aaron; 9. St Sergius Wachas; 10. St John Baptist; 11. St Anthony the abbot; 12. of the five martyrs Eustratius, Euxendius, Barbarius, Orestus, and Eugenius; 13. St John the Evangelist; 14. St Catharine; 15. and 16. two Episcopal chapels; 17. one in the garden where the friars are buried. And besides all these chapels is a mosch with a turret for the Turks, which stands near the western door of the great church; for the preservation of which they say, they have several immunities granted them from the hand of the prophet Mahomet. There is nothing else in the convent remarkable.

The Chapels of the Convent, 1906

Baedeker's *Palestine and Syria*

The Chapel of the Burning Bush, at the back of the apse (of the church), marking the spot where God is said to have appeared to Moses, is; probably the oldest part of the structure. Visitors must remove their shoes before entering. The walls are covered with slabs of porcelain. The spot where the bush is said to have stood is indicated by a plate of chased silver; over it is placed a kind of altar, within which are suspended three burning lamps. At the back of this sanctuary is a small niche adorned with figures, in a line with the apse, the semicircular wall of which encloses the whole of East end of the building. A ray of sun is said to enter this sanctuary once a year only, gaining admission through a cleft in the rock on the East side of the valley. From a cross erected there the hill has been named the Jebel-el-Salib ('hill of the cross').

The chapels surrounding the nave are dedicated to SS. Anna, the holy martyrs of Sinai, James, Constantia and Helena, Demetrius and Sergius. Adjoining the right aisle of the basilica are the chapels of SS. Simon Stylites and Cosmas and Damianus; adjoining the left aisles are those of SS. Anna, Marina and Antipas.—The chapel of the Latins, near the visitors' rooms, is now disused, as the Roman Catholics no longer make pilgrimages to this monastery.

Close by the Church stands the Mosque, which was erected in the 14th century to conciliate the Muslims. It is a building of simple construction, in bad preservation.—The stone wall of an out-building near the mosque and an arch between the mosque and the church still bear several coats-of-arms in the early medieval style, perhaps those of Crusaders.

Fifteen Chapels of the Convent, 1845

Basil Ouspensky

All over the monastery, in corners, and between the cells, we found fifteen churches without cupolas, which were built at different times by different persons . . . The most ancient of them, dedicated to the martyr St Etienne, is near the south-west angle of the hostelry, and it is believed traditionally to be by the same architect who built the monastery. In the church of St Serge and Bacchus, I have seen, on the altar of the Evangelists, in Greek, a document written on sixth century parchment, with, before each Evangelist, a short preface by Cosmos Indicopleustes.*

Escorted by a Monk, 1843

Stephen Olin

The visitor to Mount Sinai does not fail, with a monk for his guide, to make the tour of this labyrinth of antiquated chapels, crazy staircases, and low, dark passages.

* A sixth-century merchant-traveler.

There is hardly anything worth seeing; but it is not the less a duty to inspect everything in such a place, and a person who possesses some sense of the ludicrous will, at least, be able to derive a degree of amusement from the grotesque style of all that he beholds, and from the unique nonsense and absurdities plentifully offered by the loquacious cicerones. In making this indispensable tour, I was first led through a great number of chapels, dedicated to different saints and angels. They all had a very antiquated appearance, and are in bad repair. The walls are usually covered with small paintings, old and much faded, and, with very few exceptions, destitute of every species of merit. The most conspicuous niche was, of course, always devoted to the saint, apostle, or angel to whom the chapel is dedicated and our monk, who spoke only Turkish, which was interpreted in Italian, and again into English, usually entertained us in each chapel, with some tedious legend connected with the history of the patron saint, that, by the time it had received the decorations of three languages, arrived at the ear particularly flat and insipid. We visited, I should think, a dozen of these chapels, which I subsequently learned, constitute less than a moiety of the whole. They were probably the best, and selected on that account.

The Mosque of the Convent, 1815

William Turner

Of the beauty of the church I have already made mention. It has also a small Turkish mosque with a minaret, of which the interior is neat; of the building of this mosque they told me the following story:- A Turkish Sultan passing by, and seeing the convent, in the rage caused by hearing it belonged to the infidels, ordered it to be pulled down; but the monks found means to appease him by presents, and persuaded him to spare their convent, only on the condition that they should build a mosque for the accommodation of Mahometan pilgrims, and maintain an Imaum to take care of it. This Imaum accordingly lives in the convent; but as the Arabs would think it unjust to limit to one man the advantages of so comfortable a situation, he is changed every week, and the convent gives him an allowance of bread, fruit, vegetables, goats' hair for his dress, and other necessaries, of which a list is hung at the entrance, specifying the quantity of each. This is the only Arab ever admitted into the convent, on any pretext.

The Protection of Muhammad, 1816

John Lewis Burckhardt

It is a favourite belief of the monks of Mount Sinai, that Mohammed himself, in one of his journeys, alighted under the walls of the convent, and that impressed with due veneration for the mountain of Moses, he presented to the convent a Firman, to secure to it the respect of all his followers. Ali is said to have written it, and Mohammed, who could not write, to have confirmed it by impressing his extended hand, blackened with ink, upon the parchment. This Firman, it is added, remained in the convent until Selim the First conquered Egypt, when hearing of the precious relic, he sent for it, and added it to the other relics of Mohammed in the imperial registry at Constantinople; giving to the convent, in return, a copy of the original signed with his own cipher. I have seen the latter, which is kept in the Sinai convent at Cairo, but I do not believe it to be an authentic document. None of the historians of Mohammed, who have recorded the transactions of almost every day of his life, mention him having been at Mount Sinai, neither in his earlier youth, nor after he set up as a prophet, and it is totally contrary to history that he should have granted to any Christians such privileges as are mentioned in this Firman, one of which is that the Moslems are bound to aid the Christian monks in rebuilding all their ruined churches. It is to be observed also that this document states itself to have been written by Ali, not at the convent, but in the mosque of the Prophet of Medina, in the second year of Hedjra, and is addressed not to the convent of Mount Sinai in particular, but to all Christians and their priests. The names of twenty-two witnesses, followers of Mohammed, are subscribed to it; and in a note it is expressly stated that the original, written by Ali, was lost, and that the present was copied from a fourth successive copy taken from the original. Hence it appears that the relation of the priests is at variance with the document to which they refer, and I have little doubt therefore that the former is a fable and the latter a forgery.

The Coming of St. Catherine, 1816

John Lewis Burckhardt

A few years after the completion of the convent, one of the monks is said to have been informed in his sleep, that the corpse of St Catherine, who suffered martyrdom at Alexandria, had been transported by angels to the summit of the highest peak of the surrounding mountains. The monks ascended the mountain in procession and found the bones, and deposited them in their church, which thus acquired an additional claim to the veneration of the Greeks.

Monastic establishments seem soon to have considerably increased throughout the peninsula. Small convents, chapels, and hermitages, the remains of many of which are still visible, were built in various parts of it. The prior told me that Justinian gave the whole peninsula in property to the convent, and that at the time of the Mohammedan conquest, six or seven thousand monks and hermits were dispersed over the mountains, the establishments of the peninsula of Sinai thus resembling those which still exist on the peninsula of Mount Athos.

The Most Blessed Virgin St. Catherine and Her Holy Relics, 1483

Felix Fabri

During this time it had become bright day, and we went down into St Catherine's Church to see her holy relics. When we were in the church, the Father of the monastery came with all his monks, each of them bearing a lighted candle in his hand; and in like manner all of us pilgrims had lighted wax tapers in our hands, and so we stood round the holy virgin's tomb, on both sides thereof. Now came the sacrist of the convent with his keys, and essayed to open the locks of the tomb, but he could not do so, because both the locks and the keys were altogether covered with rust and out of order; howbeit at last with the help of others of the brethren, by great force and labour they opened the locks, and exposed the tomb of the sacred body.

When the marble lid which covered the tomb was taken away, the monks began to chant an antiphon, whereof both the music and the words were Greek, of which I could understand no word, save only 'apostles' and 'martyrs'; for they sang these two words repeatedly amongst others, and they are the same both in Greek and Latin, and have been taken from the Greek language into the Latin. Whilst they were singing, the Father of the monastery came to the place of the sepulchre, and after making a low bow went up to the coffin, which stands in a higher place. Here he plunged his head into the coffin, kissed that treasure house of heavenly wisdom, the virgin's sacred head, and then raising himself up again, remained standing beside the head of the coffin. After him all the monks drew near, beginning with the eldest, and kissed the holy relics in the same manner in which the Abbot had done. After the monks we pilgrims went and worshipped the relics in the customary manner, and after us our ass-drivers did the same.

When we had done this, our noblemen gave me all their jewels of gold and jewels of silver, that I might touch the holy relics with them. So I took both the jewels which had been entrusted to me at Ulm by those dear to me, and those of my comrades their lordships the knights, and put each one of them into the coffin, touching with them the noble virgin's sacred head. While I was doing this, the Father of the monastery who stood beside me, never took his eyes off me, and watched my hands most carefully, lest any of the relics should be carried off; for indeed much has been taken away in past times, both by having been stolen by pilgrims and begged by emperors, bishops, and kings, and so much has been given away in this fashion that only less than half of the sacred body is left. Now that they know of this they guard it carefully from thieves, and neither entreaties nor bribes will induce them to give any part of it away.

The greater part of it is still there—that is to say, the entire head of the holy virgin, covered with a golden crown adorned with many gems and with the symbol of sanctity; and the left hand, whose fingers are covered with exceedingly costly rings set with precious stones. The other hand, the monks told me, is in Georgia; but they of Rhodes boast that they possess it, and show it to pilgrims. We saw some of the ribs, shin-bones and many other members of the holy virgin lying in the coffin. The sacred bones seem to have lain in oil, because they are not white, but are of the colour that a bone or piece of wood contracts by lying in oil. It is the belief of the holy church that the virgin's limbs once sweated forth oil; but this miracle has now ceased for a long while, and the holy limbs are swathed in silk, pieces of which are now given to the pilgrims instead of oil. They soak these pieces of silk in the lamps which hang in the chapel of St Mary at Bush, and so take them home as St Catherine's oil.

Devotion to St. Catherine, 1498

Francis Suriano

And although they show some of her relics and bones, yet in truth they have nothing of St Catherine but the hands, white as milk, with the fingers which are long and covered with rings, although some of the joints of the fingers are missing and not one of them is entire; these I touched and kissed with unspeakable devotion.

The Relics of St. Catherine, 1722

The Prefetto of Egypt

October 1: On this day we opened a chest, kept on the right hand of the presbytery, in which are preserved the relicks of St Catharine; and the principal parts they brought out to show us, were the skull and left hand of this saint, having the flesh and skin on it, but quite dried up, and covered with beautiful rings. After we had been favoured with this sight, we were permitted to depart. Taking leave therefore of the archbishop, and the rest of the monks, we came out of the convent about noon, amidst the noisy clamours of the Arabs, by the same way that we entered.

The Exterior of the Church, 1839

John Kinnear

The exterior of the church is without any architectural beauty; but one little circumstance struck me as very interesting. This was, several shields and coats of arms rudely engraved on the stone, on each side of the entrance; memorials, no doubt, of the chivalry of the crusades, and perhaps scratched with their daggers by some knightly pilgrims.

The Exterior of the Church, and Entering . . . , 1857

James Hamilton

The church without belfry (for the Greeks use a wooden board to call the prayers) and the minaretted mosque stand side by side in the centre of the building in most edifying harmony—the latter as remarkable for its absence of ornament, as the former for its rich decoration.

Externally, the church has not an imposing effect, its pavements being several feet below the level of the court, and low, mean buildings such as disfigure so often the old churches of France and Germany, surrounding it on every side. It is well and solidly built, and its style of architecture smacks of that called Romanesque in Germany, and Lombard in Italy. The windows are double round-headed, the arches springing from a short column, and resting on a short column on each side. The doorway, to which you descend by a flight of steps, is large and simple, and leads into a *pronaos*, from which a second door of the same dimensions gives entrance to the church.

The first view of the interior of the church is striking both on account of its richness and its brilliancy, and of the picturesque grouping of the furniture with which it is filled; its cleanliness is admirable, and many of the details merit close examination.

The columns are whitewashed, and their capitals (likewise of red granite) are painted green, and carved in a style which in European art denote a date of the ninth or tenth century. At a fifth column is placed the screen, concealing the high altar and the apse; it is a heavy piece of gilding, covered with bad modern pictures of the Russian school of sacred art, and is surmounted by a gigantic crucifixion with St Mary and John. The roof is flat and painted of a bright blue, sprinkled with golden stars; amidst these are circular paintings, let in at equal distances, apparently of the seventeenth century; and just beyond the centre is observed a pierced decoration, representing the sun, the moon, and the stars, which serves to admit air into the building; from this hung down three remarkably fine bronze lustres, and a great multitude of lamps.

The Pictures of the Church, 1815

William Turner

[I]t is built by the same hand as the convent, is in the usual style of Greek churches, and is certainly very superb. Its pavement is a mosaic of fine marbles of different colours, of porphyry, and of verd antique. It is lighted by above forty silver lamps, and its walls are covered with pictures of Saints much better executed (because painted in Russia) than is usual in Greek churches; some of these are very amusing. There is one of St Christopher with a dog's head, as, said the Greeks, were all the men of the country where he was born.—One of the men ascending to heaven on a ladder, and angels pulling some of them down.—One of the last judgement, in the background of which are fishes casting out men (the sea giving up her dead) and in front an angel weighing men and devils, carrying the light ones into the mouth of a large fish. There are at least a dozen of the Virgin, and many of Christ, and John the Baptist. Seeing a large silver hand stuck on the side of one picture of the Virgin, who had besides two painted ones in the picture, I asked what it meant, and the Caloyers told me the following story.

A monk was preparing to leave the convent; one day, while he was standing alone in the church, near this picture, the right hand advanced and boxed his ear. A voice then issued from the lips reproaching him for wishing to leave the convent, and commanding him to stop and die there. He obeyed, and in sign of submission and gratitude, made an offering to the Virgin of this silver hand.

The roof of the church is painted light blue, with holes in the middle for ventilators, which are ingeniously made into sun, moon, and stars, and neatly gilt. The altar, divided, (as in all Greek churches) by a screen from the church is very handsome, and above it is a figure of Christ, and another of the Virgin represented in mosaic as large as life. There are also pictures in mosaic of Justinian and

Theodora. On a table near the altar is a box containing, say the monks, the bones of St Catherine, and in the church are a great many representations of her flight to Sinai. There are also many of Mount Sinai and the convent, on one side of which are represented processions of priests coming out of the convent, and on the other (I do not mean that the canvas is painted on both sides) Arabs firing at those who are hoisted up the rope.

The Church of the Transfiguration, 1820

Sir Frederick Henniker

From the library we adjourned to the church—a handsome building well fitted up in the Greek style, with much gilding and many portraits; among the most striking is the likeness of a saint, with a pig's face, and another with a beard as long as himself;* but Catherine is the favourite, - the founder of nunneries is the patroness of this monastery; repetitions of her portrait form the principal ornament; and her bones constitute the chief wealth of the sacristy; not but that a proper attention is paid to worldly riches; - a canvas face, on Mount Sinai, as well as in Rome is capable of receiving offerings; the Holy Lady smiles propitiously even on Turkish money, with pieces of which she is bedizened, in the same manner as an Egyptian Almah. The bones are preserved in a silver case, presented for that purpose by Catherine of Russia!

The Apse: Matthew 17: 1–3, 2004

Michael Haag

In the apse is the 6th century mosaic of the Transfiguration, one of the finest works of Byzantine art.

It is exceptional too for having survived the destructions of the iconoclasts and for being untouched by restorers. The Transfiguration is notable too for the painterly manner of its execution, unlike the more graphic style of its mosaic contemporaries at Ravenna.

The subject of the mosaic is taken from Matthew 17: 1–3, after Jesus asks his disciples who they think he is:

> *And after six days Jesus taketh Peter, James and John his brother, and bringeth them up into a high mountain apart. And was transfigured before them: and his face did shine as the sun, and his raiment was white as the light. And behold, there appeared unto them Moses and Elias talking with him.*

---

* Henniker believed this was Christopher, a saint with the head of an unclean animal; St. Nicholas, who having but a short beard, prayed that it might be lengthened.

An Observer at the Service, 1845

W.H. Bartlett

I descended to the church in melancholy mood. On entering it now for the first time, I was both pleased and surprised: although somewhat spoiled by tasteless and gaudy decoration, it is a fine simple solemn basilica, built in the time of Justinian, and is kept in the nicest care by the brethren. Leaning against the carved seat I waited through the service, I which I understood nothing, but which is described by a previous traveller as "simple, dignified, and solemn, consisting in great part in the reading of the Gospels, with the touching responses and chants of the Greek ritual." To me, it appeared impressive enough, without mummery, and the chants were very moving and devotional: the demeanour of the Superior seemed both dignified and serious. It was effecting to see some very old men come tottering in from a side passage during the service, whose beards, long to their girdles, as they knelt down swept the marble pavement, and who, after brief but earnest protestation in prayer, withdrew; failing nature being apparently unequal to the fatigues of an entire service and though the piety they nourish may be open "traditionary and degraded" it would surely be a harsh judgement which should refuse them the final rest to which through life they have aspired, if the award be according to the measure of what a man has, and not what he has not. Milton, who was no lover of monks,— "white, black, and grey, with all their trumpery"—would at least give them a place in his "Paradise of Fools," which is better than the limbo to which they and their erring piety are devoted by the more exclusive sort of sectarians.

A Service With the Monks, 1861

Edward Robinson

Sunday, March 25th Having expressed a desire to attend the service in the great church this morning, we were welcomed to it, with the remark, but this was something unusual with travellers. We had already been invited to breakfast afterwards with the fraternity in the refectory. The service commenced in the church at 7 o'clock and continued an hour and a half. It was simple, dignified, and solemn, consisting in great part in the reading of the Gospels, with the touching responses and chants of the Greek ritual. The associations of Sinai came strongly in aid of the calm and holy influence of the service; and everything tended to awaken in the breast feelings of veneration and devotion. The antique yet simple grandeur of the church is also imposing. The monks seemed each to have his particular seat or stall; and two very old men struck me in particular, who chanted the responses and *kyrie eleison* with great simplicity and apparent fervour. The service included also the high mass, or consecration of the sacraments of the Lord's Supper. But the monks did not commune; only one stranger, a Greek from Tûr, partook of it. Just at the close of the service Father Neophytus, the Prior, as a mark of special favour, called us of his own accord into the sacristy and showed us the relics of St Catherine. . . . The relics consist of a skull and hand, set in gold and embossed with jewels.

The Church of the Transfiguration Transfigured, 1938

H.V. Morton

I have mentioned the legend that the first church was built to enshrine the Burning Bush, which in the earliest Christian period was the most sacred object in the valley. St Helena is also believed to have built near this church a tower of refuge in which the monks might gather during attacks by the Saracens. No date is given for these foundations, but, if the legend is true, it must have been in 327 AD, when she was in Jerusalem seeking for the relics of the True Cross.

The original church of the Burning Bush had been standing for two centuries when Justinian built the fortress walls around it in 530 AD. At this time, or shortly afterwards, the Church of the Burning Bush was enlarged into the present church, which was then called the Church of the Transfiguration, from the exquisite Byzantine mosaic which still decorates the dome above the high altar. The apse of the old church of the Burning Bush was retained and still stands beyond the end of the present east end of the Church of the Tranfiguration, obviously part of an older smaller building, and on a lower level.

Different travellers to Sinai perceived the services in the church in different ways at different times. How they saw it depended also on their own religious experience—the Protestant, accustomed to religious service conventional and stripped down to simplicity, disturbed by the ornate foreign ritual; the Catholic, even from a Protestant tradition, more easily understanding what they saw. Time too changes perceptions. At times, of course, the rule of the monastery, though unchanging at heart, was more or less spiritual in presentation. Thus, one observer at one time might find the services offended them and wished to withdraw; another person at another time was drawn into them.

The Burning Bush and Its Chapel

The Burning Bush before the Convent, A.D. 383

Egeria

The way (down from Mount Sinai) took us to the head of this valley because there the holy men had many cells, and there is also a church there at the place of the Bush (which is still alive and sprouting). It was about four o'clock by the time we had come right down the Mount and reached the Bush. This, as I have already said, is the Burning Bush out of which the Lord spoke to Moses, and it is at the head of the valley with the church and all the cells.

The Bush itself is in front of the church in a very pretty garden which has plenty of excellent water. Near by you are also shown the place where holy Moses was standing when God said to him, "Undo the fastening of thy shoes" and so on. (Exodus 3.5; Acts 7.33)

Since it was already four in the afternoon by the time we got there, it was too late for us to be able to make the Offering, but we had a prayer in the church and also in the garden of the Bush, and as usual the appropriate passage was read from the Book of Moses. Then, because it was late, we had our meal with the holy men in the garden near the Bush, and stayed there for the night. Next morning we were awake early, and the presbyters made the Offering there at our request.

> ***The pilgrims were then taken and shown all the places which linked the area to the Old Testament, and "everything which the Books of Moses tell us took place in that valley beneath holy Sinai, the Mount of God."***

I know it has been rather a long business writing down all these places one after the other, and it makes far too much to remember. But it may help you, loving sisters, the better to picture what happened in these places when you read the holy Books of Moses.

The Chapel of St. Mary at Bush, 1483

Felix Fabri

[W]e entered barefoot into another chapel adjoining that one, passing through a little doorway which stands at the head of the great church. The pavement of this chapel was strewn with costly carpets, the walls were covered with precious polished slabs of marble, it was lighted by many lamps, and everything in this chapel was beauteous, decorated, and devout. This is the place where stood that miraculous bush of Moses, which he saw burning, and the flames rising aloft from out of it; yet was it not hurt by any fire as we read in Exodus iii. But even more wondrous was the fulfilment of this vision, when Mary, that ever-green bush, ever-flowering, and sweet-scented was kindled and impregnated by the Divine fire, while nevertheless her virginity suffered no hurt. Of this holy bush the Church sings, *Rubum quem viderat Moses incombustum, etc.* We sang this hymn there, and bowing ourselves down at the place where the bush stood, most devoutly kissed it, and received plenary indulgences.

Beneath the altar is the place where the bush is believed to have stood, and in the pavement there is a brazen plate, whereon is carved the figure of the burning bush, and Moses sitting down putting off his shoes. Many lamps hang above the place, for it is held in great respect by all men. Saracens, Arabs and Turks beg earnestly to be admitted to this place, and when they are admitted do not enter it save barefoot. Jews would be exceeding glad to enter it, but are not suffered so to do.

The Burning Bush, 1739

Richard Pococke

The convent of Mt. Sinai is situated on the north foot to Mt. Horeb,* and west of the Mount of Moses; for so I chuse to express myself, though the valley runs from the south-west to the south-east. At a well in the convent, called the Well of Moses, they say, Moses met the daughters of Jethro: That on the Mount of Moses he was feeding the flock of Jethro, his father-in-law; and that in the spot where now is the chapel of the Holy Bush, adjoining to the east end of the great church of the convent, grew that tree which appeared to Moses as if it burnt and was not consumed, and out of which God spake to him. In a garden near the fathers have planted a bramble, such as are common in Europe, and say it was such a bush in which the miracle was wrought; though such brambles do not grow in these parts; but they tell you that formerly they did.

Preparing to Enter the Chapel of the Burning Bush, 1820

Sir Frederick Henniker

Having paid the tythe, I was hastening into a small cell or chapel, which is honoured by a situation immediately behind the grand altar; my guide desired me to take off my boots, for it was on that spot that the Lord appeared unto Moses in the burning bush, and He himself commanded the prophet to loose his shoes from his feet.†

The Chapel of the Burning Bush, 1865

E.H. Palmer

Before entering the Chapel of the Burning Bush, the visitor is requested in so many words "to take the shoes from off his feet, as the place whereon he is standing is holy ground." The late Abbas Pasha (Khedive of Egypt) was so much impressed with the sanctity of the shrine that during his sojourn in Sinai he preferred saying his daily prayers upon its soft carpeted floor to prostrating himself upon the hard pavement of the whitewashed mosque. There are other chapels in the Convent designed for the use of the Latin and Armenian sects, but as only Greek and Mohammedan pilgrims now visit the place they have become entirely deserted.

. . . And In, 1872

Paul Lenoir

All of a sudden the monks who accompanied us assumed a solemn demeanour, and apprised us that we were about to be admitted into the sanctuary where God appeared to Moses. The altar in this little chapel is placed where the burning

---

* Mount Horeb is the name some travellers used, mistakenly, for Mount Sinai.

† "Put off thy shoes from thy feet, for the place whereon thou standest is holy ground" (Exodus 3:5).

bush stood. A bright light reflected in a plate of gold is the emblem of the sublime apparition; and it was with gestures of respect and awe that the monks withdrew for us the veil which hides the little flame from profane eyes. This is the most curious and richly ornamented of all the chapels. The light is softened by coloured windows; it would otherwise destroy the poetic charm of this sacred place. Our stockinged feet rested on Persian carpets, and we stood before the burning bush with our boots in our hands, in the very place where the custom originated at the command of God—"Put off thy shoes from off thy feet, for the place whereon thy standest is Holy Ground."

Celebrations

Holy Sunday, 1722

The Prefetto of Egypt

September 13. This day being Holy Sunday, we were invited to attend at church, as we usually did on other days, where the archbishop himself officiated, and sang the mass clothed in his *pontificalibus*, wearing on his head a sort of imperial crown made in silver, of exquisite workmanship; with the rest of the ministers that attended him, in very sumptuous apparel; which when ended, we dined in the common refectory of the convent, with the archbishop and the rest of the monks, who eat only of one dish. After dinner, all of us standing up, we took each a moderate piece of bread, cut from one loaf, and drank also all out of one cup, the archbishop beginning first. When all had drunk, we broke up, and departed. This ceremony is observed as a mark of mutual love and charity.

Christmas Day, 1853

Catherine Tobin

In the evening we attended vespers: the church was but dimly lighted. A silver salver and vase, containing the sacred elements, were placed in the centre of the nave; and while the Superior pronounced a benediction, the other officials walked round them in procession. At midnight we were awakened by a most discordant ringing of bells, summoning the brotherhood to prayers. This was *Christmas day*—the sixth of January—and the monks had a busy time of it! The six cannon were fired at sunrise; when, quite unable to go to sleep again, we opened the windows, and looked down upon our Arabs; who, not admitted into the convent, were sitting in a circle round a cheerful blaze outside; the camels lying near them.

The Festival of St. Catherine, 1860

William Beamont

Dec. 6—The Greek calendar differing from ours by eleven days, today is their 25th of November, and a great day here, being the festival of St Catherine, with whom the convent, though not actually dedicated to her, is associated by many legends.

To celebrate the festival the monks rose in the night. At an early hour of three o'clock my ears caught a sound they had not lately heard, 'the sound of a church-going bell', with its cheerful notes summoning the monks to prayer. Hastily throwing on my clothes, and repairing to the church, I reached it just as the nakus, or clappers, the substitute for our saint's bell, took up the summons which the bell began. The nakus, a sonorous wooden plank, ten feet long, six or eight inches deep, and three inches thick, hangs free in the middle, and being struck with a mallet produces a novel but harmonious sound. 'Bells' or 'no bells' once formed as great a distinction between Christian and Moslem as the signs of the crescent and the cross, and the latter communion resorted to the nakus as a substitute when their dominant masters had interdicted them the use of bells. From adherence to long custom, the nakus, though the reason of its use has long ceased, is still continued at Mount Sinai, where it is a very pleasant variation of the call to prayer.

The church was dimly lighted by six or eight tapers, and the monks, entering noiselessly one by one, after repeated crossings, prostrated themselves on the marble floor and kissed it, looking, in the mysterious gloom and silence, more like spectres and apparitions than creatures of flesh and blood. Rising from their prostrations they retired to their stalls, and either followed the officiating priest, who was chanting (which all the Eastern churches use instead of reading), or prayed by themselves in an under-tone.

When this had continued for some time, the reading of the gospel began, and an abundance of candles and tapers where lighted, while an acolyte circulated through the church with a censer, and censed the monks, the lay brothers, some Russian pilgrims, and ourselves, who formed the congregation.

The Russian pilgrims, four men and twelve women, wore short dark-furred cloaks, drawn over the head so as to leave only a part of the face exposed. At one part of the service, where the priest repeated the words "Kyrie eleison" so fast as to be almost out of breath, the bowings, crossings, and prostrations of the pilgrims were incessant, and as they rose and fell they looked like the waving billows of a little sea.

I remained at the service until all the extra lights and tapers were extinguished, and the church was again immersed in gloom, and then crept back to my couch by the light of the moon and Charles's Wain, which were both shining brilliantly.

The Greek New Year and Epiphany, 1892

Annette Benson*

We went to a special (Greek) New Year's service in the church, and stood or sat in the stalls along the nave for one and a half hours. These stalls are meant for standing, the divisions having flat tops for arm-rests; the seats are hinged to turn up, and then the bracket on the underside makes a little rest at a higher level than the seat proper. There was no instrumental music whatever, but the usual rich, unaccompanied singing of the Greek church. A flat loaf with a picture of the Convent impressed upon it was placed on a small table with candles, and censed and blessed; at the end it was presented to Dr. Rendell Harris; he and Dr. Hatch occupied places of honour near to the archimandrites.

After the service two silver boxes about 10 x 10 x 6 inches, were brought out to a table in the nave and opened to our view, with much ceremony and reverence; one contained the skull and one the skeleton hand of St Catherine. The hand was covered with rich rings, while flowers, gold ornaments and costly gems decorated both.

On Friday, January 19th, there was a grand burst of bells in the night, probably at about 4 a.m., each successive peal being started by a loud explosion produced by the firing of a cannon, for this was the Feast of Epiphany, a very great day, when the Baptism of Christ is commemorated, the beginning of his Gospel as recorded by St Mark; Christmas, as a festival, originated later in the West.

We had a hurried breakfast that we might be in the church by 7 a.m., when the monks rang the bells again, for they deferred part of the rites until this hour, especially the baptism of the crucifix, in order that we might be present. They themselves had continued from the first ringing, and still went on till nearly 9 a.m. There were long hymns and psalms and readings from the Gospels, and processions round the church. A table placed in the nave near the west door bore a beautiful large porcelain bowl, and also a cross, candles, censer and incense, and bunches of sweet basil. Presently many were grouped at the table, and water was poured into the bowl and blessed, and a small crucifix and the herbs were dipped together into it; then the larger cross was sprinkled, and afterwards the group of those who stood round on the right hand and the left. Finally, others came near, one by one, with bent heads, and so received the sprinkling from the wet basil.

On leaving the church we were taken to the reception room and entertained. The usual large tray was handed round with a *compot* (a delicious quince jelly on this occasion), and glasses of water and arrack followed by coffee. The two chief archimandrites wore their splendid gold chains and jewelled crosses, and all were most friendly and hospitable. They gave us sprigs of sweet basil, grown in pots (and old petrol tins)—on the roof. From the roof, outside the room we were in, we could see the monk in the bell-tower with the ropes

* Quoted by R.W. Wilson.

gathered in his hand, his hair flying out from his head as his body swayed to peel the bells, while another man on the lower story of the tower struck the horizontal wooden beam.*

The Library of the Convent

The Convent library and the important manuscripts which it holds have been the focus of much attention over the last two centuries.

The Library, 1815

William Turner

To my inquiries after manuscripts and a library, the priests answered, that they had only three bibles, and I took their word the more readily, as Pococke states that they had no rare manuscripts. But Mr Bankes [William John Bankes who visited in 1813], by persevering and rummaging, found out a library, of 2,000 volumes, of which three-quarters were MSS [manuscripts] and of these, nine-tenths were Greek. The greater part were theological but some were interesting, Mr Bankes bought away, 1—a thick MS, containing Hephaestio on the Greek Metres, an Oration of Isocrates, the Letters of Phalaris (which were the subject of much controversy some years ago); 2d. Another containing three first books of the Iliad, and part of the fourth; two Tragedies of Aeschylius, and much Greek poetry; 3d. Another thin one, containing the Medes of Euripides, and the beginning of his Hyppolitas: 4th, An Historical Work of Cedrensu (a Byzantine historian quoted in Gibbon); 5th, a very fair one, containing, it appears, all the Physics of Aristotle, probably of no remote antiquity, as it is written with contractions, which were not used in the early ages. There were also many Arabick, Syriac, and Coptic MSS. The Arabick MSS, Burckhardt says, are of little literary value.

On October 7, 1819 the traveler John Hyde wrote to William Bankes from Cairo, reporting on his visit to St. Catherine's Convent, where Bankes had visited six years earlier and borrowed some books from the library—which Hyde returned.

The Library, 1819

John Hyde

On arrival at Mount Sinai I availed myself of the first opportunity to examine the Library, and after a most indefatigable though fruitless search, through the Books

* The wooden beam was hollow and acted as the 'bell' for the monastery.

upon the floor and upon the shelves, I was compelled to give up the hope of executing the commission you trusted to me, in the perfect conviction that Slobonius' manuscript was no longer in the Library.* You mentioned to Kyriako having placed it apart from the others on its shelf, we therefore more particularly examined such Books on the floor as all answered to your description of this manuscript, but the Book was not to be found. Disappointed in our endeavours to find it, as a dernier resource, I directed Kyriako to ask for the works of some Greek historians, and amongst the rest to name Sidrinus, with a view to ascertain if the Librarian knew the book, but he appeared altogether unacquainted with the name of its Author. Since you were at Mount Sinai, several travellers have visited the Convent. It's more than probable some of them have laid their hands upon this Mss and carried it away. I regret the circumstances the more, as judging from the very friendly reception the Monks gave us, and from their apparent anxiety to do every thing in their power to oblige me, I am persuaded that if the Book had been in the Library, they would readily have permitted me to bring it away -

The last visitors who preceded us were three Halemis (they passed themselves off as Englishmen). I learnt that they spent a great deal of their time in the Library and that they mapped, measured, and took drawings of nearly every part of the Monastery, after inflicting themselves upon the poor Monks for about ten days they took their departure without leaving a Para for the Convent.† They even left the Convent the charge of paying the Arab guides who accompanied them to the neighbouring mountains. You will probably not be much surprised to find that one of these three worthies was the Chevalier!‡ who travelled under the name Amiro, which (since my return to Cairo) I have learnt is the name he tacks to poetical effusions with which he occasionally favours the World.

The four Books you entrusted to my care I saw placed upon a shelf in the Library.

The Library, 1820

Sir Frederick Henniker

The library does not contain many books of value; all that were worth moving have been lately carried to Egypt; there still remain many scrolls of parchment, on which are written prayers in Greek and Syriac, and also some damaged Aldine editions;§ - but listen, Mr Frognall Dibdin: - while I was dirtying my fingers in search of the true black letter, the superior told me to throw away the stupid *old* books, and look at some nice new ones! - They are very clean copies—they bear no mark, but that of the Bible Society, and are very carefully put on the shelf.

---

* This was one of the manuscripts reported by Bankes as being in the library.

† A para is a very small Turkish coin of almost no value.

‡ 'Chevalier' the name used by Domenico Fredianu (1783–1823) was an Italian soldier who came to Egypt in 1811 and appears in travellers' accounts until his death.

§ A modern series of popular books at the time.

The Library and the Treasury, 1846

Lord Lindsay

In the archbishop's apartment, now used as the Treasury, we were shown a most beautiful manuscript of the Gospels in Greek, on vellum, in uncial, or capital, letters of gold; I thought the good father would never have done turning over the preliminary leaves of illuminations, and arranging the silk screens interposed between them. Would that it were in the British Museum! I wonder whether it has ever been collated. The illuminations consist of full-length figures of the Apostles, and are extremely well-executed, the colours as brilliant as if laid down yesterday. It is at least twelve hundred years old.

I was disappointed in the library of the convent, finding no very ancient Greek manuscripts, or valuable printed books; a manuscript of Saint Chrysostom, in a great number of folio volumes, all apparently in the same handwriting, interested me most. There are many MSS. of the Scriptures in Greek, and some in Slavonic of portions of the Bible, - many Arabic manuscripts also, all of which were examined by Burckhardt. The books are arranged alphabetically in large cases.

The Library, 1865

E.H. Palmer

[W]e came to the library, a wretched unpainted room, containing a goodly number of worm-eaten manuscript volumes in Greek and Arabic. They are chiefly patristic or controversial literature, and of little interest, the really valuable books being securely locked up in the Archbishop's room, into which we were not at the time allowed to register. I offered to make a catalogue of the Arabic manuscripts, and had actually commenced the task, but so many difficulties were thrown in my way that I was at length compelled to relinquish it. Father Jacob, the oeconomos, looked upon the whole proceeding as fatuous from the very first. Since the affair of the Codex Sinaiticus, the monks have come to regard their manuscript treasures with a jealous eye, though not from any real appreciation of their literary value. They ought, however, to be content, for the Emperor Alexander (of Russia) has paid them handsomely for it, and presented them in addition with brand new shrine for good St Katherine's bones. Considering the worm-eaten and utterly neglected state of the books, I think that it would be greatly to the gain of literature if the whole collection were handed over to more careful guardianship.

The scandal of the removal of the Codex Sinaiticus from the library has run through the history of the Convent of St. Catherine for more than sixty years. In 1925, Mary Dobson summarized the happenings surrounding the Codex Sinaiticus.

Tischendorf and the Codex, 1912

Mary Dobson

When visiting the Convent in 1844, Tischendorf saw in the middle of the great hall, a basket full of old parchments, and was told that two similar heaps had been burned. On examining the manuscripts he found, to his astonishment, a number of sheets of the a copy of the Old Testament in Greek which bore evidence of great antiquity. He was allowed by the convent to take away about forty-five of these sheets, which he published as the Codex Friderico-Augustanus in honour of his German patron.

He returned in 1853, with little result, but when he went once more in 1859, with a commission from the Emperor of Russia, he found nearly the whole of the remainder of the manuscript. It was shown him just before he was leaving by one of the stewards of the Convent, who had it in his cell wrapped in a red cloth. Tischendorf says of the Codex:

It contains the Old and New Testament, and is written with four columns to the page. The New Testament is perfect. To the twenty-seven books of the New testament are appended the Epistle of Barnabas complete and part of the shepherd of Hermas.

He calculated that the manuscripts should be assigned to the middle of the fourth century. He considered it possible that Emperor Justinian, the founder of the Sinaitic monastery, sent it as a present from Constantinople to the monks of Sinai.

Tischendorf thus concludes the story:

"On the 27th of September I returned to Cairo. The monks and archbishops then warmly expressed their thanks for my jealous efforts in their cause, and the following day I received from them under the form of a loan the Sinaitic Bible to carry to St Petersburg and there to have it copied as accurately as possible. I set out from Egypt early in October, and on the 19th of November I presented to their Imperial Majesties in the Winter Palace at Tsarkoe-Selo my rich collection of old Greek, Syrian, Coptic, Arabic and other manuscripts in the middle of which the Sinaitic Bible shone like a crown."

The monks and archbishops never set eyes on the manuscript again.

The Case of the Codex Sinaiticus, 1938

H.V. Morton

Possibly the most tactless thing an Englishman could do in Sinai would be to inform the monks that he had subscribed to the purchase of the Codex Sinaiticus, which is now in the British Museum. I am thankful to say that no one mentioned this subject to me, for I understand that the monks have the strong feelings about it. They say that Tischendorf took away the Codex in 1859 to copy it, and that the Tsar retained possession of it by unfair means. Apparently they think it wrong of us to have bought at great cost what they regard as stolen property.

Whether may be the rights and wrongs of this question,* the subsequent fame and financial value of the Codex have caused the monks to guard their Library with the eyes of the lynx. The books are no longer neglected. They are stored in a stone room rather like a bank vault, and the more precious volumes are kept behind a locked grille. The books repose on shelves, and most of them bear paper labels on the spine, on which titles are written in Greek and Arabic. I was shown the famous Codex Aureus with its illuminated pages, and many other ancient and valuable manuscripts, now rightly kept under lock and key.

The Library, 1872

Paul Lenoir

This wonderful library is ordinarily accessible to the monks only, but our quality of painters, and the magnificent proportions of our official dromedaries (lent by the Pasha in Cairo), smoothed away all difficulties. The superior himself conducted us to the library, and brushed away the dust for us from the most curious among the store of parchment and papyrus.

A 'Life of the Saints', profusely adorned with paintings and portraits, especially attracted our admiration, by the purity of the designs, and the brilliancy of the colours. These manuscripts in themselves would richly repay the journey, and we obtained permission to study them at our leisure. We were also shown the four Gospels, entirely written, they told us, by the Emperor Theodore's hand.

Their bindings are as remarkable for taste as for richness. Some of them, in carved wood, are covered with gold and silver ornaments exquisitely wrought.

The Library, 1873

Murray's Handbook

The Library will be to the Biblical scholar one of the most interesting portions of the convent. Unfortunately the monks are not literary men, and their library has been greatly neglected. In consequence of the visits to Tischendorf and other scholars a slight improvement has taken place of late. It contains about 1500 volumes of printed books, many of which are worn, torn and dilapidated. The books are of little value and little use. But it also contains a number of manuscripts, chiefly Arabic and Greek, some of which are of very great value, and of high antiquity. Here Tischendorf discovered the now celebrated *Codex Sinaiticus*, the only complete uncial manuscript of the New Testament, and one of the oldest and most valuable. Two other beautiful manuscripts are still here. They are not kept in the Library with the other books, but are carefully locked up in a chamber called the Archbishop's Room. Of late the monks have occasionally shown some unwillingness to permit travellers to enter the library, or inspect these more precious literary treasures.

---

* Morton refers to the purchase of the Codex from the Soviet government of Russia by the British Museum in 1933. It can now be seen both there and on the museum's website.

The Library Has Changed, 1912

Mary Dobson

The Library itself is a very different place from what it was fifty, or even thirty, years ago. Time and experience have taught the monks the importance of preserving cataloguing and knowing the contents of their manuscripts and books. Carefully constructed grills now guard the precious treasures of antiquity from prying eyes and over-eager hands, while the august Librarian is the only means of access to any volume of parchment on the shelves.

In addition to all this, exacting rules are posted up in a conspicuous place at the entrance; visitors are thereby informed that they may only have access to the place for a certain number of days, and that, moreover, they may only work for a certain number of hours during those days. Together with all these limitations stands a strict injunction that no photographs at all may be taken, a proviso which struck chill to our hearts, for there were two skilled photographers in the party, and we had hoped to bring back untold treasures in the way of manuscript photographs.

The Convent Garden

In a Convent Garden, 1722

The Prefetto of Egypt

September 12. The aforesaid garden is situated on the outside of the walls of the convent, to the north-west; to which there is a passage underground from the convent, with iron gates to it. This garden is sufficiently spacious, and very well supplied with good water, with which it is daily watered, and by that means produces great quantities of all sorts of plants, and herbs, and trees; such as almonds, apples, peaches, olives, figs, pomegranates, pears and in particular most delicious grapes both red and white: and as this month happened to be the season for ripe grapes, as well as many other fruits, we gave a loose to our appetites; and the air of the place being exceedingly fine and wholesome, indulged our palates with great freedom and luxury.

The temperature of the air seemed to me as moderate as if I had been in one of the most temperate climates of France in the month of September; the heat of the day not being excessive, nor the night air insufferably cold. However, I cannot but think, that the heat of this place in summer, as well as the cold in winter, must be almost insupportable, since, during the winter season, the snow falls here in great abundance.

A Change of Weather, 1908

Elbert Farman

On our arrival at the convent, we presented our letters, were kindly received and, by invitation, pitched our tents in the gardens, which were surrounded by high walls. The camels and Arabs remained outside, camping in the desert until the time of our departure. The gardens contain but a few acres and are irrigated during the long rainless summer by waters from a reservoir which is filled in the winter. They are at the base of the mountain slope, and a high retaining wall has been built on the upper side to protect them from the torrents caused by the winter rains. They form a small oasis, the fragrance of which is refreshing and delightful to one who has been travelling for days on the desert. They produce a variety of vegetables and among their fruits are the orange, quince, almond, peach, olive, fig and pomegranate. Vines climb the walls and a number of tall cypress trees lend, during the hot summer, their grateful shade.

It had been hazy during the latter part of the day and, after the setting of the sun, the heavens were completely obscured. In the evening, a monk came to our tent to say that the Prior sent us an invitation to come into the convent for the night, adding that he thought it would rain before morning. This change would require the removal of all our beds and effects, as only empty uninviting rooms could be furnished or rooms with beds we did not care to occupy. So, after consultation, we concluded to remain in our tents and sent our thanks to the prelate for his thoughtful kindness.

At about two o'clock, we were awakened by a sharp report of thunder. This was soon succeeded by another and then peal on peal quickly followed and reverberated from mountain to mountain, the sound being heightened, sharpened and quickened by its confinement between the lofty surrounding cliffs. Our tent was intermittently as light as day. On going outside, we witnessed one of the grandest displays of nature. The heavens were ablaze. Piercing, dazzling lines of fire darted in every direction among the overhanging rocks, lighting up mountains and valleys. These were followed by sharp, deafening peals, that made the mountains tremble, as if they were rent asunder. The reverberation, at first sharp, quick and loud, slowly died away in the distance, like a roar of falling fragments crashing down the mountain sides.

Fierce thunder-storms are always impressive, and especially in childhood. The lightning, the thunder, the wind, the rain of such wild scenes remain vivid in the memory. But I have never witnessed anything approaching in its fierceness, its power, its awful grandeur, the thunders of Sinai. Their sharp crashing peals echoed from mountain to mountain, as if tearing away the summits and scattering the fragments in the surrounding valleys. I was reminded of the graphic Biblical account of the "there were thunders and lightnings and a thick cloud upon the mount, and the Lord descended upon it in fire, and the smoke thereof ascended as the smoke of a furnace, and the whole mountain quaked greatly".

Wind and rain immediately followed and soon we heard the roar of the torrents coming down the mountain side. The ground, covered with water, was softening and our tent though doubly secured began yielding to the force of the storm. Hassan and the gardener were on the outside with mallets vainly trying to fasten the stakes and hold the tent in place. It was three o'clock and the convent bells were calling the monks to the chapel for prayers.

We were already well drenched, and the little protection we had seemed about to be removed. We began to consider whether we would not have done better to accept the invitation to enter the convent. General Loring with a soldier's tenacity still strongly insisted upon remaining outside. The prelate had not forgotten us. He sent a monk to renew the invitation, and to say that there was danger of the falling of the high retaining wall under which we were encamped. This settled the question, and we removed, as best we could, through a driving storm into the convent.

In the morning, all the mountains were white with a thin layer of snow. Thus suddenly had the long, dry summer changed to winter.

Met in the Garden, 1846
George Fisk

While walking in the convent garden, a young monk—a Russian—who spoke eleven languages, introduced himself to us. He was evidently out of health. He asked me for medicine. I gave him what I thought might be useful. I saw him several times. The medicine seemed to have been beneficial. On leaving the Convent, I presented him with a little supply for future use. His smiled gratefully upon me, and kissed me on the shoulder when I bade him farewell.

Plenty in the Desert, 1872
Paul Lenoir

The next day we passed at the convent where we had not yet been admitted to the garden. All the trees were in blossom, and the red and white bunches adorning the branches contrasted strangely with the desolation which reigned around this little paradise. The rich mould which accounted for its incredible fertility had been brought from Egypt on camel-back, so we could form an idea of the time and patience which had arrived at such a result. Arbours, symmetrically arranged and covered with vines, transported us in imagination to the too formal villas in the environs of Paris.

We had come at the wrong season for tasting the fruit of this delicious garden, in which there seems to be a specimen of every kind of tree, but, judging by the flowers, the next fruit harvest will be plentiful. The fathers gave us some delicious vegetables which were most welcome, considering that we had been deprived of every kind of green thing since we left Cairo. They also presented us each with a little bag of manna, and a small tin tube filled with honey made by bees of the Holy Mountain.

The Cemetery and Charnel House

There Are in a House . . . , 1436
Pero Tafur

There are in a house certain bodies of men embalmed. Some say they are the bodies of knights who visited that holy place and died there. Others say that some knights of Greece were carried there after death, and it is a place of great devotion. The monastery derives a large income from all Greece, and a great lord of Candia (Crete) left to it, when he died, an income of 4000 ducats, but since the place is very remote, and the provisioning of it costs much money, part of the revenue is expended in maintaining an establishment in Babylonia (Cairo) and the Patriarch of Alexandria lives there. He provides for everything and the revenues are paid to him. He also elects the Patriarch who is sent to Greater India to Prester John (in Ethiopia), and while I was in Babylonia, the former patriarch being dead, he chose his successor and dispatched him thither.

The Burial Place of the Dead, 1835

John Lloyd Stephens

In the garden of the convent is the cemetery of the monks. Though not of particularly melancholy humour, I am in a small way given to meditation among the tombs; and, in many of the countries I have visited, the burial-places of the dead have been the most interesting objects of examination. The Superior had promised to show me his graves; . . . and I now reminded the old man of his promise, and he hobbled off to get the key; for it appeared that the cemetery was not to be visited without his special permission. At the end of a long arbour of grape-vines, a narrow staircase cut in the rock, which I had not seen before, led down to an excavated square of about twenty feet; on the left of which was a small door opening into a vault, where formerly the bodies of the dead monks were laid on an iron bedstead, and there suffered to remain until all the corruptible part was gone, and only the dry bones remained. Now they are buried for about three years, or as long as may be necessary to effect the same object; and, when the flesh and muscles have disappeared, the bones are deposited in the great cemetery, the door of which is directly opposite.

Within the door is a small antechamber, containing a divan and a portrait of some saint who wandered eighteen years in the desert without meat or drink. From this the door opens into the cemetery, which was so different from any I had ever seen, that I started back on the threshold with surprise. Along the wall was an excavation about thirty feet in length, but of what depth I could not tell. It was enclosed by a fence, which was three of four feet above the ground, and filled with human skulls; and in front, extending along the whole length of the chamber, was a pile of bones about twenty feet high, and running back I could not tell how far. They were very regularly disposed in layers, the feet and shoulders being placed outward alternately, and by the side of the last skeleton was a vacant place for the next that should be ready.

I had seen thousands of Egyptian mummies, and the catacombs of Kiev, the holy city of Russia, where the bodies of the saints are laid in rows, in open coffins, clothed in their best apparel, and adorned with gold and jewels . . . I had seen the catacombs of the Capuchin convent at Syracuse, where the bodies of the monks are dried and laid in open coffins, or fixed in niches in the walls, with their names labelled on their breasts; and in the vault of the convent at Palermo I had seen the bodies of nobles and ladies, the men arranged upright along the wall, dressed as in life with canes in their hands and swords by their sides; and the noble ladies of Palermo lying in state, their withered bodies clothed in silks and satins, and adorned with gold and jewels. . . .

I had seen these things, and even these did not strike me so powerfully as the charnel-house at the convent of Mount Sinai. There was something peculiarly and terribly revolting in this promiscuous heaping together of mortal relics; bones upon bones; the old and young; wise men and fools; good men and bad; martyrs and murderers; masters and servants; bold, daring and ambitious men—men who would have plucked bright honour from the moon, lying pell-mell with cowards and knaves. The Superior told me that there were more than thirty thousand skeletons in the cemetery—literally an army of dead men's bones.

Besides the piles of skulls and bones, in a chamber adjoining were the bones of the archbishops, in open boxes, with their names and ages labelled on them, and those of two sons of the King of Persia, who came hither on pilgrimage and died in the convent; their iron shirts,* the only dress they wore on their long journey from their father's court, are in the same box. Other skeletons were lying about, some in baskets, and some arranged on shelves, and others tied together and hanging from the roof. In one corner were the bones of St Stephen—not the martyr who was stoned at Jerusalem, but some pious anchorite of later and less authentic canonization.

As to the effect upon the mind of such burial-places as this, or the catacombs to which I have referred, I can say from my own experience that they destroy altogether the feeling of solemnity with which we look upon the grave.

Isabella Bird was also disturbed by her visit to the cemetery and the charnel-house.

Skulls and Sepulchres, 1878

Isabella Bird

In this garden the monks are buried, and when the flesh has returned to dust the bones are exhumed and are placed in the charnel-house. This charnel-house consists of what may be called a mortuary chapel with two long vaults attached. Here at last is peace, and the wretched remains of the holy and unholy wait the resurrection trump together. I was escorted through these capacious vaults by two lay brothers, each of them carried in one hand a candle and in the other a censer of incense wherewith to overpower the odours of corruption. To enter this place we had to crouch, but the interior must be fully eight feet high. On the right within the entrance sits the mummy of St Stephen the porter, arrayed in gorgeous robes, the leathery face turned a little to one side, and wearing an expression

* Other writers record this as chain mail as used by medieval soldiers.

of ghastly intelligence. This grim porter of the house of death in the days of his flesh sat at the 'Strait Gate' on Sinai to shrive the pilgrims who passed to the summit, repeating to each "Who shall ascend into the hill of the Lord?" If tradition speaks truly of his faith and works, "the mount which might be touched" was exchanged many centuries ago for "the heavenly Jerusalem".

For St Stephen only is the ghastly dignity of mummyhood reserved. In the same vault are many rude wooden boxes, about two and a half feet square, each containing the jumbled bones of an abbot or saint. My guides pushed aside the lids, turned the bones about, took the skulls out and exhibited them. In one box are the skeletons of two Indian princes who spent many years as hermits on Jebel Musa, wearing shirts of link armour, pieces of which are with their bones, as well as a rough iron chain, weighing fifteen pounds, made of iron nails, with which they were bound together in life.

Another box contains iron necklets, girdles and leather scourges with knots, and other instruments of flagellation, some of them apparently black with blood, pathetic relics of the time when instead of forty monks living in wealth and comfort, six thousand hermits were gathered about the mount, the majority living in dens or caves of the earth, seeking in loneliness, fasting and pain, to justify themselves with God. These boxes, to which names are attached, contain what may be termed the aristocracy of the charnel-house.

The bones of an unnumbered multitude of hermits, priests and bishops fill that crypt. At the end of the crypt is a stack of skulls, so arranged as to show the faces. Roughly guessing there may be from 3,000 to 4,000 staring with sightless eye-sockets, grinning, leering, a ghastly mockery of the dignity of death. The effect of what came to look like a concentrated mocking grin was truly horrible.

Isabella Bird went on to describe the stacks of spines and leg-bones, arms, and hands. She concluded "We do well to bury our dead out of sight." Half a century later another woman expressed much the same reaction to the sad spectacle.

The Bone House, 1912

Mary Dobson

But the spectacle which most arrests, and almost horrifies the visitor on entering, is the clothed skeleton that sits between the vault of the lay brothers and that of the priests; it is the earthly remains of St Stephanos the porter, who sits and guards the Bone House as he once guarded the way up Jebel Musa, by the archway now called the Gate of St Stephen, examining the pilgrims before they are allowed to pass on to the Confessors at the second gateway close to the chapels of Elijah and Elisha. His purple skull-cap, his rosary and staff, all are there. He sits with his head slightly inclined, while the light seems to fall into the sightless sockets, and gives a strange appearance of living intelligence. The Russian pilgrims have always taken a deep interest in St Stephen, perhaps because of his connection with the pilgrims in days gone by; they have even provided new clothing for him as necessity arose. He died in 580, and has sat in the same spot during the centuries since.

The archimandrites, as they conducted us round the vaults, seemed painfully accustomed to the whole, and instructed us with meticulous minuteness as to the life-history of the persons represented there. They removed the lids of certain boxes to show us the remains of those who were special saints. "Look," said the gentle, courtly Librarian, as he opened a coffin, and there lay before our astonished eyes two skeletons, still fastened together in death as they had been in life.

11
Convent Life and the Traveler

The Organization of the Convent

Balconies and Texts, 1846
Lord Lindsay

Father Dimitri ciceroned us over the convent two or three days afterwards. It resembles a little fortified town, irregularly built on the steep side of the mountain, and surrounded by lofty walls; the passages and courts are kept very neat and clean; balconies with wooden balustrades run round each area, on which the doors of several apartments open; texts of Scripture are inscribed on the walls in every direction—in inextricably contracted Greek.

Convent Life, 1708
Hippolyte Vichensky

Our voyageurs were made very welcome. They put two monks at our disposal to serve us. The next day we attended divine office, and their repast. At their repast they observed the rule of the desert hermits: at Christmas and Easter and feast days and on ordinary days they ate the same. Some of the several dishes served were thorn-leaves, gruel, lentils and Red Sea fish. On feast days they each had a portion of eau-de-vie of dates and a cup of wine or water.

How the Pilgrims Were Cared For, 1838

Edward Robinson

When pilgrims arrive at the convent, a caloyer or lay brother is appointed to attain on them, to prepare their provisions in a place apart, which is served in their chamber. They are shown all the chapels and offices of the convent, the library, where there are a few manuscripts, but I saw none that were rare. They have many Greek books of the first printing.

The pilgrims commonly attend the service of the church twice a day, and on some certain days they dine in the refectory with the monks and soon after they arrive, being conducted from the church to the refectory, they perform the ceremony of washing the feet, as they do at Jerusalem. If the pilgrim is in orders, a priest performs this ceremony; I had that honour done to me by the superior. One of the monks, after this ceremony is over, holds a basin and urn to wash the hands, and then sprinkles the pilgrims with rose water; if it is a lay person, one of the lay monks performs these ceremonies, the whole society sitting in the hall and chanting hymns.

On Easter Sunday I rose soon after midnight to see the ceremonies. All being over about daybreak, we went to the archbishop's apartments, where they broke their severe fast, by eating eggs boil'd hard and cheese; and coffee was served round. The monks seemed extremely pleased that their lent was over, were very cheerful, sung hymns in their chambers, and went to repose. We all dined together in the refectory about ten in the morning; and coffee being served in the passage, I was invited to the superior's room, and from there we all went to pass some time in the garden.

They had ask'd me if I would perform our service on Easter-day in a chapel that is allotted for that purpose; there being one for the Roman Catholics, and if I mistake not, another for all other professions.

The Monks, 1816

John Lewis Burckhardt

At present there are only twenty-three monks in the convent. They are under the presidence of a Wakyl or priest, but the Ikonomus* whom the Arabs call the Kolob, is the true head of the community, and manages all its affairs. The order of Sinai monks dispersed over the east is under the control of an Archbishop, in Arabic called the Reys. He is chosen by a council of delegates from Mount Sinai and from the affiliated convent at Cairo, and he is confirmed, pro forma, by the Greek patriarch of Jerusalem. The Archbishop can do nothing as to the appropriation of the funds without the unanimous vote of the council. Formerly he lived

* Some wrote Economus.

in the convent; but since its affairs have been in decline, it has been found more expedient, that he should reside abroad, his presence here entitling the Bedouins to great fees, particularly on his entrance into the convent. . . . Hence it happens that no Archbishop has been here since the year 1760, when the Reys Kirillos resided, and I believe died, in the convent. I was informed that the gate has remained walled up since the year 1709, but that if an Archbishop were to come, it must be again opened to admit him, and that all the Bedouin Sheiks then have a right to enter within the walls.

Besides the convent at Cairo, which contains a prior and about fifty monks, Mount Sinai has establishments and landed property in many parts of the East, especially in the Archipelago, and at Candia [Crete]: it has also a small church at Calcutta, and another at Surat.

The discipline of these monks, with regard to food and prayer, is very severe. They are obliged to attend mass twice in the day and twice in the night. The rule is that they shall taste no flesh whatever all year round; and in their great fast they not only abstain from butter, and every kind of animal food and fish, but also from oil, and live four days of the week on bread and boiled vegetables, of which one small dish is all their dinner.

A Monk's Life, 1822

John Carne

A venerable monk, above ninety years of age, the oldest in the convent, paid us a visit in our apartments: he had resided here seventy years; and we asked him in what manner his life had passed during this best part of a century's confinement within the convent and garden-walls. One day, he said, had passed away like another; he had seen only the precipices, the sky, and the desert; and he strove now to fix all his thoughts on another world, and waited calmly the hour of his departure. He then dwelt much on the vanity of human pleasures and the nearness of eternity, and ended by asking me, very earnestly, for a bottle of rum. We had but one left for our future journey, but gave it, however, to gratify the old father, who requested that my servant, when he brought it to his cell, would conceal it beneath his cloak, lest his brethren would catch a glimpse of it.

The Monks, 1864

Arthur Penryn Stanley

The monks were usually Greek, speaking ordinary modern Greek. There in the midst of the desert, the very focus of the pure Semitic race, the traveller hears once again the accents of the Greek tongue; meets the natives of Thessalonica and of Samos; sees in the gardens the produce, not of the desert or of Egypt, but of the isles of Greece; not the tamarisk, or the palm, or theacacia, but the olive, the almond tree, the apple tree, the poplar and the cypress of Attica and Corcyra.

Convent Life, 1839

John Kinnear

The discipline of the convent is very severe. The monks are obliged to attend mass twice every day and twice during the night. They are forbidden to eat animal food, even fish ... and are allowed neither eggs, butter, nor oil. Their food appears to be rice, bread and dates; yet they are all fine athletic-looking men; and even the old superior, who had been forty years in the convent, andwas passed his eightieth year, appeared to enjoy excellent health.

The discipline of the convent appears to have varied over the decades—some found it strict, yet at other times travelers thought it lax.

The Monks' Life, 1861

Edward Robinson

The monks of Sinai lead a very simple and also a very quiet life, since they have come to be on good terms with their Arab neighbours. Five centuries ago Rudolf de Suchem describes their life in terms which are equally applicable to them at the present day. "They follow very strict rules; live chaste and modestly; are obedient to their archbishop and prelates; drink not wine but on high festivals; eat never flesh; but live on herbs, peas, beans and lentils, which they prepare with water, salt, and vinegar; eat together in a refectory without a table-cloth; perform their offices in the church with great devotion day and night; and are very diligent in all things; so that they fall little short of the rules of St. Antony." To this day the same rules continue; they eat no flesh and drink no wine; but their rules were made before the invention of distilled liquors, and therefore do not exclude date-brandy. Yet they all seem healthy and vigorous and those who remain here retain their faculties to a great age. The lay brother who waited on us had seen more than eighty years; one of the priest was said to be over ninety; and one had died the year before at the age of one hundred and six. A great portion of their time is nominally occupied in religious exercises. They have (or should have) regularly the ordinary prayers of the Greek ritual seven times in every twenty-four hours. Every morning there is a mass about 7 o'clock; and on Saturdays two, one at 3 A.M. and the other at the usual hour. During Lent the exercises on certain days are much increased; on the Wednesday which we spent there, the monks were at prayers all the morning until 12 o'clock; and again during the night from 10 till 4 o'clock.

The pilgrims have of late years greatly fallen off; so that not more than from twenty to sixty now visit the convent annually. These, according to the Superior, are chiefly Greeks, Russians, and English; a few Armenians and Copts; and only now and then a Mussulman. The good father probably regards all visitors as pilgrims. Yet so late as the last century, regular caravans of pilgrims are said to have come hither from Cairo and from Jerusalem; and a document preserved in the convent, mentions the arrival in one day of eight hundred Armenians from Jerusalem, and at another time, of five hundred Copts from Cairo.

Coming from a Scottish Protestant background into the ornate customs of the Orthodox church, Isabella Bird found much she felt uncomfortable with, including the rituals and the demeanour of the monks.

The Monks, 1878

Isabella Bird

Of the thirty-five inmates of the monastery only seven, besides the abbot and the sub-abbot, who officiated, and the sacristan, appeared (at the service of vespers in the church), and all the seven were late. As they entered each crossed himself frequently, and, after kissing three of the pictures, took a staff and leant upon it during the service. The abbot, who is a noble-looking man, with a lofty intellectual brow and classical features, and the sub-abbot, gorgeously dressed in stiff silk brocade, blue and yellow, flowered in gold thread and silk, and adorned with old Greek lace. They remained usually at the altar within the screen, but emerged several times, swinging silver censers of ancient and exquisite workmanship three times towards each person. The service lasted for an hour and a quarter, and between the standing, the dim light, the evil odour of the clothing of the monks, the smoke and heavy scent of the incense, the airlessness and the noise, I feared several times that I should become insensible.

The Local Arabs, 1839

John Kinnear

The monks appear to be on tolerably friendly terms with the Arabs around the convent, to whom a scanty dole of bread is let down, from the window at which we entered, three times a week.

Apart from the monks and the lay brothers, there were a number of local Arabs who assisted with the work of the convent. Some of these 'local' Arabs were, according to tradition, the descendants of people who had been sent many centuries before to serve the convent.

The Servants of the Convent, 1865

E.H. Palmer

The Arab servants of the convent are fine sturdy fellows, and present a great contrast to their effeminate masters. Mohammed, the chief amongst them, is a good-looking, stalwart Arab, always ready to lend the traveller or his servants a hand; nor is Musa, the next most prominent of the attendants, less willing or obliging; and, notwithstanding the loss of a finger. Blown off by a matchlock, he is handy too. There is quite a colony of them in the convent garden, where their tents are pitched; and the pilgrim who wishes to add to his entomological stores, cannot do better than give a few piastres and a pickle bottle for the collection of Coleoptera to little Mohammed and Khidhr, the respective heirs of the two last named Arabs.

They all belong to the Jibaliyeh tribe, who are recognised as the serfs of the convent. This tribe is said to be of European origin, and to have descended from the colony of Wallachian and Egyptian slaves, placed there by Justinian, to protect the monks. They themselves have a tradition that they came from a country called 'K'lah'; and their features, differing somewhat from the ordinary Bedawi type would seem to favour the supposition.

The Jibaliyeh have an additional claim upon our interest as the representatives of the older inhabitants of Sinai. The remaining Bedawin tribes have preserved the purity of descent, and the genealogical pride, which is so curious a characteristic of the Desert races; and in names, manners, and appearance, they are now what their ancestors were in Hejjaz or Yemen. It is clear that they can have no admixture of Aramaean blood; and if any of the local traditions do still survive in the peninsula, it is to the Jibaliyeh alone that we owe their perpetuation.

Where the Travelers Stayed

Travelers were given rooms in different parts of the monastery. Some were large communal rooms, others were smaller shared or single rooms. Many of the travelers—as was the custom—inscribed their names and the dates of their stay on the walls of their room.

The Travelers' Room, 6th century

Lina Eckenstein

The convent included a hostel for the aged and for pilgrims, built by a certain Isaurus. It attracted the attention of Pope Gregory the Great (592–604), who, hearing of it, forwarded to John Climacus, who was superior at the time, woollen coverings and beddings for fifteen beds, together with money wherewith to purchase feather-beds. At the same time he wrote to Father Palladius, to whom he forwarded a cowl or tunic. . . . He seems to have made a permanent grant to the convent. A pilgrim of 1341 mentioned that the day of St Gregory was kept at the convent, since he had bestowed on it alms out of the treasury of the Church, by which the number of convent inmates was raised to four hundred.

William Turner was writing in his room when the superior of the convent came to talk to him. As was then the custom in hostelries, people wrote their names on the walls or fixed a note there for future travelers.

Messages in the Travelers' Room, 1815

William Turner

[The superior] asked many questions about the names stuck up on the wall, among which were those of Messrs Gully Knight, and Fazakerley,* with two French travellers (*Membres de la Commission des Sciences et des Arts*) in 1801, and a German one. There were great numbers of names of Greek pilgrims; he showed us specimens of talc found in the neighbourhood, by the Arabs, and several pieces of hexagonal crystal, and brought me a folio Hellenick testament, printed at Frankfurt, in 1597.

The Travelers' Rooms, 1822

John Carne

These apartments are very small, and covered with a handsome carpet and cushions, with part of the floor raised in the eastern style; and a neat lamp was suspended from the ceiling and already lighted. There was real sumptuousness in all this to our feelings, after the passage through the Desert. After all, happiness is in a great measure derived from the contrast of situations; and is, in this respect, perhaps, not unlike eastern scenery—plains and valleys blooming like Paradise, amidst naked mountains and wilds. No calm, comfortable, luxurious life in England could ever afford these vivid and transporting feelings which were ours during these journeys in the East.

The New Travelers' Room, 1846

Harriet Martineau

The monks have recently built a new set of guest chambers, in which the greater part of our company were lodged. These rooms are made as comfortable as possible, under the circumstances: and there we remained from Saturday afternoon to Wednesday morning. We were waited upon, of course, by our own people; and served, for the most part, with our own utensils and stores; while a monk was at our call, to give us guidance and information.

Who Made the Rooms? 1853

Catherine Tobin

The apartments occupied by travellers were built about nine years ago, at the joint

* Two English travelers there in about 1811.

expense of a rich Cairene cousin of the "Professor",* and a present Superior of the convent. The original "Strangers' Corridor" was on a lower story, and is now allotted to the use of Russian pilgrims only. Our little *ménage* at Mount Sinai was most snugly compact and comfortable.

We were taken into a room where the monks kept for sale—sweetmeat of dates and almonds; crystals found in these mountains; gazelle's horns; shells and coral from the Gulf of Akaba; rosaries made of black worsted; and silver rings of rude workmanship, stamped with the insignia of St. Catharine—with which every visitor takes care to provide himself, as a token of pilgrimage. There are also small round tin boxes of what is called "*the true Manna of the Israelites*", sold here. This manna is of the gummy substance, and as sweet as honey: it exudes at certain times of the year from the lesser branches of the tamarisk tree, and is produced by the bite of an insect. Vincenzo told us that he had seen it in great quantities near Baghdád, and that it dropped upon his coat as he rode along.

Accomodation and the Jebellyeh, 1906

Baedeker's *Palestine and Syria*

The traveller presents his letter of introduction and is admitted by a side-door. The Bedouins and camels remain outside. The monastery contains visitors' rooms, beds, sofas and a kitchen. The dragoman must make his own bargain with the monks, to whom the traveller may afterwards present a gift on his own account. Those who have to pay their own expenses are generally charged at least 4 shillings a day each for lodging alone.

It is healthier during the cold nights in these mountains in spring, as well as more interesting, to lodge in the monastery; but the traveller will find it more independent and less expensive to camp in some suitable spot in the lower Wadi Shu'aib—the Jebellyeh† as the servants of the monks are called, are excellent guides for the excursions and will accompany the traveller for a trifling fee, carrying the necessary provisions.

My Room at the Convent—and the Rules, 1938

H.V. Morton

My room was bare, yet crowded. An ancient iron four-poster, heavily encumbered by lace frills and a mosquito net, occupied most of the space not taken up

* Their nickname for a monk who had attached himself to the Tobins and provided answers to all their questions.

† Baedeker explains these servants: "The monks were greatly benefited by a gift from Justinian of a hundred Roman, and a hundred Egyptian slaves, with their wives and children. From these retainers are descended the Jebellyeh, who still render service to the monks, but are despised by the Bedouins, and stigmatised as 'Nazarenes' and 'fellahin', in spite of the fact that they have all embraced Islam."

with a couch, two chairs, a marble-topped table, and a washstand on which stood two tin jugs of cold water. The only picture was an ikon of the Madonna, which hung in a wooden shrine on the wall, with a sprig of dry basil lying in front of it on a little shelf. The outer wall of the room was that of Justinian's fortress, and from a small window punched in its massive stones I looked down into the entrance courtyard, and over the cypress trees in the garden to the mountains of the gorge. The bedroom ceiling had been painted green somewhere about the year 1860, by a monk who had released his knowledge of contemporary decoration in a flowery and not unpleasing wreath.

Near the bed was a framed copy of the Monastery Regulations in Greek, Arabic, French and English. I gathered from the following rules that the monks have been obliged to place things on a firm financial basis.

> Each visitor desirous to pass the night in the monastery must pay for food and lodging one Egyptian pound daily, and without food half a pound only daily. Passing the night outside the monastery (under a tent he should bring with him) he has to pay Piastres 25, for entrance fees to enter the convent. Any person wishing to visit the Monastery of the Decalogue and the Mount of St Catherine must be accompanied by a monk, and has to pay Piastres 25 for camel fares to the Mount of the Decalogue, Piastres 30 for camel fares to the Mount of St Catherine, and, moreover, Piastres 50 to the monk who will accompany them.

A few days later H.V. Morton asked Brother Gabriel to show him his own cell.

We ascended several steps to a group of wooden buildings rather like almshouses, built against the monastery wall. He pushed open a door and led the way into a clean little room where a few sacred pictures hung on the walls and a few Greek books stood on a shelf; there was a bed and a chair. As cells go, it was almost luxurious, and he said he was happy there.

Rules of the House, 1857

James Hamilton

Then visited us he, who delighted in the office of Economist; and by him we were enlightened concerning certain rules of the House. We were to enjoy a well-taxed hospitality, it seemed and this was the tariff:-

Visit to Mount Sinai	1 dollar
Two Arabs to carry coffee	14 piastres

Brother Dispenser	1 dollar
Cure, visit to the church	1 dollar
Service	1 dollar
Brother Porter	1 dollar
Hoisting luggage	3 piastres

Wood for fuel, milk, sheep, eggs, fowls, - all at prices three or four times those of Cairo, - were to be bought of the Arabs at the convent door, but "for fear the poor creatures should lose their money among the stones", we were requested to pay them only through the hands of the Oekonomos.

The establishment sells sausages of Sinai dates, with almonds, araki, villainous Cretan wine, and little silver rings, blessed by St Catharine's shrine; of this latter item we did not lay in a stock, to gratify our lady friends in Europe, because the value of the benediction and of the metal seemed so monstrously disproportioned; also were to be bought little boxes of manna, and madrepores (coral) and star-fish from Tor; all, as Harpagon says, "agreeable curiosities"

Not all the travelers slept in the convent. Some preferred to camp on the hillside and only visit the convent during the day. The convent developed a scale of charges for services they rendered to these travelers. Palmer was a member of the expedition to survey the Sinai Peninsula.

Camping on the Hillside, 1865

E.H. Palmer

Having paid our introductory visit to the monks, we proceeded to fix upon a site for our camp, a question of some importance, as we were to stay at Jebel Musa six or eight weeks. The spot selected was a pleasant, sheltered one, lying on a slight depression at the foot of Aaron's Hill. True, we were given to understand that the place was infested by hyenas, but this only added to the romance and excitement of the thing. Wonderful stories the Arabs told us of the cunning of these beasts: how, for instance, a hunter lay down to sleep with his dog and his powder-flask beside him, when the hyena, of whom he was in quest, seized the opportunity and the dog, devoured the latter, and walked off with the powder-flask, without arousing the hunter from his sleep.

One hyena attracted by the savoury odours of the cook's tent, did visit us for several successive nights, carefully selecting a moment when dinner or sleep was engrossing all our energies, and consequently always skulking off before anyone could snatch a gun. Emboldened by long impunity, he ventured into the small tent in which the stores were kept, and at last appeared before the astonished gaze of our two Arab 'helps' who had sought shelter there. Salem, one of the Arabs aforesaid, and our own most trusty guide, determined to avenge himself on the intruder, and having borrowed a gun, sat up on the following night in hopes of getting a shot at the foe. About midnight an echoing shot astonished the camp, and rushing out we met old Selim, who in triumphant whisper declared he had done the deed. Following him in an excited procession, we beheld, stretched before the door of the tent the mangled remains of an Arab cur! To this day the word *dhaba* (hyena) is an abomination to Salem's ears, and if applied to an animal of the canine species it reduces that intelligent Bedawi to the temporary condition of a drivelling idiot.

Traveling on her own with only her guide and servants, Isabella Bird refused to stay within the monastery.

Sleeping on the Hillside, 1878

Isabella Bird

I lay down after my supper, but got up again just before midnight and stood outside the tent to watch the frosty stars hanging out of the purple sky, and the dark forms of the mountains which had "trembled in the presence of God". I grudged the time which had to be spent in sleep, yet I soon slept soundly, to be awoke before daylight by a sound of exquisite beauty. Waking suddenly, I thought that it was the sound of "harpers harping with their harps", and that "the terrible journey of life was done"; but when I went to the tent-door there were the same grand mountain forms, and Orion, only changed in place, still wheeled through the purple night. The sound as of silver bells of uncanny sweetness rose and fell fitfully, and I knew then that it was the call to prayer in the convent. I long to hear it again.

When Hassan, with a rueful face, brought my stirabout it was 8 a.m., and the morning was in his glory, the red peaks flaming, and the chasm filled with blue atmosphere. The awful desolation of the region is even more impressive in the blaze of the full sunshine than yesterday evening. It is very silent; no song or cry of birds or bleating of sheep. Nothing moves. The naked granite blazes under the sun as the day goes on. The mountains look as if but yesterday they had "burned with fire", and their fiery colouring had not had time to fade.

Today I have done nothing but rest and think, and watch the mountain forms and realise where I am, and the brief but extraordinary connection of this peninsula with the world's history and the Divine plans. It is emphatically holy ground, and I am very thankful to be alone, and that there are no distracting or jarring influences. Except Hassan, and a single bee, I have not seen a living thing all day, and now the sun is sinking, and while the cool shadows lengthen across the Wady-el-Dayr the red peaks are every moment crimsoning.

April 17th, evening Last night was rather a disturbed one. Hassan had very little fuel for his watch fire, and two hyenas howled and prowled about the camp for some time before he succeeded in driving them any distance. He has insisted on watching all night—a needless precaution, I think. but afterwards a strong north-east wind sprang up, and my tent began to shiver and sway alarmingly, and it soon became evident that its pole was likely to come down. So taking things I valued most outside, I stumbled across to Hassan, who dismally said he would see about it. There was no light for seeing anything distinctly, and shortly a gust overturned the whole.

It was too dark for walking for three hours, so, dragging some blankets from under the wreck, I lay with my head on a stone till sunrise, bitterly cold, I confess, but thinking much of Jacob at Bethel and Elijah's fast near the same spot. The brief, majestic narrative of Sinai takes complete possession of one here.

A Herd of Cats, 1938

H.V. Morton

While I was having breakfast in a room on the gallery, five or six cats of various colours, no two of them alike, crept up and crouched expectantly round the door. They sprang on any scraps of food flung to them, but vanished instantly like so many witches when I invited them to come inside. If you could imagine a cat belonging to anything so plebeian as a herd, I would say that Mount Sinai has a herd of cats, for these animals are everywhere: cats that have never known the thrill of being chased by a dog, have certainly never tasted the joys of fish, and know nothing of the pleasures of milk or the abandoned ease of the fireside. The kittens are the only young things that ever enliven this place with their beauty, and the mother cats are the only representatives of their sex who dwell, or have dwelt, within the walls. The cats of Sinai share with those of London an abundant and never-ending roof line. It should be possible for a cat of agility to make his way overhead from end to end of the monastery, while for those with a fondness for tiles, there are tiles without numbers. But the cat of Sinai has his work to do: he is there to keep down the rats and snakes.

Convent Meals and the Refectory

The Diet of the Convent, 1721

Thomas Shaw

These, and the *papasses* or *presbyters*, who are commonly called *calories*, make in all about a hundred and fifty; who live a very strict and austere life, abstaining not only from flesh, but also from butter, milk and eggs; which even the pilgrims are not permitted to bring into the convent. The least mortification they undergo (which indeed is not often) is when they receive, from their sister convent at Tor, a quantity of shell-fish, crabs or lobsters, other fish being prohibited by their insti-

Refectory at the Convent

tution.* For bread, or biscuit, is the main article of their sustenance; to which is added, according to the course of their stated days, half a pint of date brandy, together with a small portion of olives, oil and vinegar, salad or pot-herbs; or else of dates, figs, almonds, parched pulse, and such like food as was the dry diet of the primitive Christians. Their bread, biscuit, oil, olives, pulse, and figs, are brought to them monthly from Cairo; but their dates, brandy, salad, and pot-herbs are chiefly from their own gardens and plantations.

The Refectory, 1739
Richard Pococke

* Peter the Deacon in his twelfth century *Book on the Holy Places* described the harvest of the sea: "You have all the sea-food you could want: there are trumpet-shells and oysters of various kinds, white-shells, and several kinds of large snail. And the different things you find along the shore are bigger and prettier than any other sea. Also there is a great deal of coral on this shore. The Red Sea is part of the Ocean."

to prepare his provision, to see it served up in his chamber, to shew him all the chapels, offices, and the library, wherein are deposited some of the first Greek books that were ever printed, and some few manuscripts. But none of them are curious, or if they are, they fell not within the reach of our uthor.

The feet of all pilgrims are washed, from after their arrival here, by some of the lay brothers; but those of a priest are washed by one of the same rank in the church; and our author had the honour of being attended in this ceremony by the superior of the convent. When it is over one of the community brings water for the pilgrim to wash; and then sprinkles him with rose-water, the whole society sitting all the time in the hall, chaunting hymns.

At some certain days, they dine in the refectory with the monks, and one of them, during that time, reads from a desk certain lessons, in which he is directed, by another's ringing a bell, when it is proper for him to stop. After dinner the pilgrim is refreshed with coffee, and a small collation, in the archbishop's chamber; and he enters his name, with the value of what he chuses to bestow upon the convent in the book of benefactors.

This time of Dr. Pococke's being here, was just after Easter, and he had the satisfaction of being present at all the ceremonies performed in holy week; and of dining, with the whole convent in the refectory, about ten o'clock in the morning on Easter Sunday, when the monks appeared all very cheerful, and well pleased that their Lent was passed. He was also left at liberty to perform the devotions of the season, either conjunctively with them, or in a separate apartment, destined to the use of people of a different profession.

The Refectory, 1865

E.H. Palmer

We next visited the refectory, a narrow room approached by a long dusty corridor on the southern side of the building. It contains two ancient tables, of rude but elaborate construction, which extends along its entire length, as well as a small pulpit and a gaudy altar at the other end. The scene when the monks are at dinner is indescribably quaint, and seems to carry us back centuries, to the times of the Crusaders, whose arms and crests are scratched with their dagger points upon the doors. There they are, some twenty long-bearded men with serge dresses and rosaries, Justas you may see them in the paintings of the old Italian masters, eating their vegetable diet in silence on the uncovered board, while a priest from the pulpit is drawling out in a monotonous tone the life of some saint appropriate to the day. Behind them stand the servitors, only to be distinguished from the rest by being, if possible, a little dirtier and a little more villainous than their brethren; and at the lower table some half-dozen or so of the pilgrims are munching lettuces with faces expressive of mingled hunger and awe.

When the monks have finished their repast the cats of the convent (and their name is legion) assemble at the ringing of a bell and receive their rations from the scraps that are left.

Near the door is the kitchen, and a little further on the distillery, where that most important adjunct of a recluse's life, the araki is made. A carpenter's shop, a bakehouse and other offices, numerous small chapels situated in odd corners of the convent, and one or two pretty little oriental wells, complete the category.

Reverend Edward Robinson and his traveling companion, Eli Smith, attended a service with the monks in the church and then joined them in the refectory for a meal.

Dining with the Monks, 1838

Edward Robinson

We now repaired to the refectory, and were seated at the long table next below the priests; the lay brethren and pilgrims taking their seats still further down. The table was neat, and without a cloth; some of the larger vessels were of tinned copper; but the plates, spoons, basins, mugs and porringers for drinking were all of pewter. An orange and half lemon lay by each plate, with a portion of coarse bread. After a grace, a large basin of soup or stew, made of herbs and a species of large shell-fish, was set on; from which each helped himself at will. This with a few plates of olives and raw beans soaked in water till they sprout, formed the whole repast. The good monks seemed to eat with relish; and some of the very old ones set away their plates with the remains of these tit-bits in drawers beneath the table. During the meal the young monk or deacon, whom we had met with on the way, read from a small pulpit a sermon or homily in modern Greek, in praise of Chrysostom. On rising from the meal a taper was lighted on a small table at the head of the room, around which all gathered, and a prayer was said over a piece of bread and a very small cup of wine. These were then carried around to all standing; every one (including ourselves) breaking off a morsel of the bread and tasting the wine. This was explained to us as a sort of love-feast, a mere symbol of the enjoyment of wine, of which the monks are not permitted by their rules to drink. The ceremony however has no reference to the sacrament of the Lord's Supper; as has been erroneously supposed by some travellers. After this, on leaving the room each one received separately the benediction of the Superior; and we all retired to the adjacent ancient piazza, where coffee was handed round; the deacon following and continuing his reading the whole time.—There was a simplicity and seriousness during the whole repast and its accompaniments, which were quite pleasing.

Isabella Bird camped on the hillside near the convent, but was invited to dine with the monks on one of her visits.

The Refectory, 1878

Isabella Bird

The tables in the refectory were arranged for supper, with a bottle of Medoc by each plate, though wine is forbidden! The refectory is an ancient room with some badly-painted pictures of saints on the walls. The table is of carved oak. Meat is forbidden as well as wine, but dishes of a savoury stew were being carried in as I came out, and I longed to eat for my soul was loathing the light food which is my sole diet. The rule is nominally very strict, for, during fasts, oil, milk and even butter are forbidden.

As I left the building, monks with their handsome faces, picturesque dresses, and sandaled feet were gliding about, their long shadows thrown upon the sunny walls, for it seemed, as most things seem in the desert, not a novelty, but a memory.

All travelers knew of the manna upon which the Israelites were able to sustain themselves. There were various explanations of what it might be.

A Dainty Discourse Concerning the Manna We Found, 1483

Felix Fabri

On the twenty-second, which is the feast of St Maurice and his companions, we rose very early, loaded our beasts, followed the star to the blessed virgin St Catharine, which seemed to be standing close to us, and went up the mountain-wall by which we were encompassed. When we were come to this rocky wall, we found a narrow cleft in the rock which afforded us an entrance, through which cleft Moses passed with his flock into the innermost parts of the wilderness. A loaded camel could scarcely squeeze through this narrow pass. When we were within, we entered another and exceeding fair plain, wherein were grass, shrubs and bushes. Here we refreshed ourselves with the falling dew, which were sweeter than honey, altogether different to that dew which we tasted as aforesaid; for the dew which now falls about these holy places shows us how sweet was the manna which there was given to the patriarchs.

At this day manna, or dew of manna, falls round about Mount Sinai for two months—to wit, August and September. The Arabs collect this manna, and sell it to pilgrims. I myself have seen and eaten much of this manna. Vincentius, in his *Speculum Naturale*, Book V, chapter lxxxv, says that manna is dew that falls upon leaves or stones, where it thickens like honey, grows dry like gum, becomes sticky, and afterwards is gathered. . . . When it is pure and not mixed with other things, it is exceeding aromatic and precious; it is of a whitish colour, and sweeter than anything else in the world. It is of an exceeding pleasant savour, and it has to be of the same kind whereon the Hebrews lived in the wilderness for forty years, which manna was formed there by Divine miracle, whereby its appearance and taste were changed for the better; for this natural manna falls far short of that miraculous manna, seeing that the natural manna is not to be found every night, or every season of the year, whereas the other was found every morning, wheresoever God's people sojourned. It is likewise found in some parts of Greece.

12
Pilgrimage to the Neighboring Holy Places

Most travelers took only a day to rest from their long journey and then wished to climb to the heights above the convent. When considering the holy places around the convent, knowledge of the Old Testament story of Moses led travelers to interpret what they saw. Monks who attended them on their climbs were willing to link the sites to the Old Testament, which early travelers knew so well. The Convent of St. Catherine was created by Justinian in A.D. 527, but centuries before the valleys of Sinai had attracted hermits and pilgrims. One of these was the nun Egeria who arrived here to climb Mount Sinai in A.D. 383 and visit other sites in the area.

Mountains and Hermits, 383

Egeria

So this was our plan. When we had seen everything we wanted and come down from the Mount of God, we would come to the place of the Bush (the present place of the Monastery). Then from there we would return through the middle of the valley now ahead of us and so return to the road with the men of God, who would show us each one of the places mentioned in the Bible. And that is what we did.

So, coming in from Paran, we said the prayer. Then, going on, we made our way across the head of the valley and approached the Mount of God. It looks like a single mountain as you are going round it, but when you actually go into it there are really several peaks, all of them known as "the Mount of God", and the principal one, the summit on which the Bible tells us that "God's glory came down." (Exodus 19:18–20) is in the middle of them. I never thought I had seen mountains so high as those which stood around it, but the one in the middle where God's glory came down was the highest of all, so much so that, when we were on the top, all the other peaks we had seen and thought so high looked like little hillocks far below us. Another remarkable thing—it must have been planned by God—is that even though the central mountain, Sinai proper on which God's glory came down, is higher than all the others, you cannot see it until you arrive at the very foot of it to begin your ascent. After you have seen everything and come down, it can be seen facing you, but this cannot be done till you start your climb. I realised it was like this before we reached the Mount of God since the brothers had already told me, and when we arrived there I saw very well what they meant.

Late on Saturday, then, we arrived at the mountain and came to some cells. The monks who lived in them received us most hospitably, showing us every kindness. There is a church there with a presbyter, that is where we spent the night, and pretty early on Sunday, we set off with the presbyter and monks who lived there to climb each of the mountains.

They are hard to climb. You do not go round and round them, spirally up gently, but straight at each one as if you were going up a wall, and then straight down to the foot, till you reach the foot of the central mountain, Sinai itself. Here then, impelled by Christ our God and assisted by the prayers of the holy men who accompanied us, we made the great effort of the climb. It was quite impossible to ride up, but though I had to go on foot I was not conscious of the effort—in fact I really hardly noticed it because, by God's will, I was seeing my hopes coming true.

All there is on the actual summit of the central mountain is the church and the cave of the holy Moses. No one lives there.

As one reads Dr. Richard Pococke's account one can hear him questioning the veracity of the explanations given by his guides—their accounts did not seem to him to match either the Old Testament or the reality of the places he was shown. Unlike others at the time, there is a real scepticism in his reporting.

The Environs of the Convent, 1739

Richard Pococke

At a well in the convent, call'd the well of Moses, they say, Moses met the

daughters of Jethro; that on the mountain of Moses he was feeding the flock of Jethro, his father-in-law; and that in the spot that now is the chapel of the Holy Bush, adjoining to the east end of the great church of the convent, grew that tree which appeared to Moses as if it burned and was not consumed, and out of him God spake to him. In the gardens near the fathers have planted a bramble, such as are common in Europe, and say it was such a bush in which the miracle was wrought; though such brambles do not grow in these parts; but they tell you that formerly they did. . . .

The vale to the west (of Mount Sinai) is certainly the vale of Rephidim, where the Israelites encamped when they came out of the deserts of Sin. Here they show the rock which, they say, Moses struck and the waters flowed out, where God told him he would stand before him upon the rock in Horeb, which was afterwards call'd Massah and Maribah; it is on the foot of Mt. Serich, and is a (very large) red granite stone. . . . The Arabs call this the stone of Moses; and they put herbs into the 'mouths' in the rock and give them their camels, as a sovereign remedy, as they think, in all disorders.

It was in this valley that Israel fought with Amalek; and at the south west end of it, at the foot of Mt. Sinai, in the convent of the forty martyrs, where the fathers have only a servant who has care of the large garden. Here are the only fruit trees in all these parts, which they have of almost all sorts.

From there they ascend very high to the south west, up to the mountain of St Catherine's, and on the summit of it, pretend to show the print of the rock where the body of that saint lay; which being tied to a wheel at Alexandria, under the Emperor Maxentius, in order to be put to death, it is said the wheel snapp'd in pieces; and being afterwards beheaded, her body (according to her prayer, that it should not come into the hands of the infidels), they say, was carried by angels to the top of this mountain, and was brought to the convent by the monks, soon after it was finished.

About a third of the way up is the spring of the Partridges, which the caloyers (local employees) say was discovered by partridges, who flew after the body; when the monks resting there, who brought it down, and suffering with thirst, the birds all went to this spring, by which marks, they say, they found the water.

This mountain is higher than any other in these parts; and when one is at the top of it, Mt Sinai north east of it appears but low. From the top of this high mountain I saw both the arms of the Red Sea, and on the east side, a part of the sea, south of the promontory; on the other side into Arabia Felix.

A Creature of Sinai, 1582

The Merchant Triphon Korobeinikoff

Here, near the monastery of Sinai, exists a bird—the ostrich. In height he reaches the shoulder of a man; his head is like that of a duck, and his feet are like cloven hooves, and his legs are long, like those of a crane, and his wings seem made of leather. He walks on the ground and flies little.

Mount Sinai

The Ascent of Jebel Moosa, 1873

Murray's Handbook

Several paths lead up to the summit of Jebel Moosa, but the one usually followed goes up a rude glen at the back of the convent, and is called Sikket Seyyidna Moosa—'the path of our Lord Moses'. A lay brother, or an Arab, is furnished by the convent as a guide. There is a flight of rocky steps nearly the whole way, which renders the ascent easy.

The first object of interest is Ayan Moosa ('the fountains of Moses'), a delicious spring of cool water which rises beneath a huge granite boulder, and is surrounded by a fringe of maiden-hair fern. According to the Bedaween it was here that Moses watered Jethro's flocks; monkish tradition makes it the abode of St Stephen the cobbler. The path leads up through narrow ravines, over large boulders of granite to what is called the Chapel of the Virgin of the Oeconomous, or Bursar, a small building of unhewn stone, erected to commemorate the miraculous extirpation of fleas from the convent—a miracle which most visitors to the convent will agree in thinking needs repetition.

The road now turns to the right, and ascends sharply to a cleft in the rock, spanned by a circular arch with a cross on either face. Here sat St Stephen the porter and his successors and shrived the pilgrims who passed on repeating Psalm xxiv, 3,4: "Who shall ascend into the hill of the Lord etc." A little further on is another gateway, and then a small plain at the foot of the peak of Jebel Moosa is reached. Here is a ruined garden, a solitary cypress-tree, and a building containing the chapels of Elijah and Elisha. Monkish tradition points out a small grot in which the former lived (1 Kings xix, 8,9). From this point a stiff half hour's climbing takes one to the top of Jebel Moosa.

How the Pilgrims Ascended the Holy Mountains, 1483

Felix Fabri

[W]e rose three hours before sunrise and celebrated Masses in the Latin chapel. When these were over a monk, the sacrist of the monastery, named Nicodemus, came to guide us up the holy mountains. He passed all the pilgrims in review, and looked narrowly at each one of them. He would on no account suffer those who he thought to be sickly to set out with us, for he said that the pass was a steep and very laborious one. So some sickly pilgrims stayed behind; yet some, albeit that they were sickly, yet altogether refused to stay behind.*

We took our scrips with our food, our bottles full of wine, and jars of water, enough to last us for two days, and gave them to our ass-drivers to carry, for they were ready to go up with us to wait upon us. When we had made these arrangements, Brother Nicodemus led us out of the monastery by the gate through which we had come in, and we went down in a southerly direction at the foot of the holy mount of Sinai and Horeb, on the side whereof the monastery is built. Indeed, this holy mount has two names; from the monastery to the chapel of St Elias it is called Sinai and from thence to the top is called Horeb. . . .

As the monks climbed they saw places they knew well from the evidence of the Old Testament and they recalled the stories and words related to each place. They recalled how, almost at the top of the mountain, Moses desired to see the face of God, and the Lord replied: ". . . It shall come to pass, while my glory passeth by, that I will put thee in a cleft in the rock, and will cover me with my hand."

So out of devotion we all laid ourselves in the hollow place wherein the Lord laid down Moses upon his belly. In imitation of the prophet we laboriously wormed ourselves into this hole. The hole is a little way above the ground and is low, not lofty, so that a man standing on the ground can get his outstretched arms and his head into it. If he wishes to get his breast also into the hole, he must raise himself from the ground, and then his arms, breast, and head are indeed within, but his legs hang outside, together with all the hinder parts of him, as far as his navel. Thus the man lies as though he was between two mill-stones, for he lies his belly resting upon the stone below, and the stone above touches

---

* Later Friar Felix tells of a piece of luck he received as a result of the sickliest among the party not being able to climb with them. One of the sick knights brought him a new pair of shoes which he had bought in Jerusalem, and said, "Lo, Brother Felix, I bought these shoes meaning to climb the holy mounts in them; but now seeing that I cannot climb thither, I pray you take them." Friar Felix's own shoes certainly would not have held together during his ascent and he gladly accepted the knight's gift.

his back. If a man chose, he could draw himself altogether into the hole, for it is a deep one; but I can hardly see how he could get out again without help, seeing that he cannot get out by moving himself backwards like a crab. . . .

Friar Felix, who had a strong sense of the ridiculous, continued to explain the necessary contortions, and concluded that "Should anyone wish to know what the face and the back parts of God may be, let him consult Nicholas de Lyra in this passage." The pilgrims then went on to climb to the summit of Mount St. Catherine.

At last, since 'shrewd toil overcometh all', we came to the head or the top of the holy mount. When we were there, so harsh, cold, and strong a wind was blowing, that we could neither say our prayers nor do any good thing without a fire. The Arabs straightaway collected faggots, made a pile of them, and lighted a great fire, beside which we stood until the sun, which now had been risen for some time, grew higher, and the chilliness of the wind grew far less keen. When we were warmed, and in some sort revived, we went to the tomb to which the angels bore the glorious virgin St Catherine, where we merely chanted the service of praise appointed in the 'Processional' of the Holy Land, prayed exceedingly devoutly, meditated for a very long while in silence, and received plenary indulgences. . . .

(Then) we bowed ourselves to the earth before the place in which the virgin lay, and placed ourselves therein, not out of presumption or curiosity, but out of piety. We measured our bodies against the form of the hollow, and inferred that she must have been of tall stature. At last, after we had paid all due honour, or at all events all the honour which we were able to pay to this holy place, we turned away to view other things.

Egeria took four hours to climb to the mountain's summit.

The Summit of Sinai, A.D. 383

Egeria

All there is on the actual summit of the central mountain is the church and cave of holy Moses. No one lives there. So when the whole passage had been read to us (on the very spot!) we made the Offering in the usual way and received Communion. As we were coming out of the church the presbyters of the place gave us "blessings", some fruits which grow on the mountain itself. For although Sinai, the holy Mount, is too stony even for bushes to grow on it, there is a little soil round the foot of the mountains, the central one and those around it, and in this the holy monks are always busy planting shrubs, and setting out orchards or vegetable-beds round their cells. It may look as if they gather fruit which is growing in the mountain soil, but in fact everything is the result of their own hard work.

Egeria asked the monks to point out all the different places. The holy men willingly agreed.

They showed us the cave where holy Moses was when for the second time he went up into the Mount of God and a second time received the table of stone after breaking the first ones when the people sinned. They showed us all the other places we wanted to see, and also the ones they knew about themselves.

I want you to be quite clear about these mountains, reverend ladies my sisters, which surrounded us as we stood beside the church looking down from the summit of the mountain in the middle. They had been almost been too much for us to climb, and I really do not think I have seen any that were higher even though they only looked like little hillocks to us as we stood on the central mountain. From thence we were able to see Egypt and Palestine, the Red Sea and the Pathenian Sea (the part that takes you to Alexandria), as well as the vast lands of the Saracens—all unbelievably far below us. All this was pointed out to us by the holy men.

To the Summit, 1762

Carsten Niebuhr

I wished to choose from among the Arabs who had gathered about us, a guide to conduct me to Sinai. This, however, our Ghafirs would not permit; which occasioned a quarrel among them and the other Arabs. Next day, however our Schiecks brought me an Arab, whom they qualified with the title of the Schieck of Mt. Sinai, to procure him some profit from us, by the right which he thus arrogated to himself of attending strangers who came to visit the mountain.

Under the conduct of this newly created lord of Sinai with our Schiecks, I attempted, on this same day, to clamber to the summit of that mountain. It is so steep, that Moses cannot have ascended on the side which I attempted. The Greeks [the monks] have cut a flight of steps up the rock. [Richard] Pococke reckons three thousands of these steps to the top of the mountain, or rather bare, pointed rock.

Five hundred steps above the convent we found a charming spring, which, by a little pains, might be improved into a very agreeable spot. A thousand steps higher stands a chapel dedicated to the Blessed Virgin; and five hundred above this, two other chapels, situated in a plain, which the traveller enters by two small gates of mason-work. Upon this plain are two trees, under which, at high festivals, the Arabs are regaled at the expense of the Greeks, My Mohometan guides, imitating the practices they had seen the pilgrims observe, kissed the images, and repeated their prayers in the chapels. They would accompany me no farther; but maintained this to be the highest accessible peak of the mountain; whereas, according to Pococke, I had yet a thousand steps to ascend. I was therefore obliged to return, and content myself with viewing the hill of St Catherine at a distance.

The Mountain of Moses, 1816

John Lewis Burckhardt

May 20th: We were in motion before sunrise for the Djebel Mousa or Mountain of Moses, the road to which begins ascend immediately behind the walls of the convent. Regular steps were originally cut all the way up, but they are now either entirely destroyed, or so much damaged by the violent torrents as to be of very little use. After ascending for about twenty-five minutes, we breathed a short time under a sharp impending rock, close by which is a small well of water as cold as ice; at the end of three quarter's of an hour's steep ascent we came to a small plain, the entrance to which from below is through a stone gateway, which in former times was probably closed; a little beneath it stands, amongst the rocks, a small church dedicated to the Virgin. On the plain is a larger building of rude construction, which bears the name of St Elias; it was lately inhabited, but is now abandoned, the monks repairing here only at certain times of the year to read mass. Pilgrims usually halt on this spot, where a tall Cyprus tree grows by the side of a stone tank, which receives the winter rains.

On the Mount of Law, c. 1335

Lina Eckenstein

On the Mount of the Law stood the small church which at one time contained the relics of St Katherine, and which continued to contain bodies of saints as late as 1384. Near it was the cavern in which Moses stood when the Lord passed. Beyond it was the small mosque which the Saracens sought in pilgrimage. . . .

The relative position of these buildings and sites is shown on the topographical sketch made by Jacopo, which is here reproduced. On it we note the convent church with its tower, and we are told that inside the convent walls there "stood likewise a mosque with a tower of its own, from which the *cazes*, or priest of the Saracens, proclaimed the Mohammedan faith," . . . The sketch of Jacopo further shows the path leading up from the convent to the Mount of Law "where the law was given to Moses", with the chapel "where the Blessed Mary appeared"; the church of St Elijah; and the mosque of the Saracens. There is also a garden with a fountain, and a zigzag path leading up to a higher mountain where "lay the body of the Blessed Katherine." From the summit of this mountain Jacopo saw the Red

Sea, and watched the ships that carried pepper, ginger, cinnamon, and other spicery from India.

Mount Sinai and the Troubles, 1822

Joseph Wolff

Nov. 8: The priest asked us whether we desired to take a view of the remarkable antiquities surrounding Mount Sinai. We desired to see the spot where it is believed that Moses went up while the elders tarried for him and Joshua.

They all regretted they could not accompany us, because of the tribe of Arabs with whom they were at war, on account of provisions which they demand, and which they are not able to give to them.

The Arabs who were in the service of the convent were to accompany them.

They dissuaded us from going to the summit of St Catherine, on account of the danger to which we should be exposed, and its being hardly worth seeing . . . .

On the summit of Mount Sinai: I read to the company in English, and for myself in Hebrew, Deuteronomy xxxii, Exodus xx and xxiv, some Psalms, and some parts of the New Testament. . . .

After this we went to a house which belonged to the convent called *Arbain*, and I sent back my servant with the servant of Mr Carne, who was attacked by a violent fever, and we continued to mount St Catherine.

On their return the next day the party were attacked by Arabs who threatened to hold them hostage until the convent gave them the letter they demanded. They were urged to write a letter to the English consul at Cairo to plead the Arab's cause and Wolff urged them to pray to God "and God will hear them as well as the Greeks. They replied that God never minds the prayer of an Arab." Treated throughout with great civility and kindness, Wolff and his party were eventually allowed to return to Egypt, and they started on their journey on November 15.

Mount Sinai, 1845

Richard Lepsius

24th March 1845: Today we ascended Gebel Musa. In my own imagination, and by the descriptions of former travellers, it formed the actual centre of the whole range; but this is not the case. Both in elevation and in the planimetrical projection of the whole mass of the primitive range, it forms part of the north-eastern slope. The convent in a direct line is *three times* as near the eastern border of the range as the western. Even Gebel Katherin, situated situated immediately to the south, is loftier than the almost concealed summit of Gebel Musa, which is invisible to the whole of the surrounding country. Still higher mountains rise on the farther side of Katherin, but in steps, as for example, Um Riglin, Abu Schegere, Qettar, etc., as far as Um Schomar, which towers up over all the others, and stands in the centre of the eastern and western slope of the whole elevation, forming the principal and most northern vertebrae of the long backbone of the range, which passes down to the south, and determines the direction of the whole Peninsula.

The Remarkable Places upon the Mountain, 1721

Thomas Shaw

The summit of Mount Sinai is not very spacious; where the Mahometans, the Latins, and the Greeks, have each of them a small chapel. Here we are shewn the place where *Moses fasted forty days, Exod. xxxi, 18;* where *his hand was supported by Aaron and Hur, at the battle with Amelek, Exodus xvii, 9, 12; where he hid himself from the face of God;* the cave, as they pretend to shew it, having received the impression of his shoulders; besides many other places and stations recorded in Scripture.

Ascent of Mountains, 1878

Isabella Bird

This day my pilgrimage has been crowned with success, for I have ascended Jebel Musa, the highest point of the Sinaitic ridge, and Ras Sufsafeh, the presumed Mount of the Law, under the auspicious circumstances of solitude and superb weather, leaving the camp shortly before sunrise, dismissing my guide on the mountain top, and returning in the evening twilight. I took my frugal breakfast by lamplight, and just as the first rosy flush tinted the east, and the last star withdrew, my guide arrived, a wretched Bedaween, one of the convent Arabs, scarcely erroneously called convent serfs, a dried-up, wizened creature not more than five feet three inches in height, lean, shiny, clothed in a girdled cotton garment which had once been white, a dirty turban, and goat-skin sandals, at once pathetic, stupid, and melancholy-looking, a quiet, harmless man, whose energies seemed concentrated on the search for vermin, a query only too successful. Hassan stayed below to watch the tents.

As the early rose-flush gave place to day, each mountain peak, sun-kissed, turned rosy, and the red granite peaks which confront Sinai became vermilion-coloured. The splendour of the morning was almost overwhelming, and the day has been perfect, absolutely cloudless, while the heat of the sun has been tempered by a keen north wind, which here, as elsewhere, gives a peculiar brilliancy and clearness to the atmosphere.

The road is steep, but the only difficulty was that it was impossible for a person of my low stature to climb the biggest of the boulders (arranged in the rough similitude of steps) without being dragged up by the Bedaween by means of two straps.

The Sinai range is one mass of *shivers*, great and small boulders, and fragments altogether sharp-edged. Soon after beginning the climb we halted at *Mayan Musa*, the Fountain of Moses, a cold crystal spring, beneath a great granite boulder, According to Bedaween tradition it was here that Moses watered the flocks of his father-in-law Jethro. Eight varieties of small flowering plants, including a lovely little blue forget-me-not, fringe this "spring of waters whose waters fail not", and the fragile fronds of the maidenhair fern bend over it. Some confervae of a peculiarly brilliant green abound within its rim, and the larvae of mosquitoes.

If Bedaween tradition errs not, the great Lawgiver, toiling up this ascent to the awful communings above, drank of this spring. Still climbing the cleft, among and over huge boulders of granite, among which I counted many flowering plants, we rested at a rude building of unhewn stones, called "The Chapel of the Virgin of the Economes". This commemorates "the miraculous extirpation of fleas from the convent". According to all visitors, the plague has returned in full force.

After this the steps turning to the right, ascend with much abruptness to a narrow cleft in a battlement of rock, spanned by a circular arch, with a rude cross on either face. The arch is very narrow, and there is a certain solemnity in passing under it, for there in the days of mortal life sat the pious St Stephen, the Porter, whose ghastly mummy guards the gate of the charnel-house, and after him sat a long line of successors and shrived through many ages the long succession of pilgrims who passed upward to "the holy place of Sinai" on repeating Psalm xxiv, 3,4, "Who shall ascend into the hill of the Lord?" . . . Near this arch is another crystal spring, at the side of which a blue forget-me-not was struggling into flower.

A little further on is another rocky wall with a rocky gateway, and then a small and most rugged plateau of shivered rocks, on which are a solitary cypress tree and a rough ruinous building containing chapels dedicated to Elijah and Elisha. Near this is a small cave which tradition regards as the the place of Elijah's temporary abode. As far as this plateau no part of the which gives access to it some evidence in the shape of rough and Cyclopedean steps that human agency has attempted to lessen the difficulties of the ascent. Beyond this the way is steeper and less defined.

Miracles on Mount Sinai, 1914

Oliver Brockbank

We went through the gateway at the back of the monastery courtyard, and commenced the ascent of the mountain by way of the Pilgrim Steps. It appears that St Helena originally provided the money for the making of this easy route for pilgrims, and that quite recently a wealthy Greek has emulated her example, and, at his own expense, re-made the road and steps, so that the climb is a most easy and comfortable one—a great contrast to that of Mount Serbal.

Our pace was necessarily slow, for it was nearing the end of Lent, and our monk guide was still fasting and quite off colour. After a quarter of an hour we began to get very fine views of the monastery down in the valley below us, with the morning sunlight creeping towards it, and tingeing the mountain side with a lovely golden yellow.

Our first halt was at a little hermit's cave, containing a tiny spring, fringed with green maidenhair fern. Father Modistus told us that the hermit had once been a shoemaker, and that when he came to live in the cave he found it a difficult task each day going down to the valley for water—he therefore prayed, and the spring was miraculously sent.

The next shrine, some distance further up the mountain, was dedicated to the Virgin, and here again our guide had a miracle to relate. He said, "That long years ago a plague of fleas visited the monastery, and rendered the life of the fathers a burden to them. To add to their miseries food supplies were cut off by robbers, and they were threatened by starvation. Driven to despair the monks decided to abandon the monastery, and before doing so took their last pilgrimage to the summit of the beloved mountain. The Abbot had gone on ahead with the other monks, but the Economos lingered behind, and just at the place where this little chapel now stands he suddenly met a Bedouin woman carrying a baby, and accompanied by an old man. The woman asked whither he was going, and on hearing his tale of woe, told him to go back to the monastery and live there, and promised that the curse of fleas should be removed. On his way down the mountain the monk caught sight of camels, coming with abundant supplies of wheat from Akaba, and no flea has ever dared to show its nose within the walls of St Katharine since. It then appeared that the Bedouin woman must have been the Virgin and her Child, and St Joseph; and a chapel was built in her honour.

In another ten minutes we saw ahead of us a little arch across the rock staircase, and beyond it another. At these two portals pilgrims stop to confess on their way up the mountain.

The Summit of Jebel Musa, 1820

Sir Frederick Henniker

On the very summit are two dilapidated chapels, on one side rises the rock of St Catherine, more lofty and more picturesque than that of Sinai, but all the rest is a sea of desolation, It would seem as if Arabea Petraea had once been an ocean of lava, and that while its waves were running literally mountains high, it was commanded suddenly to a standstill.

Breakfast on the Summit, 1846

George Fisk

Before we prepared to descend, our friends Angelo and Nicodimo (two monks who accompanied them) led us to a charming clear well, near the summit; from which delicious water was drawn for immediate refreshment, and for the purpose of furnishing us with coffee. A fire was soon kindled, and the coffee made; and it was a study for a painter as we all sat together, partaking of a convent meal, brought in a rough-dressed goat skin, which was spread on the rock for our tablecloth. We occupied one side—Angelo and Nicodemo the other, and behind, a little apart, sat Hassenein and the Bedaween. Our breakfast consisted of very coarse brown bread, goat's-milk cheese, black olives dressed in oil, delicious coffee, fresh water from the spring, and a little flask of date spirit to qualify it. We did ample justice to our rude repast, after so much toil; and commenced an extremely difficult descent, by the deep rocky valley of El Ledja, formed by Gebel Musa, and Gebel Katarina, which runs nearly parallel with the ravine in which the convent is situate.

While passing along El Ledja, the monks pointed out to us a huge mass of granite, lying as if hurled by some mighty hand from the masses above; and this they affirmed was the stone which, when smitten by the rod of Moses, gushed forth with water. They bade us notice several curious fissures, from which they say the water miraculously issued. But, after all, I feel fully persuaded that this is purely legendary. The ravine of El Ledja, cannot, I think, be the vale of Rephidim. Moreover, there is reason to believe that the present tradition had not its commencement till about the fourteenth century.

From the Summit, 1854

R.W. Stewart

Summoning my guide, I set myself to study the leading points in the surrounding scenery. He was an elderly man; had been with Ibrahim Pasha through all his Syrian campaign;* and having been long quartered at Tor, and often on the top of Gebel Musa, I found him very intelligent, and well acquainted with all the most remarkable mountains within sight.

Nearest to that on which we stood, with only a deep ravine between, rose the dark frowning crags of Ghebel Katerin, bearing S. by W. It is said to be 1000 feet higher than Ghebel Mousa, which . . . is 7034 Paris feet above the level of the Red Sea, and 1700 feet above the level of the Wadi er Rahah. In the same direction, though hidden by Katerin, is Um Shomer, said to be the highest mountain in the peninsula, on whose summit no European has ever yet set foot, nor I am aware that, since Burckhardt's failure (in 1816), any one has made the attempt; and beyond it, on the sea-shore, as the name denotes, is Tur el Bahr. To the NW, the highest peaks of Mount Serbal were distinctly seen,† and beyond them, in the far distance, the blue range of Abou Deraj, on the African coast. Between Katerin and Serbal, still to the NW, lies Gebel Tineh, on which the Pasha's palace was being built.§ Below us, directly north was the narrow valley in which was the Chapel of Elijah, and beyond it Ghebel Lejah and Ghebel Safafeh, which are generally represented as shoulders of Ghebel Mousa, though in reality entirely separate from it; and by these the view of the plain of el Rahah and Wadi es Sheikh was completely shut out. A little farther to the north was the pass of Howa, through which we had arrived the previous day.

To the north-east, there was close at hand Ghebel Fureia, rising in the angle formed by the junction of Wadi er Rahah and Wadi Sheikh, while the horizon line in the same direction was formed by the chain of Ghebel et Tih. In the same direction we had the peaks of Ghebel ed Deir peeping through the clefts in the Safsafeh ridge, with Ghebel Monejah a little more to the east; while between them and the horizon rose the mountains which skirt the western shore of the Gulf of Akabah.

To the east and south of east there was a view of the distant blue mountains of Arabia beyond the Gulf, the water of which was shut out by intervening hills. But on turning a little further SE, a broad expanse of smooth water glancing in the sunshine, with the island of Tiran in its midst, was seen a little to the north of Ras Mohammed, which divides the waters of the Red Sea into two separate gulfs.

---

* Ibrahim Pasha was the Pasha of Egypt, Muhammad 'Ali's son and general.

† There was, Stewart admitted, some dispute about this from other travelers.

§ Muhammad 'Ali's grandson, Abbas Pasha, determined to create a health resort for himself in Sinai and much preparation was made including the road which other travelers describe. The Pasha died before the completion of his project.

From the Summit, 1878

Isabella Bird

Upon the plateau stands the peak of Jebel Musa, a grand pile of naked grey granite without other vegetation than stains of orange and dark-blue lichen. I was three quarters of an hour in climbing this last peak. For how many years, from early childhood upwards, have I thought and dreamt about this mountain top, and have imagined its aspect! It is like and unlike—like it in absolute desolation, but unlike in its grandeur and majesty. The summit is very small and shivered into boulders, and leaves little space for aught but two rude buildings, a chapel and a mosque, built out of the ruins of an earlier convent. Beneath the mosque is a cave in which Mahometan tradition says that Moses passed the forty days and nights. Quite near is a deep cleft in the rock to which my Bedaween pointed and said something in Arabic, which I have since learned is the name signifying the "cleft in the rock" in which Moses was hid when the glory of God passed by. An empty champagne bottle profaned this summit, and I threw it with indignation over the southern precipice more than 1,000 feet in depth.

Mount Saint Catherine

Climbing Mount St. Catherine, 1816

John Lewis Burckhardt

May 21st. We left our resting-place before sun-rise, and climbed up a steep ascent where there had formerly been steps, which are now entirely destroyed. This side of Djebel Katerin or Mount St Catherine, is noted for its excellent pasturage; herbs sprout up every where between the rocks, and as many of them are odiferous, the scent early in the morning, when the dew falls, is delicious. . . . In the month of June when the herbs are in blossom, the monks are in the habit of repairing to this and the surrounding mountains, in order to collect various herbs, which they dry, and send to the Convent at Cairo, from whence they are dispatched to the archbishop of Sinai at Constantinople, who distributes them to his friends and dependents; they are supposed to possess many virtues conducive to health. A botanist would find a rich harvest here, and it is much to be regretted that two mountains so easy of access, and so rich in vegetation, as Sinai and Libanus, should be still unexplored by men of science.

As we approached the summit of the mountain we saw at a distance a small flock of mountain goats feeding among the rocks. One of our Arabs left us, and by a widely circuitous road endeavoured to get leeward of them, and near enough to fire at them; he enjoined us to remain in sight of them, and to sit down in order not to alarm them. He had nearly reached a favourable spot behind a rock, when the goats suddenly took to flight. They could not have seen the Arab, but the wind changed, and thus they smelt him.

Gebel Catherina, 1923

William Beadnell

The ascent to the summit of Gebel Katherina, the highest point in Egyptian territory, has been many times described. It presents no difficulties by the regular route, which is a winding track of easy gradient, made for the many pilgrims—men and women—who come from the countries of south-eastern Europe. A feature of the neighbourhood is the abundance of running water in the gullies. Most of the streams are brought under control at the base of the main slopes, and used to irrigate the outlying gardens of the convent, which, with their cypresses, poplars, apples, olives and almonds, have a Grecian rather than an Egyptian aspect.

There was little snow left when I made the ascent on March 11, but we passed many frozen rain-pools on the way up and the early morning was keen and chilly. Precariously perched on the summit, at 8,681 feet, is a tiny Christian chapel dedicated to St Katherine, a weird and homely erection of white plastered walls, roofed partly with tiles, partly with corrugated iron. The view on a clear day embraces the greater part of the peninsula proper, but at the time of my visit haze hid the more distant portions of the country. After leaving the summit we dispensed with beaten tracks, and by making a long detour to the east got across to Gebel Musa without descending to the monastery, whence the usual pilgrim routes proceed. This peak we climbed by way of a joint on the rather steep eastern side, eventually reaching camp shortly before dusk.

Gebel Musa—the reputed Mountain of the Law—is held in veneration by Christian and Moslem alike. On the summit chapel and mosque stand side by side, while nearby is the cleft into which, according to Arab tradition, Moses sank at the words of the Almighty, "Creep thou into the rock, O Moses, for thou canst not bear my glory."

Other Sites

The Forty Martyrs, 1820

Sir Frederick Henniker

We descended (from Mount Sinai) by the same path as far as the cypress tree, and thence turned towards the convent of the forty martyrs; it is situated on the opposite side of the mountain from that which we had left in the morning, and to reach it employed about six hours; we met with several springs, aromatic herbs, and small solitary cells, which were once the residences of Sts: St Gregory and others. The convent of the forty martyrs is now in the forcible possession of the Arabs, but who still allow the monks to sleep there in their pilgrimages to the top of the neighbouring mountain, St Catherine; the same privilege was offered to me, as it is impossible to perform the double labour in one day; I however declined it altogether, for my Cicerone confessed that there is nothing to be seen but a spring of water, resorted to be partridges, stones, bearing marks resembling trees, and the burial place of the saint. Some authors talk also of an impression of the saint on stone, but I have already seen one specimen of lithography.

In approaching the convent, Harriet Martineau's party took a different way from others who passed this place.

El-Erbayn, the 'Forty,' 1846

Harriet Martineau

We passed three gardens and a chaos of boulders and at last sat down in the pleasant olive grove belonging to the small convent of El-Erbayn, "the Forty" so named from the forty martyrs who perished here; - monks or anchorites slaughtered by the Bedoueens. There are no clear particulars told on the spot; but Dr. Robinson points out that these forty martyrs were probably the thirty-eight killed, and two mortally wounded, of the hermits who were attacked by the Saracens in the fourth century, when the holy Superior Doulas retired, with a few companions, into a tower on the mountain. The story is that when the Saracens endeavoured to attack the tower, the whole of the summit of the mountain became fiery; on seeing which, the enemy fled, leaving the monks free to come down and bury their dead.

We were invited into this convent by our servants; and we entered it through a little orchard of blossoming trees. Mats were spread for us in the gallery; and there we were served with coffee, palm brandy and dates preserved in oil – which some of the party found highly offensive, and others rather liked. The convent and garden are in the charge of the Arab dependents of the Christians; and a few of the monks occasionally live here. About ten o'clock, we began to climb the mountain. As we were on the opposite side from that which we ascended yesterday, we were, of course, in the sunshine; and blazing and broiling sunshine it was, till we reached the highest ravine. Here was no path, nor any steps like those which had so aided us on the other side of the mountain. It was rough and toilsome till we reached the little plane on which grows the little cypress then, after descending a little, we ascended the ravine which few travellers have, I believe, attempted, and where no women had probably set foot.

When we reached our point, we thought no more of our fatigues, nor of our doubts how to get down again.

Our convictions was strengthend that, on some of the adjacent cliffs, was the spot where the Lord "descended in fire" and proclaimed the Law.

They Showed Us the Bible, 383

Egeria

All along the valley, below Mount Sinai, the local monastics serving as guides showed us how each Israelite had a house, and they were round stone houses, as you can still see from the foundations.

They showed us where holy Moses ordered the children of Israel "to run from gate to gate" (Exodus 32:27) when he had come back from the Mount. They also showed us where holy Moses ordered them to burn the calf which Aaron had made for them, and the bed of the stream from which, as you read in Exodus, holy Moses made the children of Israel drink (Exodus 32:20). And they pointed out the place where a portion of Moses' spirit was given to the seventy men (Numbers 11:25), and where the children of Israel had their craving for food (Numbers 11:4). They showed us also the place called the Fire" (Numbers 11:3), a part of the camp which was burning, where the fire stopped when holy Moses prayed. And they showed us where the *manna* and the quails descended on the people (Numbers 11:6, 31). So we were shown everything which the Book of Moses tell us took place in that valley beneath holy Sinai, the Mount of God.

The Remarkable Places Round about This Mountain, 1721

Thomas Shaw

The monks, likewise, shew us several other remarkable places; as where *Aaron's calf* was molten, Exodus xxxii, 4 (but the head only is represented, and that very rudely) where the *Israelites danced* at the consecration of it, Exodus xxxii, 19; where *Carah and his company were swallowed up*, Numbers xvi, 32; where *Elias hid himself*, when he fled from Jezebel, 2 Kings viii, 9. But the history of these, and of other places, which I have mentioned, upon the mount, is attended with so many *Monkish* tales and inconsistencies, that it would be too tedious to relate them.

Until the mid-nineteenth century it was accepted virtually without question that Mount Sinai was where Moses presented to the world the laws. Increased religious scepticism and widening scientific knowledge began to make some people reconsider this assumption.

Doubts about the Site, 1865

E. H. Palmer

But, imposing and grand as the spot undoubtedly is, a single glance at the valley beneath is sufficient to show that it is not in any way adapted for the encampment of so large a host as that of the Children of Israel, nor for the battle of Rephidim; for the monks most inconsistently place the scene of the encounter with the Amelekites and the reception of the Law in one and the same spot. The summit itself is, moreover, invisible from any part of the spacious plain of Er Rahah, situated at the other end of the block, but there the mountain terminates in a magnificent bluff, called the Ras Sufsafeh, which fronts the plain and commands a view of its entire extent. This bluff is divided by a deep cleft, to approach which you cross a basin similar to that which the cypress and chapel of Elijah are situated. At this secluded spot Moses may have separated from the Elders who had accompanied him thus far on his ascent, and it requires but little imagination to believe that from the cleft itself the Ten Commandments were proclaimed.

I have already alluded to the traditional evidence in favour of the identification of Jebel Musa with Mount Sinai; I will now endeavour to show how far the physical aspect of the mountain satisfies the requirements of the Sacred Narrative.

An Amazing Stage Set, 2004

Michael Haag

On the plain of Raha, where the Children of Israel are said to have camped, the Egyptians have thoughtfully built a tourist complex of small chalets, somebody's idea of Bedouin tents in stone. The view is up the Wadi el Deir, with two mountainous shoulders on either side. The scene seems pure Cecil B. de Mille and is familiar. Then you realise it is familiar because it is Cecil B. de Mille: here Charlton Heston came down from the mountain clutching the Ten Commandments. For once a gigantically imposing set did not have to be built; the location chosen by God and Moses for their famous encounter had satisfied a Hollywood film producer's demand for spectacle.

13
The Return from Sinai

Travelers wrote surprisingly little about their return journey. Those who went on east to Akaba and Petra and thence to Jerusalem naturally continued to write about their new experiences, but those who turned around and retraced their tracks hardly mentioned the experiences they had.

Not This Way, 1873
Murray's Handbook

From Sinai direct to Palestine via Nahkl is a route which presents no object of interest to the ordinary traveller: he had much better return to Suez, and go thence, via Port Said to Jaffa.

The travelers through the ages desired to leave a mark of their visit at the Convent. Early travelers wrote or carved their name in their room or pasted a note of their presence there. Later travelers were offered a book—the Book of Strangers—in which they could inscribe their names.

The Penciling of Visitors, 1820

Sir Frederick Henniker

The travellers' room in the convent of Mount Sinai, like the travellers' room in a public house in England, bears the pencillings of its visitors; the memorandum in themselves differing as widely as the places are distant from each other. Here, instead of laughing at the amatory complaints of bagsmen, we pause before the useful notices of those who journey in pursuit of knowledge; and in lieu of passing by such names as Green, White, Brown, we are reminded of men whose labours have benefited mankind. Seetzen,* on a vessel of paper, pasted against the wall, notifies his having penetrated the country in a direct line, between the Dead Sea and Mount Sinai, a route never before accomplished. This was the most interesting to me as I had previously determined to attempt the same, it being the shortest way to Jerusalem.

The Book of Strangers, 1836

Joseph Wolff

I found in the Book of Strangers the following lines written by that extraordinary Trappist, Marie-Joseph de Geramb:- "Je suis arrive le 25 Fevrier, 1833, au Convent du Mont Sinai; le 28 J'ai couche ma front dans la poussiere sur la montagne sainte. L'Eternal, qui dans sa miesericorde donna a Moise les plus anciens des Historiens, le plus sublime des Philosophes, et le plus sage des Legislateurs cette Loi fondement necessaire de la notre. Parti le 3 de Mars, Marie-Joseph Geramb."

Time to Leave, 1872

Paul Lenoir

On the day before our departure, we went to pay a farewell visit to the good monks. We had taken their photographs, and exchanged pledges of eternal friendship, and now we were about to conform to custom, and enter our names on the register in which the names of all the pilgrims who visit the convent are inscribed. We found ourselves in familiar company when the scroll was opened, though the French are in the minority among visitors to Sinai, where the English are much better known. On that occasion we were shown the signature of General Bonaparte, at the end of a firman written by his own hand, by which the convent is entitled to a protection which has not yet quite lost its prestige among the tribes of the Peninsula.

At last, we were obliged to tear ourselves away from our hospitable entertainers. Our pockets were crammed for the last time with uneatable sweetmeats, our bakshish was gratefully accepted, and we parted with mutual regard and regret.

"When you come back," said the Superior, "you shall taste a special wine I made myself."

---

* Ulrich Jasper Seetzen (1767–1811). Henniker noted "On the margin is written—Seetzen died at Acaba; supposed to have been poisoned." Other sources suggest that his mysterious death happened near Mecca.

Taib! Taib! Taib!

"When you look in at Bougival, you shall have a row in the Seine, and we will show you great things."

The presence of the Superior was not without its useful influence in inducing our camel-drivers to start. They were to be taken far away from their tribes by our journey to Akabah, and they were not particularly zealous when it came to the loading of the camels with out formidable luggage.

The Visitors' Book, 1938

H.V. Morton

It was my last night in Sinai. As I sat alone after supper, in the little room next to my bedroom, a monk brought in the visitors' book for me to sign. As I turned its pages, famous and interesting names revealed themselves in the light of the lamp. It is strange that many a bad hotel in much frequented portions of the earth has a visitors' book bound in precious vellum, while the monks of Sinai, whose visitors are as unnumbered as the sands and include pilgrims of all ages and of all countries, content themselves with an exercise book.

This visitors' book is a modern touch in Sinai, for it begins only in the year 1860. Burckhardt has told us that when he visited the monastery in 1816 he found the walls covered with scraps of paper on which visitors had written their names, so that the present book is evidently what is termed "a long-felt want".

The first entry is that of Johan Thomas Olaf Neergaard of Copenhagen, who stayed there from March 19–21, 1860. The first English entries in that year are those of C.M. Nickels, S.H. Moore, and William Howard Doughty, who left fifty francs for the benefit of the monastery.

On April 5, 1871, was this item:

We beg to acknowledge with many thanks the kindness and courtesy received from the monks during four days' visit to the convent. Cunningham Graham, Scotland

At an unspecified date in 1875 the book was signed: "Charles M. Doughty".

On March 1, 1894 the book was signed "Pierre Loti".

On May 10, 1903 an entry appears from the first Franciscans to come here to this holy spot after many centuries. "May God bless this holy house and all who dwell therein. F. Godfrey, OFM, W. Mowbray, Fra Fidelis da Boston.

The Pilgrim Certificate 1, 1822

John Carne

[T]he memorable print kept in the convents of Sinai and Cairo, which is given to all pilgrims to carry to their homes. . . . In this print is a lofty and vivid representation of Mount Sinai, rising up like a huge tower; Moses is seen toiling up the steep, with a long beard and staff, and nearly arrived at the top; beneath is the convent of Mount Sinai, out of the windows of which is pushed the bald head of a monk, who is engaged in relieving the wants of the wicked Arabs, who, drawing their bows, cover the sands below; the arrows are seen flying, the loaves of bread falling at the same moment: the rock of Meribah, though some distance off, is brought in sight, and the water gushing forth. In the background, though near two hundred miles off, is seen the passage of the Red Sea by the Egyptians; and Pharaoh, who leads them on, is shown sinking in his chariot, to hasten which catastrophe, Moses, who stands on the shore, has just aimed a tremendous blow at him with a cudgel.

A century later, the pilgrim certificate had been renewed and changed.

The Pilgrim Certificate 2, 1912
Mary Dobson

Every pilgrim who comes to the Convent is presented with the pilgrim certificate, which is a most interesting document. It has grown more elaborate as the years have gone on, but gives an excellent idea of the events supposed to have taken place at or near Jebel Musa throughout the ages. Three mountain peaks are shown: Jebel Katerina, Jebel Musa, and Jebel Moneja. At the summit of Jebel Katerina two angels are laying Catherine to rest; on Jebel Musa, Moses receives the tables of the law from the hand of the Lord, while near the head of Jebel Moneja stands the once-time Convent of St Episteme.

Beyond the peaks of the mountains the sea is seen, and on the foothills Moses tends his flocks. Various other events besides are expressed as taking place on the three great peaks' and, with curious disregard of geography, scenes, such as Elijah feeding the ravens on Jebel Moneja, are depicted. At the foot of the picture is the old Convent fortress, foursquare, out of which rises the Burning Bush; its flaming foliage encloses the Holy Child with His Mother. The pent-house with a descending basket is also shown; and, while Arabs are aiming their crossbows at the building, a party of ecclesiastical officials proceed in state from the great door on the other side.

Departure 1, 1820
Sir Frederick Henniker

It is customary, previous to embarking on an expedition of danger, to demand the Arab assurance of fidelity, and I now had an opportunity of witnessing this ceremony. On mentioning the subject to the elder of the party, he immediately drew his sword, placed some salt upon the blade, and then put a portion of it into his mouth, and desired me to do the same; and "Now, cousin," said he, "your life is as sacred to me as my own;" or, as he expressed himself, "Son of my uncle, your head is upon my shoulders." My head being upon his shoulders rendered us consanguineous, by eating together we became friends, and that friendship was to be maintained by the naked sword. Salt is considered by the Arab as so necessary to life, that he often carries a portion of it about his person.

The camels were speedily laden and I bade my adieu to the convent. The journey was calculated at ten days, and for this the monks had supplied me with that food of the desert—loaves and fishes; I was provided also with rice, coffee and sago. My guides had pledged their faith, so that if I had previously felt under any apprehension, I was now willing to accredit the usual character of the Bedouin.

Departure 2, 1835
John Lloyd Stephens

Twice since my arrival there had been rain. In that dry and thirsty desert, every drop of water falls upon the earth like precious ointment and "welcome", says the Arab "is the stranger who brings rain."

I turned my back upon the rising sun and felt by comparison on the way home; but a long journey was still before me; I had still to cross "the great and terrible desert" of the Bible which spread before the wandering Israelites its dreary and eternal sands, from the base of Sinai to the Promised Land.

Departure 3, 1845
W.H. Bartlett

October 20. I had now spent several days within the convent walls—had become in a state of mental and bodily lassitude, half reconciled to its dull routine, and, not withstanding the smallness of our stock of ideas and topics in common, had by little and little established a decidedly friendly feeling with the superior, the Ikonomos, the Librarian, the cook, and the old gardener; meeting them every evening on the convent terrace overlooking the garden, when the sun declined and the shadows crept up the surrounding peaks, and all was hushed and cool, and reciprocating our little store of comforts and luxuries, I felt half loath to leave them and to launch again upon the burning waste. Thus it is with the traveller; no sooner does he begin to grow anything, than he is rudely torn from it; he no sooner begins to love, than he must hasten to forget; and few are the friendships that outlive the feverish hurry of his vagabond course. I began therefore reluctantly to collect all my movables, accept a skin of that confection of dates and almonds of which the convent is famous, as well as a box of manna; (for which little presents of course and equivalent was given) distributed small donations of tea and other trifles, and, after bestowing the customary and very moderate sums on the cook and others, conveyed to the Superior the hundred piastres, which is the minimum of what is usually given, as an offering for the hospitable shelter of the convent. With a supply of bread for some days already been furnished, which was of course also paid for.

If our arrival at the convent was unnoticed, this could not be said of our departure, for it was graced by a tumult and uproar which might have awakened the dead. Immediately on first reaching it, Umbarak and his Arabs had, as I have already said, dispersed to their tents in the mountains, with the understand that they were to reassemble in a few days. Knowing that they had arrived, I despatched Ibrahim to negotiate for four camels instead of five; our reduced stores rendered the fifth animal quite unnecessary, as in fact it had been from the beginning; and he returned with the message that four camels should be ready on the following day. It was noon when Komeh, in a great passion, came running in, to say that Umbarak and a whole posse of his Arabs was beneath the gate, requiring that we should take five camels as before, and refusing to proceed unless we did so. I went to the aerial portal, and looking down below, saw the whole space blocked up with Umbarak's friends and camels; the Arabs, in fact, had combined to get a hundred piastres out of me. Resolved, notwithstanding, to make a strong demonstration before yielding, I held tight by the rope, and leaning out, made a spirited but useless oration, which Ibrahim translated as well as he could. Hereupon ensued a tremendous uproar, in the midst of which the baggage was lowered; and parting from all the inmates of the convent, I went out by a back way with the Superior.

Departure 4: The Loading, 1853

Catherine Tobin

[Our guide] then led us along a subterraneous passage, and across part of the nearest garden, to front of the convent—where the camels were loading. Shivering from head to foot, we seated ourselves on the edge of a large stone reservoir of water; into which, at one corner, is a descent of stone steps. Fortunately, we had amusement enough in watching our *belongings*, animate and inanimate, as they were—one by one, by means of a thick rope—let down from the high door. It was, as may easily be supposed, a tedious business so far as *time* went. When the crate of fowls descended with *cackling sounds* the anxious face of the cook was seen watching over its safety.

Our Arabs made noise sufficient for the whole legion of brigands. Two of them fought desperately, in a dispute as to which of their camels was to have the additional weight of a carpet bag; but Vincenzo's strong arm speedily settled the quarrel, by throwing the *bag* of contention in the face of each combatant; giving them, at the same time, a few blows with his *coorbash*. He then turned towards the Sheikh—who behaved disgracefully in not preserving better order—and gave *him also* a good beating! By degrees a crowd of mendicants gathered round us, urging all sorts of unreasonable claims for *backsheesh*—every one having been already paid to his utmost desert.

Harriet Martineau's group continued on toward Akaba, Petra, and eventually to Jerusalem.

The First Days Out, 1846

Harriet Martineau

We left the convent on the morning of the 10th of March, at ten o'clock and travelled till three, when we encamped in a wild place among shivered rocks. By the middle of the next day, we had left the granite, and found ourselves among sandstone, red and white. As I had a rough-paced camel, I walked this morning fourteen miles, in excessive heat. When we came to heavy sand, at two o'clock, I was obliged to mount. The heat here was too much for our sociability. At luncheon, some of the party crowded under the scanty shade of a thin acacia, whose thorns, strewing the ground, made the resting-place uneasy enough. One gentleman might be seen crouching alone, with his luncheon, under an angle of the rock, where there was just shade enough to thrust his head into. Another lay on a shelf a few feet above the sand, with a red handkerchief over his head, thus introducing a nice bit of colour' into the landscape; while I sat apart, quietly bearing the sunshine for a breath of air from the wadee, and be spared the trouble of speaking. Our encampment was delightful after this; in a wide water-course, among the most fantastic rocks of white sandstone, and surrounded by tufts of tamarisk and innumerable bushes of flowering white broom.

Returning, A.D. 383

Egeria

From this point [where they emerged from the mountains] we went our way back by the way we had come, and it was from the same point that the children of Israel "went their way", as we are told in the Books of Moses. We returned by the same route and the same staging-posts to Clysma [Suez], and there we had to have a long rest, as the way through the desert had been so sandy.

News from Home, 1892

Agnes Smith Lewis

Next morning we saw the one well that now remains in Elim, a mere hole dug in the sand, where the water sometimes runs very low. In the afternoon we were cheered by the arrival of three travellers, the Rev. Dr. McCallum of Glasgow, and Messrs Morrow and Small, of Philadelphia. . . . They were the first who gave us news from Europe since we had left Suez two months previously, and we of course, took charge of their letters.

The next two days were spent in a dreary journey over sandy plains, where we suffered greatly both from heat and thirst. As no rock, with its welcome shade, was to be expected, we insisted on the kitchen tent being taken and pitched for us during our mid-day rest. From within it we became covered with wind-blown sand. . . . We were at our wit's end to get anything drinkable. Khalil became very ill with the effects of the unfiltered water, which, in this limestone district, contains a strong infusion of Epsom salts.

Our last encampment was between Wady Sadur and Ain Mousa. The wind blew straight onto us from the sandy plains from the sea, which was about two miles distant; it shook the tent and even shook my bed all night. . . . Next day, at half-past ten, the Bedaween raised a shout of triumph, almost equal to Miriam's, as the crest of a sandy ridge brought us a fine view of the oasis of Ain Mousa, with a glimpse of the Gulf of Suez on the horizon. They almost ran and so did the camels, and we were consequently well shaken before being deposited (and photographed by my sister) beneath some stately palm tree.

In mid-December, William Beamont returned to the hotel where he had stayed on his way to Suez weeks earlier. It must have seemed like paradise.

Home Comforts, 1860

William Beamont

After our desert sojourn this hotel seemed a real oasis of civilization. Numbers of Arab boats were unloading their cargoes near the quay, and the sailors were singing at their work. Their songs were for the most part monotonous chants, but there was one which was singular and not displeasing.

I left Suez by the railway at a quarter past two, and having passed through a portion of the desert very similar to that which I have before described, I reached Cairo at six o'clock.

When a vessel quits the port her sails are snowy white, her tackle is in order, and the pennon flies at the mast-head; but she returns with her canvas torn, her tackling damaged, and her paint and gilding soiled by the sea-water. We have not returned from the desert as we set out; our habiliments have suffered, and buckles, straps and buttons have been missing when they were wanted. Our chins, too, where the hair has been allowed to grow as a protection against the sun, who has taken an ample revenge for being excluded from the south side of the face, by blistering the rest, "show like a stubble land at harvest home." I am glad to have seen the desert, and thankful to be once more in the regions of civilization!

The End, 1722

The Prefetto of Egypt

October 16. This day we entered the city, in good health, by the port of Baab el

Nassar; and I arrived at my own house: thanks be to God, who brought me thither safe from mischief.

Traveling eastward and then northward, Oliver Brockbank reached Jerusalem on May 1.

The End, 1914

Oliver Brockbank

We had spent exactly five weeks and a day under canvas in the Desert of the Exodus and Arabia, and during that time had covered over 400 miles on camel and 700 miles on horseback. Not a single accident or day's illness had befallen any of us, and I could not help but feel that God's good hand had been upon us all the time.

A Beginning, 1912

Mary Dobson

Any pilgrim who at length visits a place he has long desired to see, and who, in that place, meditates long on the events which are in his own soul connected therewith, comes, at last, to the point where he feels as if he belonged to that spot in a special manner, and as if that part of the globe were an intrinsic part of him. He even comes to instinctive conclusions, the reasons for which he cannot give fully to the world, but which are often perfectly right; and these things happened to some of us during our stay on Sinai, as we roamed the mountain-sides and heard great sounds, and saw great sights, which only those who go to Sinai can ever hear and see.

The Travelers

Brief Biographies

Ammonius was a fourth-century monk from Canopus near Alexandria who journeyed to the Holy Lands "inspired by a desire to survey the venerable places." He visited Sinai at the time of the martyrdom of the "The Forty," a group of monks near the present monastery. His account was translated and published in 1912 by Agnes Smith Lewis.

William John Bankes (1786–1855) was a well-to-do and clever traveler and antiquary who never published his own work. He lived in Egypt and around the Mediterranean from 1815, traveling up the Nile twice, recording inscriptions, and collecting an obelisk in Philae, which now stands in the park of his Dorsetshire home. During his first visit to Egypt in 1815 he went to Sinai, where he borrowed some manuscripts that were later returned.

Samuel Colcord Bartlett (1817–1898). Apart from his account of his travels through Egypt and Palestine and his journey in the Sinai Peninsula, there appears to be little information about S.C. Bartlett.

William Henry Bartlett (1809–1854) earned his living as a topographical artist at first in Britain and later around the world illustrating a number of books. He traveled widely in the

Near East and by the 1840s was also writing the text for his books. Bartlett's *Forty Days in the Desert on the Track of the Israelites* includes his travel in Sinai. He died at sea while returning from Asia Minor.

Said Ibn Batrick (fl. 877–969/70), otherwise known as Eutychius or Said Ibn Batriq, was Patriarch of Alexandria 877–940. He reported in a full account the building of the convent. His writings were translated by Edward Pococke in the seventeenth century because of their interest as early Christian documents in Arabic.

H.J. Llewellyn Beadnell (1874–1944), for three decades, worked as a British official in Egypt, surveying the deserts of the country including two surveys of the Sinai Peninsula 1921 and 1923–24 and published from these experiences *The Wilderness of Sinai* (1927). His survey work is recorded in the *Desert Surveys* and reports of the Geological Surveys of Egypt.

William John Beamont (1828–1868), a Church of England clergyman and fellow of Trinity College, Cambridge, toured Egypt, Sinai, and Palestine in 1854. He spent some time in Jerusalem helping in the education of intending missionaries to Abyssinia and later acted as chaplain to camp hostels in the Crimea. Back in Cambridge, he was active in various initiatives linked to education and the church. He published *Catherine, the Egyptian Slave* (1852) and *A Concise Grammar of the Arabic Language*, and his account of his Eastern travels (both in 1862). His early death was partly attributed to a fever acquired in the East.

Pierre Belon du Mans (c. 1517–1565), a French naturalist and traveler, journeyed in the Eastern Mediterranean in 1546, reaching Egypt and Sinai in 1547, and traveling on through Syria to Constantinople. Back in France he published an account of his observations in 1553–58: *Les Observations. en Grece, Judee. Egypte, Arabie et autres pays* (Observations of Several Singular and Memorable Things Found in the Near East and India, 1555). After all his travels to inaccessible parts of the world, he was killed by thieves in Paris.

Isabella Bird (Bishop) (1831–1904) began her travels and travel writing in her early twenties (*The English Woman in America*, 1876). She visited Australia and New Zealand, crossed the Pacific to the Sandwich Islands (Hawaii) and on to America (1873), writing accounts of the places and her adventures. In 1878 she visited Japan, China, and Malaya and on her way home went on Easter pilgrimage to St. Catherine's Convent. She only published an account of this in journal articles. Soon after she married Dr. Bishop and until he died, she traveled very little. Then she started traveling again and continued to do so to the last year of her life.

Horatius Bonar (1808–1889), a Free Church of Scotland minister, evangelist, and writer of numerous religious books, sermons, biographies, poems and more than 600 hymns, visited Palestine and Sinai in 1856 and is said to have composed hymns as he crossed the Sinai Desert. His anthology of poems of the Holy Land, *Palestine*, was published in 1858.

Oliver Brockbank (fl. 1920) traveled from Manchester, England, direct to Suez where he had made arrangements for a long-planned journey—one of the last to be made by a civilian before World War I.

John Lewis Burckhardt (1784–1817), also known as Johan Ludwig Burckhardt (1784–1817) or Sheikh Ibrahim, the Swiss-born scholar-traveler Burckhardt moved to England in 1806 and, failing to find employment, offered his services to the Africa Association to follow the pilgrim caravan across Africa to explore the source of the Niger. He lived as a Muslim for his remaining years in Syria and Egypt, traveling and writing. In 1816 he traveled to Sinai and returned to Cairo, spending the final months of his life writing up his notes. He died in Cairo of dysentery at the age of 33. The account of his travels in Sinai was published in *Travels in Syria and the Holy Land* (1822) and *Notes on Bedouins and Wahabys* (1830).

John Carne (1789–1844) visited the Eastern Mediterranean in 1821 with his cousin after leaving Cambridge. T hey went to Sinai with the Reverend Joseph Wolff and were taken hostage by Bedouins near St. Catherine's Convent, but were released after a number of days. He published two books about his journeys and other works.

Robert Clayton (1695–1758), the Church of Ireland Bishop of Clogher, was ambitious and eager to reach high office and rewards, but not then thought "to attend upon the resulting duties." However, in later years he gained recognition as a theological writer with ideas that bordered on heresy. He did not travel to Sinai, but translated the account of the Prefetto of Egypt's (Claude Sicard's) journey with members of the Propaganda Fide. Clayton added notes on the hieroglyphs and mythology.

Francis Conyngham (fl. 1869) went in 1867 with his wife "to see the scenes of The Arabian Nights in real life." They traveled up the Nile and in March 1868 to Sinai in the company of an unnamed English clergyman, journeying on to Jerusalem.

Charles Didier (1805–1864), born in Geneva, became a journalist, travel writer, and poet in France. His first venture to the Arab world was to Morocco, then Egypt (*Cinq Cents Lieues sur le Nil*, 1856). Having spent in Cairo one of the most enchanting winters he could remember, in January 1854 Didier set out (at first with Richard Burton) for Sinai and Arabia. Not long after he returned from his Arabian journey, he became completely blind. He committed suicide in Paris in 1864.

Augusta Mary Rachel Dobson (1872–1923), a cousin of Dr. Rendell Harris, the biblical scholar (1862–1951), traveled in India—"to the frontiers of Tibet"—

as a missionary worker, and had a working knowledge of Arabic. This experience encouraged her to offer her services to her cousin on a mixed British-American expedition to Sinai in 1922. She spent most of her days there in the library among the great collection of Arabic manuscripts, which went unmentioned by most other travelers.

Alexandre Dumas (1802–1870), a prolific French writer, is best known for his novels (*The Three Musketeers*, *Black Tulip*, *Count of Monte Christo*, and *The Man in the Iron Mask*) but also wrote histories, memoirs, and later in life, about cookery. He traveled widely within Europe and wrote about his journeys in Spain, France, and Switzerland. In 1835–36 he wrote as if he had traveled in the East, including a journey to Sinai, but in fact his account was based on the travels of others.

Lina Eckenstein (fl. 1920–1940) worked with Flinders Petrie at Serabit in the winter of 1905–56 as he undertook the examination of the Egyptian remains in Sinai. She had long been interested in the hermit life of the peninsula and the growing belief that Gebel Musa was not the Mountain of the Law. She turned her attention to the history of the region, which led to *A History of Sinai*, 1920.

Egeria (fl. 360–400), probably a French woman of some social importance (she was helped in her travels by the higher clergy and Roman soldiers, which were provided to accompany her during a dangerous section of her journey), wrote an account of her pilgrimage through the holy lands which was only rediscovered in the late nineteenth century. Her writing is always lively and entertaining, though "like so many tourists, she was often misinformed" (M.L. McClure and C.L. Peltoe). After Sinai she went eastwards to Mesopotamia before returning home through Constantinople. A later traveler, C.W. Wilson, commented on the topography of her account.

Felix Fabri (c. 1441–1502), born in Zurich, became a monk of the Dominican Order on the feast of St. Catherine (November 25, 1453). Mainly based at Ulm in Germany, he traveled widely in Europe and went twice on pilgrimage to the Holy Land, first in 1480 and again in 1492 on the journey in which he also went to Sinai. He published accounts of his travels which were brought to a wider modern audience in *H.F.M. Prescott's Jerusalem Journey* (1954) and *Once in Sinai* (1958).

Elbert Farman (1831–1911) served as American Consul in Egypt c. 1868–75. He traveled through Egypt at that time and, in 1877, returned to accompany retired President General Ulysses Grant along the Nile. He wrote descriptive and political accounts of his Egyptian experiences.

George Fisk (fl. 1840s) titled his account of his travels as "A Pastor's Memorial" of his journeys with a clergyman friend through the Holy Lands in 1842.

John Gadsby (c. 1809–1893), a British printer and publisher, visited Egypt frequently for his health from 1846. He collected Egyptian antiquities, many of which are in the British Museum. He traveled to Sinai and wrote *My Visit to Sinai and the Holy Land*. He gave 'Biblical and Oriental lectures.' His two volume *My Wanderings in the East* was published in 1855 and 1860. He later traveled to and also wrote about Canada and Spain.

Margaret Dunlop Gibson (1843–1920) appears to have lived in the shadow of her twin sister, Agnes Lewis (1843–1926). She was an Arabic and Syriac scholar who traveled with her sister during 1892–1906 in the Near East. She wrote *How the Codex Was Found* (1893) based on their researches at Sinai.

Basil Gogara (fl. 1634), a native of Kazan in Astrakhan, traveled to the Holy Land in 1634. He spent three days in Jerusalem before traveling on through Cairo to Sinai. He eventually returned to Moscow in 1837.

Louis Golding (1895–1958), a prolific writer born in Manchester to an Orthodox Jewish family, started to travel for his health in the 1920s, first in Europe and then in the Near East. In 1935 he began to follow Moses journeys from the bulrushes of the Nile to Mount Pigah. This journey appeared in *In the Steps of Moses the Conqueror* (1943).

Michael Haag has done much to bring twentieth-century descriptions of Egypt to the public eye. He has written several guidebooks about Egypt, has republished E.M. Forster's *Alexandria: A History and a Guide*, and he has written *Alexandria: City of Memory*, a portrait of the cosmopolitan city.

James Hamilton (fl. 1850–58) left almost no trace of himself apart from two now little known, but well considered, travel accounts: *Wanderings in North Africa* (1856) and *Wanderings around the Birthplace of the Prophet* (1852–53) (1854). Robin Bidwell ranked particularly his account of Jeddah as "the best since Burckhardt thirty years before." He spoke Arabic, understood commerce, and argued strongly for great British involvement in the region.

Sir Frederick Henniker (1793–1825), as a young aristocrat, traveled in the Near East in 1819–20. He was the first known European to climb to the apex of the Second Pyramid at Giza and journeyed through Egypt and Sinai with intelligence and light-hearted pleasure. He died young of a severe and painful illness. He traveled with Francis Grey (1794–1854) who copied inscriptions from Wady al-Makkatib, which he later published.

Emily Hornby (fl. 1899–1901) traveled twice to Egypt and Sinai with her two sisters. After her death, one sister published her journals in 1907 in a book illustrated with the watercolors of her other sister.

John Hyde (d. 1825), a Manchester gentleman, traveled in the Eastern Mediterranean region in 1819–20, mainly on his own but joining other parties along the way. He traveled as far south in Egypt as the second cataract and also visited Sinai and Jerusalem. He kept a detailed record of his journeys, but died in India not having published his travel accounts. His diaries are now in the British Library.

Ibn Battuta (1304–1377) set out on pilgrimage from his homeland in Tangier in 1325. Although his initial objective was to go on a pilgrimage to Mecca, his passion for travel took him on a tour of the world that lasted decades. He toured Egypt, East Africa, Spain, West Africa, Asia Minor, the Crimea, Constantinople, India, and China.

Claude Scudamore Jarvis (1879–1953), a soldier and administrator, joined the Egyptian Frontiers Administration in 1918, becoming governor of Sinai 1922–36. He was "a legendary figure" for his knowledge of the Bedouin customs and law. He wrote several books about the region including *Yesterday and Today in Sinai* (1931).

Alexander Kinglake (1809–1991) was a British traveler who went on a tour of the east in the middle decades of the nineteenth century. The account of his trip, *Eothen*, soon became a best seller and later provoked much controversy. He also wrote a history of the British campaign to the Crimea.

John Gardiner Kinnear (fl. 1830–1850), a Scotsman traveling to Egypt as an extension of "an entirely commercial" trip to the Levant, in 1839 met the Scottish artist David Roberts and diverted to travel with him in Sinai. His book of his journey includes remarks on the government of Muhammad 'Ali. He wrote two further books on the crisis of currencies and competition and of the Scottish-English systems of banking.

N.P. Kondokoff and the merchant **Triphon Korobeinikoff** (fl. 1582–1594) were among the many Russian pilgrims to Jerusalem, Egypt, and Sinai over the centuries.

Leon de Laborde (1807–1869), the son of Count Alexandre de Laborde, who was well known for his "sumptuous and valuable works on Spain, Austria, etc.," distinguished himself as "a diligent antiquarian and skilful artist," both drawing and making the engravings for the illustrations of his own books of travels, journeying to Sinai with the artist Linant de Bellefonds.

Paul Lenoir (1826–1881) states clearly that members of his expedition of 1872 were not interested in history: "Our object in going to Egypt was to look out for subjects for pictures and to paint them." His account is one of amused cynicism and delight. His descriptions of the Fayoum are particularly interesting, as few travelers seem to have lingered there. His book is illustrated with photographs rather than paintings: including photographs of the monks and his Bedouin companions and a few drawings.

Richard Lepsius (1810–1884) was to become an important Egyptologist. In 1842–45 he led the very well prepared Prussian expedition to Egypt. He traveled as far south as Khartoum and also to Sinai and Palestine. He sent home many Egyptian antiquities. Returned home, he became professor in Berlin and co-director of the Egyptian Museum. He revisited Egypt in 1866 and 1869. A significant scholar, his *Letters from Egypt 1842–5* are scholarly but entertaining in their personal observations.

Agnes Smith Lewis (1843–1926) traveled with her twin, Margaret Dunlop Gibson (1843–1920), traveled throughout the Near East from 1866 onwards. The Scottish-born ssiters studied Greek and Agnes wrote about their travels in Greece. After Margaret's husband died, they moved to Cambridge, where Agnes married Reverend Samuel Lewis. When he died they made a planned journey to Sinai where they searched to identify manuscripts in the Convent library. They learned the skills necessary for recording and translation and made important discoveries. Their work in the 1890s led to scholarly recording and to accounts of their work.

Alexander William Crawford Lindsay (1812–1880), a wealthy young aristocrat, traveled in the Near East in 1836–37 with his friend William Ramsay. Later he traveled widely in Europe and became profoundly interested in Christian art and art history. He built up a noted library and picture and manuscript collection. He succeeded his father to become the twenty-fifth Earl of Crawford.

Pierre Loti (1850–1923), a long-serving French naval officer, wrote descriptive and sometimes flamboyant accounts of his journeying around the world. His private life included various romantic adventures and relationships. His literary work was recognized when he was made a member of the French Academy in 1891.

Sir John Mandeville (fl. 1357) was the supposed author of an account of his alleged travels around the known world, which appeared in many editions and was published in several languages. The narrator of these 'travels' claimed to be English-born, to have left England in 1322 and circled the world for many years, writing the book in about 1357. There is much skepticism about whether such a single person existed or took these journeys, or simply drew on other's experiences and written sources. The book includes a description of the Holy Land and the routes thither, and provides known information about Sinai.

Samuel Manning (1822–1881), born in Leicester, England, became a Baptist minister in Somerset (1846–61) and was for some years editor of the *Baptist*

Magazine. In 1863 he became the general book editor and later Joint Secretary at the Religious Tract Society. He proposed to them a series of illustrated books of travel published by the Society. He wrote and illustrated some of these books and must have traveled widely. The titles included *The Land of the Pharaohs* (1875, with a new edition in 1924), *Lands of Scripture* (1879), *Those Holy Fields—Palestine* (1874), and books on America, Switzerland, England, and Italy.

Harriet Martineau (1802–1876), partly from economic necessity, became a writer and commentator on the political economy. She was partly deaf from childhood—her hearing aid an ear trumpet—and suffered long periods of ill health. Despite these difficulties she became acquainted with many eminent people, writing of herself that she had "for a long course of years influenced public affairs to an extent not professed or attempted by many men." She traveled widely in Europe, America, and in 1846 in the Near East; she wrote novels (including *Deerbrook*, *The Hour and the Man*, and for children, *Feats on the Fjord*), works on social, political, and religious matters, and *Eastern Life Past and Present*, the account covering her journey to Sinai.

H.V. Morton (c. 1890–1975) worked on several major British newspapers. From 1927 onwards he wrote a number of travel books under the title In Search of . . . , starting in Britain and spreading out across the world. He wrote five travel books about the Near East: *Through Lands of the Bible*, *In the Steps of St Paul*, *In the Steps of the Master*, *Women in the Bible*, and *Middle East*.

Shams al-Din Abu Abdallah Muhammad Ibn Abu Bakr al-Muqaddasi (c. 946–1000) was born in Jerusalem and educated in Iraq. He traveled extensively in the Arab lands where he met scores of scholars and mingled with the different Arab peoples. His writings are considered a hallmark in the history of Arab travelers and geographers. He lived the life of the community he traveled to, adding to his knowledge and experience of the different peoples and their lands.

G.W. Murray (1885–1966) was a British surveyor and explorer who worked for the Survey of Egypt and related organizations from 1907 until 1951. He served in Sinai 1916–19. He wrote many articles about his work and published one book about the life of the people.

Carsten Niebuhr (1733–1815), born to a simple family in Denmark, was determined to become educated, choosing to study mathematics and astronomy at Gottingen University, where Professor Michaelis persuaded the King of Denmark to send an expedition to find the answers to questions raised in the Bible. In 1761 the youthful but scholarly expedition set out. In August 1762, after a year in Egypt, Niebuhr and the philologist traveled to Mount Sinai to discover whether reported inscriptions were by the hand of Moses. During its work in the East, the expedition suffered loss but also success and reached places not seen by Europeans for a century or more and wrote detailed journals in their various specialties of philology, biology, zoology, and surveying. Niebuhr reached home in November 1767, the only survivor of the expedition. His resulting account was dry and obscure, though truly 'first' for the European record, and in 1792 Robert Heron (1764–1807) issued a shortened, readable version in English.

Stephen Olin (1797–1851), an American cleric and academic, rose to become president of Wesleyan University, Connecticut. He published his two volumes of travels in Egypt and the Holy Land in 1843.

H. Ouspensky (fl. 1800) is one of the many Orthodox Russian pilgrims to Sinai.

Edward Henry Palmer (1840–1882) packed extraordinary experiences into his short life. In 1867 he joined the survey of Sinai for the Palestine Exploration Fund, principally to collect correct place names. In 1870 he and Tyrwitt-Drake walked and explored the 600 miles from Sinai to Jerusalem. He then settled to scholarship as professor of Arabic, to marriage, translating, and writing. In 1881 he abandoned academic life for journalism. Following the Arabi Rebellion, he became chief interpreter to Her Majesty's forces in Egypt. In 1882 he was killed while on a secret mission to Egypt.

H.S. Palmer (1838–1903) spent his career between the Royal Engineers and the British Ordnance Survey. He planned a survey of the Sinai Peninsula with the agreement of his uncle who was head of Ordnance Survey and carried it out between October 1868 and April 1869 with C.W. Wilson. He worked also in Canada and later spent much time in Japan.

Peter the Deacon (c. 1107–1140), a monk of Monte Cassino in Italy, traveled on pilgrimage to the Holy Land.

William Flinders Petrie (1853–1942), after an unusual private informal education including archaeological work with his father, went to Egypt in 1880–82 to make a survey near the Pyramids. He dug for the Egypt Exploration Society from 1884–86, but then worked independently until rejoining the EES in 1896–1905. He became first professor of Egyptology in England 1892–1933. In 1904–05 he dug at Wadi Maghara and Serabit in the Sinai Peninsula. He published his work extensively—his Sinai work in *Researches in Sinai* with C.T. Currelly (1906). He died in Jerusalem.

Joan Plowden (Lady Charles Julien) (fl. 1920–40) Little appears to be recorded of the life of Joan Plowden apart from her own account of her travels to Sinai in 1937. On her first visit to Egypt she decided to return to travel in 'Arabia Petraea' the name given to the northwest corner of Arabia including Sinai. Then she read Leon Laborde's account of his journey and determined to following in his footsteps. She was the great-niece of Walter Chicheley Plowden (1820–60) who traveled widely in Ethiopia (than known as Abyssinia) in 1843–47.

Richard Pococke (1704–1765), a scholar-traveler who became a Church of Ireland bishop, traveled in the Near East from 1737 to 1740, visiting Egypt, the Holy Land and Sinai, Cyprus, Asia Minor, and Greece, and published his significant two-volume *Description of the East* in 1743 and 1745. He was later noted as a person who said very little. He traveled a great deal in the British Isles, carefully noting all he saw. His manuscripts of these journeys were not published until after his death.

The Prefetto of Egypt (Pere Claude Siccard) (1677–1726) was a French Jesuit who went as a missionary to Syria in 1700 and twelve years later moved to Cairo where he lived for the rest of his life. He made extended tours in the region, including visiting Sinai in 1720, both to make converts and to observe and record the monuments. He was the first modern European traveler known to have reached Aswan. He died of plague in Egypt. His account of Sinai was translated by Robert Clayton, Bishop of Clogher.

Procopius (fl. 535), a Greek historian and secretary to Emperor Justinian, wrote an account of Sinai, describing the life of the monks as "a careful study of death."

David Roberts (1796–1864), a prolific Scottish scene painter and acknowledged artist, visited the East in 1838–39 and published the resulting work in a series of volumes with commentary from his diaries in 1846–49. His works are still widely available in books and postcards in the places to which he traveled. In Egypt he met a fellow Scot, John Kinnear, and traveled with him in Sinai. His work appears on the cover of this book.

Edward Robinson (1794–1868), professor of Biblical Literature in the Union Theological Seminary in New York and author of a Greek and English Lexicon of the New Testament, traveled to Sinai in the footsteps of Moses in 1838 and again in 1857, publishing *Biblical Researches in Palestine and the Adjacent Regions* in 1856.

Philip Schaff (1819–1893), an American traveler, journeyed through 'Bible Lands' in the late 1870s.

Thomas Shaw (1694–1751), appointed as Chaplain to the English factory in Algiers 1720–33, traveled widely in North Africa and Egypt and visited Sinai. He published his *Travels* in 1738 on his return to England. They are well illustrated with maps and plates, and include descriptions of 640 plant species. He became principal of St. Edmund Hall in Oxford in 1740 and Oxford's Regius professor in Greek.

Dean Arthur Penryn Stanley (1815–1881), after a brilliant career at Oxford, was ordained into the Church of England in 1839 and began to travel. In 1852–53 he went to Egypt and the Holy Land, including Sinai in his journey—then only visited, according to the Dictionary of National Biography "by the most intrepid of European travelers." His account of his journeying in *Sinai and Palestine* (1856) was an immediate and continuing success. He became Regius professor of ecclesiastical history at Oxford, in which role his influence long continued. He returned to the Middle East with the Prince of Wales in 1862 and published the sermons he preached in the East. He was installed as Dean of Westminster in 1864.

John Lewis Stephens (1805–1852), after training as a lawyer in New York, went on the Grand Tour to Europe in search of health. Overwhelmed by what he saw, he pressed on East to the Levant and Constantinople in 1835. He then traveled north to Moscow and back again to reach Cairo in 1836. He traveled widely and seriously in Egypt where he met an English couple who suggested he visit Sinai and Petra where they had been. Dressed in the 'disguise of a Cairo merchant' he set out for Sinai. He traveled on through the Holy Lands and eventually home to write *Incidents of Travel in Egypt, Arabia Petraea and the Holy Land* (1838). Later, with the British architect Francis Catherwood, whom he first met in Egypt, he would travel in Central America.

Francis (or Francesco) Suriano (fl. 1450–c. 1529), a Venetian, traveled widely in the eastern Mediterranean in his uncle's trading ship as a young man. Then at twenty-five he decided to become a Franciscan. He spent 1481–84 and 1493–1515 in the East where the Franciscans had worked since 1219, during the lifetime of their founder, St. Francis. Suriano became 'Guardian of Mount Sion' and presided over the eastern convents. Returning to Europe, he continued to extend the work of the order. His treatise on the Holy Land was published in Venice in 1524.

Pero Tafur (c. 1410–c. 1484), a Spanish knight and gentleman, born in Cordoba, traveled from Spain to Venice towards the end of 1435 and onward to the Holy Land on May 17, 1436, returning two years later. He traveled within the Holy Land as a pilgrim and sightseer, disguised himself as a Moor and penetrated the Haram Schereef, the Muslim sanctuary in Jerusalem. Intent on going to St. Catherine's Monastery, he traveled via Cyprus and Cairo. After several further adventures, a sojourn in Constantinople and a tour of Europe, he reached home and a quieter life. His *Travels* were first published in Madrid in 1874 and translated and published in English in 1926. He later took a prominent role in public life.

Catherine Tobin (fl. 1840–1860) twice visited the Middle East and Sinai with her husband. The first time she wrote, illustrated, and published an account of her travels; the second trip was to help heal the loss of her only son in Lucknow at the time of the India Mutiny in 1857. After this journey she wrote and illustrated her second book. Earlier she had translated an illustrated account of discoveries in Nineveh.

William Turner (1792–1867) joined the British diplomatic service and in 1811 went with Sir Robert Liston's embassy to Constantinople. Liston gave him leave to travel freely in the Near East for some years and he wrote of his travels in *Journal of a Tour in the Levant* (1820). He returned to Constantinople from 1824 and was posted to Columbia in 1829. He retired early from the diplomatic service and lived quietly with his family in Warwickshire.

Hippolyte Vichensky (fl. 1800) was one of the many Russian pilgrim to Sinai.

Sir Charles William Wilson (1836–1905) was an army officer who became involved with the Palestine Exploration Fund and the scientific exploration of the Holy Lands in 1864–65, and surveyed the Sinai Peninsula with H.S. Palmer in 1868–69. He joined the somewhat moribund Ordnance Survey Department and did much to resurrect it. After other postings, he became director general in 1885.

Joseph Wolff (1795–1862), among the most colorful of travelers, was a German Jew who converted to Christianity, became an Anglican minister, and set out in 1821 to become a missionary to the Jews. He married into the British aristocracy (and his wife often traveled with him). He traveled twice to Sinai, once with John Carne and the second time in 1836 on his own. His other journeys included sorties into Central Asia, India, and Ethiopia, but he eventually retired to an English country parish, where he dictated his memoirs to a friend.

Robert Walter Stewart (fl. 1850–1860) was a clergyman based in Leghorn, Italy, when he wrote his travels. His purpose was to gain "better comprehension of the topography of the Scripture" using the reserach of Dr. Edward Robinson and his own experiences.

Bibliography

Bartlett, S.C. *From Egypt to Palestine through Sinai, the Wilderness and the South Country*. New York, 1877 (1817–98).

Bartlett, W.H. *Forty Days in the Desert on the Track of the Israelites*. London, 1846.

Baedeker, Karl. *Palestine and Syria*. London, 1906.

Beadnell, H.J.L. *The Wilderness of Sinai*. London, 1927.

Beamont, William. *To Sinai and Syene and Back* (1860–61). London, 1871.

Belon du Mans, Pierre. *Voyage en Egypte*. Paris, 1547; *Voyage en Egypte de Pierre Belon de Mans*, S. Sauneron, ed. Cairo, 1970.

Bird, Isabella. "A Pilgrimage to Sinai," *Leisure Hour*. London, 1886.

Bonar, Horatius. *The Desert of Sinai: Notes of a Spring Journey from Cairo to Beersheba*. London, 1858.

Brockbank, Oliver. *Diary of a Journey, through the Sinai Peninsula and Mount Sinai*. London, 1914.

Burckhardt, J.L. *Travels in Syria and the Holy Land*. London, 1822.

Carne, John. *Letters from the East*. London, 1826.

Conyngham, Francis. *Leaves from My Journal*. Dublin, 1869.

Didier, Charles. *Sojourn with the Grand Sharif of Makkah*. Paris, 1857; trans. Richard Boulind. Cambridge, 1985.

Dobson, Augusta Mary Rachel. *Mount Sinai, a Modern Pilgrimage*. London, 1925.

Dumas, Alexandre. *Impressions de Voyage*. Paris, 1837; *Travelling Sketches in Egypt and Sinai including a visit to Mount Horeb, and other localities of the Exodus*, English trans. London, 1839.

Eckenstein, Lina. *The History of Sinai*. London, 1920.

Egeria. *Egeria's Travels*, trans. John Wilkinson. London: SPCK, 1971.

Fabri, Felix. *The Book of the Wanderings of Brother Felix Fabri*, trans. A. Stewart, 1897.

Farman, Elbert. *Egypt and its Betrayal*. New York, 1908.

Fisk, George. *A Pastor's Memorial of Egypt . . . the wilderness of Sin . . . Mount Sinai and the Holy Land in 1842*. London, 1843.

Gadsby, J. *My Visit to Mount Sinai and the Holy Land*. London, 1870.

Gibson, Margaret Dunlop. *How the Codex was Found: A Narrative of Two Visits to Sinai, 1892–3*. Cambridge, 1893; re-issued Brighton and Portland, 1999.

Golding, Louis. *In the Steps of Moses the Lawgiver*. London, 1938.

Haag, Michael. *Egypt*. London: Cadogan, 2004

Hamilton, James. *Sinai, the Hedjaz and across to Soudan: wanderings around the birthplace of the Prophet and across the Ethiopian Desert*. London, 1857.

Henniker, Sir Frederick. *Notes during a Visit to Egypt . . . Mount Sinai and Jerusalem*. London, 1823.

Hornby, Emily. *Sinai and Petra: the Journeys of Emily Hornby in 1899 and 1901*. London, 1907.

Ibn Batutta. *Travels in Asia and Africa* 1325–54, trans. Sir H. Gibb. London: Routledge and Kegan Paul Ltd., 1958.

Jarvis, C.S. *Desert and Delta*. London, 1938.

Kinglake, Alexander. *Eothen*. London: J. Ollivier, 1844.

Kinnear, John. *Cairo Petra and Damascus in 1839*. London, 1840.

Leon de Laborde, Marquis. *Journey through Arabia Petraea to Mount Sinai and the Excavated City of Petra*. London, 1836.

Lenoir, Paul. *The Fayoum or Artists in Egypt*. London, 1873.

Lepsius, Richard. *Letters from Egypt, Ethiopia and the Peninsula of Sinai*. London, 1853.

Lewis, Agnes Smith. *The Forty Martyrs of the Sinai Desert*. Cambridge, 1912.

———. *In the Shadow of Sinai, a story of travel and research from 1894 to 1897*. Cambridge, 1898; re-issued Brighton and Portland, 1999.

Lindsay, Lord. *Letters on Egypt, Edom and the Holy Land*. London, 1838.

Loti, Pierre, *Desert*. London, 1895.

Mandeville, Sir John. *The Travels of Sir John Mandeville*. London: Penguin, 1983.

Manning, Samuel. *The Land of the Pharaohs: Egypt and Sinai Illustrated*. London, 1875.

Martineau, Harriet. *Eastern Life Past and Present*. London, 1846.

Morton, H.V. *Through The Lands of the Bible*. London, 1938.

Al-Muqaddasi, Shams al-Din Mohammed Ibn Abu Bakr. *The Best Divisions for Knowledge of the Regions*, trans. Basil Anthony Collins. Reading: Centre for Muslim Contribution to Civilization, Garnet Publishings Ltd., 1994.

Murray, G.W. *Sons of Ishmael: a study of the Egyptian Bedouin*. London, 1935.
Murray's Handbook Egypt. London, 1873.
Niebuhr, Carsten. *Travels through Arabia and other Countries of the East performed by M. Niebuhr*, 2 vols, trans. Robert Heron, Edinburgh, 1792; re-issued with introduction by Dr. Robin Bidwell, Garnet, 1994.
Olin, Stephen. *Travels in Egypt, Arabia Petraea and the Holy Land*. New York, 1843.
Palmer, E.H. *The Desert of the Exodus—Journeys on foot in the Wilderness*. London, 1871.
Palmer, H.S. *Sinai from the 4th Egyptian Dynasty to the Present Day*. London, 1878.
Petrie, Sir Flinders. *Researches in Sinai*. London, 1906.
Plowden, Joan. *Once in Sinai, the record of a solitary venture*. London, 1937.
Pococke, Richard. *Description of Egypt and some other countries*. London, 1743.
Prefetto of Egypt (Pere Claude Siccard). *A Journal from Grand Cairo to Mount Sinai and back again*, trans. Robert Clayton, Bishop of Clogher, 1772.
Robinson, Edward and E. Smith. *Biblical Researches in Palestine and the adjacent regions in 1838 and 1852*. London, 1867.
Schaff, Philip. *Through Bible Lands*. New York, 1878.
Shaw, Thomas. *Travels and Observations relating to Several Parts of Barbary and the Levant*. London, 1738.
Stanley, Dean Arthur Penryn. *Sinai and Palestine in connection with their history*. London, 1868.
Stewart, Robert Walter. *The Tent and the Khan: A journey to Sinai and Palestine*. Edinburgh, 1957.
Suriano, Francis. *Treatise on the Holy Land*, trans. T. Bellorini and E. Hoade. Jerusalem, 1983.
Stephens, John Lloyd. *Incidents of Travel in Egypt, Arabia Petraea and the Holy Land*. London, 1838; re-issued University of Oklahoma Press, Norman, 1970.
Tafur, Pero. *Travels and Adventures*, 1435–39. London: Broadway Travellers, 1926.
Tobin, Catherine. *The Land of Inheritance or Bible Scenes Re-visited*. London, 1863.
———. *Shadow of the East or Slight Shadows of the East or Silent Sketches of Egypt, Palestine, Syria, Turkey and Greece*. London, 1855.
Turner, William. *Journal of a Tour in the Levant*. London, 1820.
Wilson, Sir Charles. *Picturesque Palestine, Sinai and Egypt*. London, 1884.
Wolff, Joseph. *Missionary Journal and Memoir of the Reverend Joseph Wolff*. London, 1824

Index of Travelers